Socio-Economic and Political Vision of Dr. B.R. Ambedkar

About the Editor

Professor S.N. Mishra, a prolific writer and established scholar had been Professor almost for two decade and half at the Indian Institute of Public Administration, New Delhi. On his retirement, he was appointed Ambedkar Chair Professor of Social Justice at IIPA, New Delhi. Professor Mishra's interest areas had been Indian Political System, Development Administration, Panchayati Raj and Rural Development.

Apart from being the Editor of Lokprashashan, Indian Institute of Public Administration, and member of Executive Council, IIPA, Professor Mishra has successfully guided 32 scholars for their Ph.D. and D.Litt. degrees. He has to his credit more than 250 research papers published in various journals and edited volumes, both in India and abroad. He has also published 34 books and is still pursuing his academic interest with greater devotion and commitment.

Professor Mishra is presently busy with a series of volumes on different facets of Dr. Ambedkar.

Socio-Economic and Political Vision of Dr. B.R. Ambedkar

Edited by

S.N. Mishra

CONCEPT PUBLISHING COMPANY PVT. LTD.,
NEW DELHI-110 059

ISBN-13: 978-81-8069-674-9 ISBN-10: 81-8069-674-X

First Published 2010

Published and Printed by

Concept
Since 1974

Concept Publishing Company Pvt. Ltd.
Regd. Office:
A/15-16, Commercial Block, Mohan Garden
New Delhi-110059 (India)
Phones: 25351460, 25351794, *Fax*: 091-11-25357109
Email: publishing@conceptpub.com
Website: www.conceptpub.com

Editorial Office:
H-13, Bali Nagar, New Delhi-110 015, India.

Cataloging in Publication Data--*Courtesy:* D.K. Agencies (P) Ltd. <docinfo@dkagencies.com>

Socio-economic and political vision of Dr. B.R. Ambedkar / edited by S.N. Mishra.
p. cm.
Contributed articles.
Includes bibliographical references (p.).
Includes index.
ISBN 13: 9788180696749 ISBN 10: 818069674X

1. Ambedkar, B. R. (Bhimrao Ramji), 1891-1956--Political and social views. 2. India--Politics and government--20th century. 3. India--Economic conditions--20th century. 4. India--Social conditions--20th century. 5. Constitutional law--India. 6. Social justice--India. I. Mishra, S. N. (Sudisht Narayan), 1942-

DDC 954 22

Dedicated to

Shri T.N. Chaturvedi

Former Governor of Karnataka

Acknowledgements

On my retirement, the idea of bringing out edited volumes was given by Shri T.N. Chaturvedi, Former Governor, Karnataka. Throughout my academic career, Shri Chaturvedi had been a source of inspiration and encouragement. No words are adequate to express sincere thanks and indebtedness to Shri Chaturvedi but to dedicate the volume.

I am equally thankful to the learned contributors of the volume, who on my request spared their valuable time and wrote for the present volume. Their contributions, no doubt, have enriched the existing literature on Dr. Ambedkar. Once again I would like to thank and express my gratitude to them.

I am also thankful to my wife, Ms. Nirmala Mishra, who spared me from household work and allowed me to devote for the present volume. My daughter, Dr. Sweta Mishra, Assistant Professor, Department of Political Science, Gargi College (University of Delhi), was always available to share her thoughts with me and helping in bringing out the present volume. My grand-children, Sanstuti and Sansriti, are also claimants of my thanks for being deprived of my love and affection for quite a long time.

Last but not the least, my thanks are also due to Shri Ashok Kumar Mittal, Concept Publishing Co. Pvt. Ltd., New Delhi, for bringing out the volume in record time and in beautiful shape.

S.N. Mishra

Contents

List of the Contributors

A.N. Panda, Reader, PG Department of Political Science, Panchayat (Govt. Lead) College, Bargarh, Orissa.

Anil Dutta Mishra, Deputy Director, National Gandhi Museum, Rajghat, New Delhi.

Ashok Kumar Singh, Reader, Department of Political Science, Y.N. College, Dighwara (Saran), Bihar.

Bindeshwar Pathak, Founder, Sulabh Sauchalay, Action Sociologist and Social Reformer, International Expert on Cost-effective Sanitation, Biogas and Rural Development.

Jai Narain Sharma, Chairman, Department of Gandhian Studies and Honorary Director, Gandhi Bhawan, Panjab University, Chandigarh.

Jaytilak Guha Roy, Professor, Indian Institute of Public Administration, New Delhi.

M.P. Singh, Professor, Department of Political Science, University of Delhi, Delhi.

P.K. Chaubey, Professor, Indian Institute of Public Administration, New Delhi.

Ramashray Roy, Former Director, Centre for Studies in Developing Societies, Rajpur Road, New Delhi.

Ruchi Tyagi, Associate Professor, Department of Political Science, Kalindi College (University of Delhi), New Delhi.

S.N. Mishra, Professor (Retd.), Indian Institute of Public Administration, New Delhi and is Editor, Lokprashashan, IIPA, New Delhi.

Sunita Gulati, Deputy Librarian, Indian Institute of Public Administration, New Delhi.

Suresh Misra, Professor, Indian Institute of Public Administration, New Delhi.

Sushma Yadav, Professor, Dr. Ambedkar Chair in Social Justice, Indian Institute of Public Administration, New Delhi.

1

Introduction

S.N. MISHRA

Born in nineteenth century, Dr. Ambedkar shines like a luminous star in the galaxy of great men. He played a crucial role in shaping the destiny of free India, and left indelible imprints on our national life and the state organization. Dr. Ambedkar rose to the zenith of his glory not by fluke but by dint of his undaunting struggles, valuable sacrifices, immense erudition, solemn dedication and abiding faith. Very few can stand in comparison with Ambedkar, whose life was full of a series of struggles and consequential enviable successes. The personality of Dr. Ambedkar was at once dynamic and multifaceted. He was a popular leader, erudite scholar, zealous social reformer, innovative educationist, expert lawyer, eminent writer, influential teacher, great patriot, distinguished politician, noted economist, able administrator, genuine humanist and fearless journalist. Along with all this, he was a champion of *'Samaiva Dharma'*, a worshipper of human feelings and experiences, a votary of women's right and the messiah of the depressed sections of society. He inherited the qualities of nobility and resolution from his father and self-reliance and dutifulness from his mother. His heart was full of love and compassion. Being the youngest of the fourteen brothers and sisters, he was loved dearly by all the members of his family. He had to suffer the agonies of privation and hardships because of his lowly birth. The social conditions of those days were callously hard pressed. There was acute dearth of carnality and cordiality in society. The conditions of depressed classes were almost hellish. The poor, underdogs were very often tyrannized and exploited. As a member of the low caste family he had to eat the humble pie, for he was, time and again, insulted and disregarded. Owing to all pervasive stigmas of social discrimination and untouchability, he could never relish the kindly feelings, humanistic sympathies and genial cordiality. His heart was excessively charged with pathos when he found inhuman, discriminatory behaviour being practiced between man and man in the then society. He resolved against the social evils, and to eradicate them from the orthodox, traditional society, he kept on striving hard without being disheartened or shaken.

Great men like Karl Marx, Lenin, Gandhi, Mao and Ho Chi Minh have all necessarily been epoch-making luminaries, but so far as the case of Dr. Ambedkar's relentless struggles against the callous injustices done to the depressed, low caste people is concerned, he naturally emerged as an apostle figure. He was one of those great men, who from the cradle to the grave, had spent their life in fermenting state of insult, anguish and oppression. The disgrace, borne by him, was comparatively more intolerably inhuman and painful than what was meted out either to Gandhi or to any other world leader. He was noted for his exceptional fearlessness and outspokenness. He was endowed with infinite patience, tolerance, humility and compassion. An iconoclast Dr. Ambedkar thought it irrational to idol the rituals, traditions, blind belief and outworn values, for he was fully convinced that it would beget jealousy, fear and religious bigotry in society.

Shri Anantsayanam Iyengar, the then speaker of the Lok Sabha, while paying glowing tribute to Dr. Ambedkar, said,

> The personality of Dr. Ambedkar was Himalayan and dynamic. Rising from the very grass root level, he became the champion leader of the scheduled caste people. He was an erudite scholar and eminent writer. More than this, he was a vociferous orator. He was a pathfinder to our constitution. In the field of social reform, he launched many welfare schemes. India has truly lost an illustrious son in his death.

S. Nijalingappa, greatly enchanted by Dr. Ambedkar's personality observed: "Dr. Ambedkar, during pre- and post-independence was a unique leader in India's life. He remains quite incomparable."

Various positions held by Dr. Ambedkar are suggestive of his multifaceted personality. It is obviously clear that Dr. Ambedkar was an epoch making doyen in the multifarious walks of life. His personality was at once gigantic and dynamic. If not impossible, it is, of course, very difficult to focus on all aspects of the Himalayan personality of Dr. Ambedkar.

He was one of the architects of our constitution, which has survived the test of time without any major change. Keeping in view the nature of the constitution, Dr. Ambedkar himself said: "The constitution of a country is a fundamental document, which carries clear documentation of the powers and privileges of all the three constituent bodies of a state—Executive, Judiciary and Legislature. Not only this, it also defines the mutual relations and rights of citizens, and executive and judiciary, as it has been worked out in the chapter, 'Fundamental Rights' in the Constitution of India. Actually, the aim of the constitution is not only to formulate the constituent bodies of a state but also to delimit and ascertain their rights and powers. If a Legislature enjoys full freedom to making ordinances and the executive has a free hand in their implementation, a state of anarchy is most likely to crop up. It is, therefore, essential that not only the tri-lateral relations of the constituent bodies of the state but also the mutual relative rights and prerogatives of the citizens and the state should be clearly envisaged and defined in the Constitution." Dr. Ambedkar admitted that "though it was almost difficult to frame up a new constitution, however, I studied good many constitutions of the world and built up our own constitution. It was no more an outcome of bare imitation. It has rather its own specific features. To elaborate these features here is not feasible. The greatest speciality of our Constitution lies in the provision of amendment incorporated in it."

While commending the monumental achievement of Dr. Ambedkar, Dr. Rajendra Prasad, the first President of India, observed:

> While occupying the Presidential Chair and reviewing the day-to-day workings, I have experienced that the exhibition of uncanny zeal and dedication by the chairman of the Drafting Committee, Dr. Ambedkar, despite his ill health, is unparalleled. He not only justified his selection as the chairman of the Drafting Committee but has also gloriously shown his superb constitution making ability.

Recalling the key-role, played by Dr. Ambedkar in the making of the Constitution, the first Prime Minister of India, Pt. Jawaharlal Nehru said:

> We recall him for many things, but more specially we recall him for the key role, he played in the making of our Constitution, and perhaps in comparison to his other feats, this accomplished achievement of his will continue to be remembered for very long.

Thus, the law experts, constitution makers, diplomats and statesmen not only of India but also of the world at large spoke highly of the Constitution. Duly recognizing Dr. Ambedkar's exceptional merits, the University of Columbia conferred on him the degree of LL.D. The Constitution was held as modern *Manu Smriti* and Dr. Ambedkar was accorded a pride of place of modern Manu.

Another good quality of Dr. Ambedkar is that he was a great educationist. Multi-linguist Babasaheb Ambedkar was well-versed in as many as fourteen languages. He had a command over each of these languages. A scholar asserts:

> One who knows one language is like a bird, having a long wing and one who knows two languages struts like a cock, but one, who commands three languages,

> becomes the shelleyan skylark that simultaneously sings and soars to the sky.

Dr. Ambedkar was fully convinced that the education is one of the best resources to connect the destitute with the main stream of national development. Hence, he laid utmost stress on the expansion and promotion of education. The introduction of free and compulsory system of primary education in the Constitution of India is the happy result of this objective.

The view expressed by Dr. Ambedkar about education is worth quoting "the education that makes us neither competent nor teaches us lessons of equality and morality is no more education." He believed that education is good only if it promotes and preserves the interests of mankind as a whole. True education, he argued, creates equality in society, provides food to the hungry people and satisfies thirst for knowledge. He was convinced that it is only education that breeds and nourishes the noble sentiments of unity, fraternity and patriotism. Education alone humanizes man. Man, without education, is no better than beast. He wanted to strengthen the national unity and integrity through education. He was of the view that education is such an indispensable thing that it should necessarily be within easy reach of all. It should be cheap also so that the poorest of the poor may acquire it. He thought so highly of education that in his tri-worded slogan—'Educate, organize and struggle', he gave top priority to it. To help and encourage the students belonging to the scheduled caste, he established a number of hostels and provided books and clothes free of cost.

Dr. Ambedkar had a deep passion for books, hence he kept on gleaning golden books on a rich variety of subjects till he breathed his last. His personal library was so spacious and richly slacked that it could be compared with any very good library. There was no book in his library without notes supplied by him with pencil. This evidently bears rich testimony to his wide, varied and profound reading. He was a distinguished authority on the subjects such as Theology, Sociology, Law, Economics, Politics etc. The institutions, Siddhartha College of Arts and Science, Bombay, Milind College, Aurangabad and the People's Education Society etc. established by him not only to symbolize his insatiable thirst for knowledge but also immortalize his name.

Another good quality of Dr. Ambedkar is that he was a fearless Journalist. Through his sharp, pointed, fiery journalistic writings he not only opposed the callous British policies but also awakened the depressed, exploited people of India towards their lustful, genuine rights. Keeping in view, the welfare of the public, he took the Journalistic Mission with ample sincerity and dedication. He practiced Journalism solemnly, producing model example for posterity, as it was a mission and not a profession for him.

Fully aware of the despicable nature of the then society, Dr. Ambedkar thought that papers and magazines run by the capitalists, feudalists and orthodox conservative minds, published only such articles which necessarily served and protected their selfish ends. Dr. Ambedkar stood firmly for the democratic, progressive and reformatory causes. Though the general trends of the Indian press towards his views and thoughts was jaundiced, he, however, remained undeterred and kept on carrying the flag flying.

To provide the voice to the poor, hapless people, Dr. Ambedkar launched a Marathi fortnightly magazine, *Mook Nayak* on January 31, 1920. The low caste people enthusiastically welcomed Dr. Ambedkar's views on democracy and liberal humanism, published in this periodical. Through his writings Dr. Ambedkar tried hard to eliminate the superfluous, unnecessary ritual and evil religious practices prevalent in Hindu community. But due to the paucity of fund this magazine ceased its publication. Therefore, Dr. Ambedkar found it very difficult to make his humanistic views reach the exploited society. Thereafter, he founded *Bahiskrit Hitkari Sabha* on July 20, 1924 and began the publication of a journal named *Saraswati Vilas*. By now, his scope of action had become enormously wide and varied. To make his views and opinions reach the common masses, he launched yet another fortnightly, namely *Bahiskrit Bharat* on April 3, 1927. Being the editor in chief of the periodical, he achieved considerable success in uniting the depressed classes together and in making them conscious of their justful rights. He also forced them to relinquish the evil social customs. The orthodox and conservative minds, among the Hindus, were so awfully dissatisfied that they declared him the destroyer of the Hindu culture and the enemy of Brahmins. In December 1930, he launched a periodical, *Janta* replacing *Bahiskrit Bharat*. Through this publication, he gave vehement expression to the agonies and aspirations of the suffering humanity.

To make the grievances of the hapless poor known to speaking people, he started the publication of a paper in English language. In conformity to his views, the paper was named *Equality*. During his long journalistic career he contributed a large number of articles and gave rich dimensions to India. Even at the fag end of his life, he could not sit idly, hence he started the publication of *Prabudha Bharat* a Marathi weekly in association with his compatriot. Through this weekly mostly he expressed the sermons and rich humanistic message of Buddha.

Dr. Ambedkar in addition to his other qualities was a great writer. His works were not only held significant during the time of their publication, but even now, they are considered as relevant and authoritative in their respective fields. He wrote more than twenty-four books and scores of articles. These monumental works of Dr. Ambedkar, besides unravelling literateur in him, manifested his versatility and acumen in the field of art of writing.

The loving memories of Dr. Ambedkar—the liberator of the exploited, downtrodden of the society, the crusader against the social evils and the architect of the Constitution of India—are struck so deep in the national ethos that the entire country recalls him reverentially. He was greatly influenced by the thoughts of Lord Buddha, Saint Kabir and Jyoti Ba Phule. This is why, he wanted to build up a society based on the noble principles of 'equality', 'liberty' and 'fraternity'. He always encouraged the people of the depressed, exploited and oppressed classes.

Since Dr. Ambedkar was a votary of human liberty and rights, he not only plunged into the Freedom Movement, but also made strict provisions in the Constitution to safeguard them. He opined that man, being the living, vibrant member of society, cannot be robbed of his freedom. Man is privileged to live a free and independent life. Considering this point, he argued that no man, belonging to a developed or advanced country, enjoys a right to enslave another man.

Dr. Ambedkar fought throughout his life against injustice, tyranny and exploitation. Though revolutionary at heart, he wanted to find solutions to the social problems exclusively on the constitutional basis. He was convinced that if it were not so, it would pave way to anarchy in society. He was not only in favour of promoting the scheduled caste people but wanted to ameliorate the wretched conditions of the backward caste people too. He was a staunch supporter of women's right also. The Hindu Code Bill, introduced by him, evidences his serious concerns in this regard. He made no discrimination between son and daughter in Hindu family. He did not like to remain confined within the utopian world but chose to come out daringly to brave the sea of problems which were very complex, and critical in nature. His personality was endowed with fiery revolutionary traits. The agitation and movements, such as *Manusmriti Dahan* and Gandhi-Ambedkar controversy testify to his revolutionary spirit.

Dr. Ambedkar was a staunch upholder of national unity. He devoted his entire life to the noble cause of national unity and communal harmony. He was advocate of equality and socialism. Keeping these noble objectives in view, he rose above the narrow barriers of religion, caste, language and region and laid emphasis on strengthening the national unity. He affirmed that in the absence of universal human religion these can survive neither unity nor democracy. He maintained that if a state guarantees and safeguards the fundamental rights of the citizens and allows them full freedom in the observance of rites, customs and religion, it will of course ensure and strengthen the national unity and communal harmony.

Dr. Ambedkar was not opposed to Hindu society or Hindu religion, he rather thought that Hindu society should be reorganized on the basis of two cardinal principles of equality and castelessness. He demanded that the prevailing system of priesthood and *purohitism* should be democratized so that everyone may enjoy the freedom in the choice of his profession according to his liking. He was convinced that this process would not only do away the evils of casteism, untouchability and discrimination between the high and the low but also foster the feelings of unity and equality in society. This is how we can build up and perpetuate our national unity. He claimed that nationalism cannot be attained unless national feelings were awakened and strengthened. He held social reform quite essential for achieving this noble end, and as such, he declared: "without social reform true feeling of nationalism cannot be evolved".

Dr. Ambedkar's abiding patriotic fervour stirs clear in the speech, he made in the Constituent Assembly, on 5 February, 1950. He said: "India has achieved freedom after centuries of struggle. Now our first and foremost duty is to safeguard our freedom. Any dissension, in our society, will snatch away our freedom." He sighted that some of our social deformities like economic disparities, backwardness, casteism etc. have perhaps been the bye-products of our centuries old slavery. He sternly warned that if any alien power, in view of our social evils, wishes to rob us of our monopolies, we would sort it out ourselves cordially. But we have to remain constantly vigilant to spot out Jai Chandras amongst us. The statement made by Dr. Ambedkar still holds its significance and relevance as it did during those days.

He fought throughout his life for the rights of the discarded, neglected and oppressed and helped them in regaining their justful, adequate place and position in the socio-constitutional life of India. He always wielded his weapons against tyranny, injustice and exploitation. Dr. Ambedkar, in the truest sense, was a stalwart and national leader and an Indian par-excellence. To brand him as a leader of the scheduled castes is not only meant to undermine his titanic personality but also to do injustice to him and to us as well.

He held religion quite essential for the national unity and the sublimation of man. But he abhorred it if it engendered exploitation, injustice and inequality. Since these were inevitably pernicious evils in Hindu religion, he made Herculean efforts to abolish them, for he thought, they were detrimental to national unity. But when it did not so happen, he adopted Buddhism on October 14, 1956.

In regard to national language, Dr. Ambedkar avowed that it is only one particular language that can be the national language of India. He advised his countrymen that if they are willing to remain united and integrated as a whole and want to develop a common harmonious culture, they should make all out efforts to adopt and develop Hindi as a common language, acceptable to all. He went to the extent of saying: "An Indian, who does not accept Hindi as the national, is not worthy to be called Indian". He wanted to strengthen the roots of unity and nationality on the basis of one common language. Dr. Ambedkar's patriotic fervour rings clear when he remarks "The dire need of the hour today is to instill the popular spirit of nationality among the people—not a spirit—that makes them feel that they are first Indians and thereafter Hindus, Muslims, Sindhis and Sikhs—but a spirit that keeps them absolutely Indians. His words, in the present day context of India, hold greater relevance.

Dr. Ambedkar was the saviour of depressed classes. He was one of the most illustrious sons of mother India, born during the age of Indian Renaissance. He dedicated his entire life for the upliftment of the depressed, backward and outcaste people of India, and thereby emerged as a messiah of undying fame. He once declared: "I am solemnly pledged to lay down my life while serving the *Dalit* Community in which I was born and bred and I am still living". Dr. Ambedkar's name reigns supreme among those who emancipated the depressed people from their hellish life and kindled in them hopes for better, renewed life. Though long before him, Saint Ravi Das, Saint Kabir Das, Guru Nanak Dev and Swami Dayanand had done their best to ameliorate the wretched conditions of the depressed people, and liberate them from the heinous stigma of untouchability, yet Dr. Ambedkar's magnanimous efforts made on the political, constitutional and social planes have proved to be epoch-making.

The resultants of Poona pact, were reservations in the Provincial and Central Legislatures and removal of disabilities of the depressed classes in regard to election to local bodies and the appointment to public services. These were embodied in the Government of India Act, 1935. In a sense it was a solemn contract between Gandhiji and Dr. Ambedkar. As far as the Scheduled Castes are concerned, this pact is an important and historic event in the annals of their struggle for emancipation. Most people who talk of need to review reservation policy towards Scheduled Castes would do well to remember this solemn pledge and contract. With the dawn of Independence and the adoption of Indian Constitution the safeguards were further enlarged and strengthened for the advancement of the Scheduled Castes and Tribes. The point to be remembered and is being posed today is whether all these provisions and safeguards are being implemented and fulfilled properly and fully today.

No doubt much has been done. But much more remains to be done. Mere political freedom without social and economic freedom is not true freedom for the scheduled castes and tribes. While several measures have been taken by the Government—the declaration of the year 1990-91 as the year of social justice is of particular importance. Dr. Ambedkar strove his best to secure "Social Justice" for the oppressed people. His intense zeal to give a fair deal to women and workers is well known. His work as a Legislator and Parliamentarian, as a Member in the Viceroy's Executive Council, as a Law Minister, as the Chief Architect of the Indian Constitution and his struggles bear ample testimony to this.

Dr. Ambedkar was a versatile personality. With a brilliant mind, keen intellect, deep knowledge and scholarship, he strode on the political and social scene as a colossus for several decades. He was a jurist, thinker, debater, writer, rebel, radical reformer, patriot, constitution maker and above all the liberator and leader of the downtrodden and suppressed millions in the country. He is one among the very few illustrious figures in the World History who fought and succeeded in rescuing and rehabilitating vast masses of humanity along suppressed and exploited.

At a time when the nation honoured him with *"Bharat Ratna"* thirty-one year after his passing away and in the beginning of twenty-first century when the country is passing through a critical phase in its history, it is but proper to recollect and remember what Dr. Ambedkar had said on some of the vital issues which we face today.

He believed that without economic and social justice, political independence would not give national integration and social homogeneity. He wanted restructuring of society by liquidating the caste system and ushering in a society based on liberty, equality and fraternity. He was a staunch advocate of unity of the nation. He sought to achieve these through the following measures. In this monumental effort he had the understanding and cooperation of Jawaharlal Nehru, Sardar Patel and other leaders.

1. The Democratic and Parliamentary System of Government and making the Indian Constitution strong enough to hold the country together with in-built resistance and flexibility.
2. Provision of special safeguard to minorities, Scheduled Castes and Tribes and the other socially and educationally backward classes. Articles 16(4) and 355 of the Constitution are important in this regard.
3. Awakening the Scheduled Castes and Tribes and instilling in them a sense of self-respect and dignity and making them equal partners in the governance of the country.
4. Enunciation of salutary principles of one man, one value and one vote. The individual citizen instead of village was accepted as a unit in the affairs of the state.
5. Incorporation of fundamental rights.

6. Directive Principles to serve as guidelines for orderly establishment of economic and social democracy in the country.
7. Abolition of untouchability and forced labour.
8. Right to Constitutional Remedies to uphold and assert one's right instead of employing unconstitutional and violent methods.

On November 25, 1949, while speaking in the Constituent Assembly, Dr. Ambedkar observed as follows:

> I feel, however, good a constitution may be, it is sure to turn out bad because those who are called to work it, happen to be a bad lot. However bad a constitution may be, it may turn out to be good if those who are called to work it, happen to be a good lot. The working of the constitution does not depend wholly upon the nature of the constitution. The constitution can provide only the organs of state such as the legislature, the executive and the judiciary. The factors on which the working of these organs of state depend are the people and the political parties they will set up their instruments to carry out their wishes and their policies, who can say how the people of India and their parties will behave? Will they uphold constitutional methods achieving their purposes or will they prefer revolutionary methods however good the constitution may be? It is, therefore, futile to pass any judgement upon the constitution without reference to the part which the people and their parties are likely to play.

How prophetic and relevant are these observations, considering the present political situation in our country.

The legacy that Dr. Ambedkar left to his followers and his countrymen is lustrous and lasting. His relevance in today's context is very important. He was a popular and dedicated leader during his lifetime but his teaching qualities and contributions are more relevant today. For example, being the architect of the constitution, the provisions he made in the constitution, are the greatest integrating force today and with the help of different amending provisions it has stood to the test of time.

As messiah of untouchables he made a lasting contribution by way of provisions of removal of untouchability in the body of the constitution. Though we have failed to bring about total untouchability in the country yet it is not a mean achievement that the downtrodden and untouchables have started realising their real status in free and independent India and are prepared to fight for that.

He stood for the unity of the country. As a result through provisions of strong centre, we have been able to hold India together which shows his relevance in present context.

In the backdrop of above statements, Dr. Anil Dutta Mishra in his article "The Man and the Life" touches on various facets of Dr. Ambedkar. In his opening remarks, Dr. Mishra, mentions about his childhood and the misfortune that followed Dr. Ambedkar from the very childhood. Subsequently he discusses about his education both in India and abroad as also the achievements which he had in his life and also contribution to the making of the Indian Constitution as Chairman of the Drafting Committee. He also mentions about the frustration Dr. Ambedkar had from the caste ridden Hindu society and absence of social justice which ultimately forced to be attracted towards Buddhism. In appendix Dr. Mishra also provides a datewise chronology of events of Dr. Ambedkar's life.

The learned Professor Ramashray Roy in his article 'Political Thinking of Dr. B.R. Ambedkar' emphasizes that the significance of political thinking of Dr. B.R. Ambedkar does not rest so much on its distinctive perspective on man and his world as it on its emancipatory power that focused on a group of people in India who exemplified "the wretched of the earth". These people are the untouchables of Panchamas, Harijans, Dalits. These epithets apply to those who condemned for ages, to the most demeaning bottom of Hindu social order, shorn of worldly possessions, and oppressed by obnoxious ritual abasement inspired by considerations of purity and pollution, have endured indignities, humiliations and insulting discrimination. Ambedkar's political thinking has proved for these people a *mantra* of great potency in emancipating them from their abject existential condition; it has seemed as a greatly efficacious political weapon for them to beat their tormentors with and win for them a foothold in the social universe. This, in turn, can serve as a springboard to gain self-determination, dignity, and self respect.

Prof. Roy further says that it should be added that political thinking of Ambedkar is by no means a philosophical cogitation of an arm-chair philosopher; it is the outcome of a close interaction between thought and action that took place over a long conflict-ridden life of a political activist. As such, Ambedkar's thinking is a guide to experience as well as chiselled by experience. Tempered in the fire of political struggle, his thinking forged a political weapon which helped him to emerge as a leader of Dalits transcending the role of the Messiah of Mahars. As a consequence, his movement that helped Mahars to emancipate themselves unfolded later to embrace the Dalits at large. It is his thinking that constitutes the impulse of inspiration for the Dalit movement even today.

Prof. M.P. Singh in his article "Political Thought of B.R. Ambedkar: The Constitutional Structure of State in India" first points out about two models of political mobilization and participation of Hindu society variously called the *panchmang*, i.e. the fifth class beyond the four *varnas*. He further states that if the Harijan identity formation and Jagjivan Ram in Congress politics in the mid-1930s represented the first model, Bahujan-Dalit identity formation and Bhimrao Ramji Ambedkar since the late 1920s represented the second model.

Ambedkar entered in the Constituent Assembly as the leader of the All India Scheduled Castes Federation, a party founded by himself in 1930. While participating in the debate in the constituent assembly, Dr. Ambedkar said "Draft Constitution is recommending the parliamentary system or has preferred more responsibility to more stability". His role in various preparatory committees and piloting the Draft

Constitution in Constituent Assembly have been examined in brief.

Prof. Singh feels that the problems of the scheduled castes were always uppermost in the thought and action of Ambedkar, especially prior to his deep involvement in the making of the Constitution of India. While concluding Prof. Singh says that Ambedkar's political thought may well be the gateway to the constitutional architecture of the State of India. He further says those who have surveyed the entire spectrum of his social and political thought would probably find it difficult to determine whether he can be said to be primarily a theorist of the Hindu social structure with special reference to the formerly untouchable castes and their emancipation or primarily a comparative political theorist of constitutional engineering and constitutional government. To Prof. Singh he was, on the balance, a statist in both the social and political domains.

Prof. J. Guha Roy's article "Dr. Ambedkar's Contribution in the Framing of India's Constitution" analyses the role played by Dr. Ambedkar in framing the Constitution of independent India. According to Prof. Guha Roy, Dr. Ambedkar held a unique place among the builders of modern India. His most notable contribution could be traced to the framing of independent India's Constitution which laid the foundation of resurgent modern India.

Prof. Guha Roy is of the view that although the Constituent Assembly was adorned with a galaxy of jurists, scholars, statesmen, social activists and political leaders, yet it had the privilege to have Ambedkar as one of its members who played a leading and historic role in the framing of India's Constitution. He entered this august body like a belligerent 'protestant', but was soon destined to hold a key position—the Chairman of the Drafting Committee. Prof. Guha Roy further points out that Ambedkar's unique idea of social justice, his dynamic political thought, his liberal views on constitutionalism, his progressive concepts of rights of the people, his vision of an ideal society, and above all, his concern for the welfare and development of the poor, little Indians, the dumb millions, or the Dalits, were not only echoed during his illustrious deliberations in the Constituent Assembly but also reflected in each and every part of the Constitution of India.

In his article entitled "Ambedkar on Economic Development: Visioning and Reasoning" Prof. P.K. Chaubey highlights the Economic Thought of Dr. Ambedkar. He classifies the economic contributions of Dr. Ambedkar in three broad areas: (i) monetary system and monetary policy, the role they are supposed to play in furthering welfare of people, (ii) fiscal federalism, the manner in which revenue be collected from the social economy, as Ambedkar calls it, for fiscal operations and the manner and principles on which should base the relationship between provincial government and the central government so that a kind of coordinated relationship is established, and (iii) economic transformation of the Indian economy from its exclusively agrarian character to substantially industrial one in order to create productive employment to idling masses on the one hand to raise productivity of agriculture on the other, and ultimately to end crushing poverty.

However, Prof. Chaubey confines himself to the third proposition in his present paper primarily persuing the work of Ambedkar published full ninety years ago in 1918, basically because this aspect in his opinion has been most neglected one. It is here that Ambedkar says industrialization of India is the soundest remedy for the agricultural problems of India. Prof. Chaubey in his concluding observation says that though Ambedkar continued working in economics and economics of India, it seems, till 1925 he did not pursue the theme of industrialization. It is possible he had occasions to depose before committees and commissions on the issues. But after he became Labour Member of Viceroy's Council in 1942, he again picked up the thread and developed it further till the making of Constitution. In the numerous meetings of the Ministries and reconstruction committees, he did not forget to point out water for industrial use and power for industries. In equally numerous addresses in different forums and writings in the form of monographs, he made it clear that industrialization is a means to improve the lot of the poor and to do that active state intervention is the need of the hour.

Prof. Jai Narayan Sharma's article "Economic Ideas of Dr. Ambedkar" analyses the various economic ideas of Dr. Ambedkar expressed at various occasions in the Constituent Assembly and earlier as a serious student of economics. He is of the view that an important aspect of Dr. Ambedkar's versatile personality does not, however, seem to have attracted enough attention especially in the light of his achievements in the field of social justice and drafting of the Constitution that he was an eminent economist. However, it would be grossly unfair to relegate his economic ideas to a secondary status.

His economic ideas should be seen in the context that nearly one-third population of the country, if not more, still live below the poverty line and substantial number of people are landless and the state must, therefore, continue to play dominant role to bring in economic equality. Dr. Ambedkar's economic thought stood for the progressive transformation of society, removing glaring social and economic equalities.

Prof. Sharma is of the opinion that Dr. Ambedkar extensively contributed to various economic issues covering concrete economic problems. Further, what is creditable is that though most of his economic writings related to the pre-independence period, they reflect not only unique freshness but also his deep insights into the problems. He approached and examined the economic issues with such foresight that his analysis and treatment of some of them is very much relevant even today.

India had a hoary tradition of economic studies in ancient times as classics will attest Dr. Ruchi Tyagi in her article 'Ambedkar's Contributions to the Study of Indian Economy' highlights that Ambedkar was among the first set of Indians who were trained in economics systematically and practiced it professionally.

She stresses that Ambedkar belonged to the group that received education abroad under some of the most eminent economists of the time. His contribution as an economist has by and large remained unnoticed. Various memoranda and statements that he submitted to the government (under the British rule as well as in the independent India) are indicative of his deep insights into India's economic problems. He was probably the first thinker to analyse economic dimensions of social maladies in India.

Finally, she concludes that as a strategy of economic development of India, Ambedkar emphasized the eradication of poverty, elimination of inequalities and ending exploitation of masses, weaker sections and *dalits* in particular. He preferred industrialization for absorbing surplus agricultural labour and land reforms to increase agricultural production. He considered agriculture as industry, and gold standard for maintaining stability of the value of Indian currency, smooth centre-state relations for coordinated economic development and state intervention for an orderly growth of the Nation. Thus, Ambedkar's economics is a vivid combination of *dalit* emancipation, socialism and nationalism.

In her article "Dr. B.R. Ambedkar and the Vision of Social Justice", Prof. Sushma Yadav first discusses about social equalities in Indian society existed since time immemorial. She rightly mentions that Indian society has been caste ridden. In the past, there existed no such area of social existence and governance where caste as political, social, economic, educational and cultural factor was not present. Even today, after more than five decades of introduction of Republican Constitution, the caste factor is dominant in every sphere of life of the people of this country.

As Prof. Yadav suggests one of the key themes of writings of Dr. B.R. Ambedkar was the attainment of Social Justice and establishment of a just society, which for him, was essentially also a casteless society. He not only provided a ruthless criticism of the existing social order but also came up with an alternative vision and alternative model of social order based on justice, liberty, equality, fraternity and annihilation of caste. Prof. Sushma Yadav feels that Ambedkar was convinced that a good social order or society has to go through two tests, namely 'the test of justice' and the 'test of utility'. His judgemental analysis of the caste based Hindu social order was based on these two tests.

Prof. Yadav concludes that Ambedkar's conception of political power was aimed at securing social justice for the deprived on more equitable and honourable terms. But for him, political justice was not enough for the welfare and well-being of the untouchables. He considered socio-economic justice as the pre-condition for redeeming political justice. Moreover, his vision of social justice involves a normative element also inasmuch as its aims at the desirability of goodness in social life, dignity of individual, equal rights of man and woman, promotion of social progress and better standards of life with peace and security in all spheres of human life.

Dr. Ashok Kumar Singh in his article "Dr. Ambedkar on Annihilation of Caste" emphasizes the views of Dr. Ambedkar on caste system. Dr. Singh starts with the message of Dr. Ambedkar which he sent to Gandhiji for the first issue of his journal, *Harijan* and quotes Ambedkar "the outcaste is a byproduct of the caste system. There will be outcaste as long as there are castes. Nothing can help emancipate the outcaste except the destruction of caste system. Nothing can help to save Hindus and ensure their survival in the coming struggle except the purging of the Hindu faith of this odious and vicious dogma" (February 7, 1933).

Dr. Singh further points out that Dr. Ambedkar never compromised either with Hindu social order or with the Hindu philosophers and social reformers who attempted to seek reasons and justifications for the iniquitous and inhuman social order: *varnashram*. He again quotes Dr. Ambedkar "to me the *chaturvarna* with its old labels is utterly repellent and my whole being rebels against it". It is this vision against the unjust system that placed him as the foremost among the pioneers and social reformers in India. No author, scholar or reformer has written so many volumes on the subject of caste and untouchability as did Ambedkar.

Prof. Suresh Misra in his article "Making of Panchayati Raj Institutions and Dr. Ambedkar" points out that the Chairman of the Drafting Committee of our Constitution,

Ambedkar was very much opposed to provide a place to village Panchayats and did not provide a place to it in the draft of the Constitution. In the draft of the Constituent Assembly, Dr. Ambedkar said, "I am therefore surprised that those who condemn provincialism and communalism should come forward as champions of the village. What is the village but a stink of localism and a den of ignorance, narrow-mindedness and communalism?" He further said, "I am glad that the draft Constitution has discarded the village and adopted the individual as the unit".

Prof. Mishra believes that Dr. Ambedkar was opposed to any role for the village Panchayat in the new set-up because he saw them as institutions of oppression and inequality. While concluding he says that we have to evaluate Dr. Ambedkar's contribution to Indian polity and society in terms of his desire to give a place of dignity and self-respect to the downtrodden in this country. He was a product of unjust and inequal social system which was hierarchical and discriminatory. His opposition to the village and the village Panchayats has to be seen in this backdrop.

Dr. A.N. Panda in his article "Ambedkar: A Champion of Human Rights" points out that the name of B.R. Ambedkar will be recorded in the history of modern India as a champion of the rights of backward people of the country. Dr. Panda further says that Ambedkar felt that the downtrodden people had no right as ordinary human beings and state and religion were against their interests as these were controlled by the higher caste people. Dr. Ambedkar wanted to bring reformation in both these institutions. His commitment for the protection of human rights can be known from his perception of state and religion. He regarded political power as a means for achieving the end of annihilation of the caste system and monopoly of the upper castes. His conversion to Buddhism may be viewed as a reaction to the prevailing situation in Hinduism and the Indian society.

The theme of Dr. Bindeshwar Pathak's article is "Relevance of Dr. Ambedkar in Present Day Context". Dr. Pathak is of the view that all his life Dr. Ambedkar, the architect of India's Constitution and messiah of the downtrodden, fought against caste-based discrimination and inequalities which were responsible for step-motherly treatment and suffering of more than three-fourths of country's population for over 2,000 years.

Untouchability and discrimination based on caste system exists even today in spite of sixty years of introduction of our Republican Constitution and here lies the relevance of Ambedkar in present day context. Dr. Pathak concludes his article with one of the most famous statements of Ambedkar that "Many Hindus regard me as their enemy. But I have personal friends amongst even the Brahmin community. Situated as I am, it has fallen to my lot to lash the anti-social actions of the Brahmins who treat my people worse than dogs and impede their progress. I hate injustice, pompousness and humbug and my hatred embraces all those who are guilty of them. I want to tell my critics that I regard my feelings of hatred as a real force. They are the reflex of the love I bear for the causes I believe in and I am in no way ashamed of them."

Dr. Ambedkar was a great humanist and advocated the principles of human rights. Today we see that the whole world is fighting the cause of human rights and wherever there is violation of human rights the UN agencies come to the help. But it is sad to note that some political parties in our country to serve their own interests play Dr. Ambedkar's card and try to belittle the personality of that great man. However, they cannot affect the relevance of Dr. Ambedkar in building a strong and humanist India.

2

The Man and the Life

ANIL DUTTA MISHRA

Introduction

The story of **Dr. Babasaheb Bhimrao Ramji Ambedkar** is the story of a person who not only changed his own destiny but the destiny of millions and millions of powerless, downtrodden, voiceless, poor and deprived people of India. A true socialist and democrat, Dr. Ambedkar, sought to establish social democracy instead of political which could satisfy the economic, social, educational and cultural needs of the people. Dr. Ambedkar was a born revolutionary as he fought against the unjust social system since his very childhood till the end of his life. In fact, he was one of those who helped to accelerate the process of social change in the pre- and post-independent India through nonviolent means. Dr. Ambedkar rose himself from the lowest rung of the society to an enviable position in Indian political arena by his incredible diligence and noble self-denial. Shakespeare said that there is a tide in the affairs of men, which taken at the flood, leads to fortune. This is true in the case of Dr. Ambedkar.

Dr. Ambedkar was multifaceted genius, who changed the course of history by thought and deeds. He was a distinguished economist, a learned professor, a brilliant lawyer, a reputed author, a nationalist, a reformer and a great political leader, but above all he left the mark as to how one could attain the height of glory through self-help, dignity, introspection, self-respect and self-esteem. Acting on these principles gradually he rose to a leader of eminence in India, and exhorted untouchables to follow his principles for removing untouchability from India and bring the untouchables in the mainstream of the society. He had played the part of destiny in the liberation of suppressed and oppressed humanity in India.

PART-I

Childhood and Early Education

Born on 14th April,1891, at Mhow in Madhya Pradesh, Bhimrao Ramji was the fourteenth child of his parents of the Mahar Hindu community. His father, Shri Ramji Maloji Sakpal, was a Subedar Major in the army. Shri Ramji Maloji Sakpal was a Kabirpanthi. He was a vegetarian and teetotaller. Kabir was a radical saint of India who was against religious dogmas and belonged to *Bhakti* school of thought, found consolation in the human attributes like compassion, benevolence and resignation to God. His *dohas* are radical and famous among Indian masses. Bhim's mother, Smt. Bhimabai, hailed from a rich family from the village of Murbad in the Thana District of Bombay State. Fair by complexion, she had a broad forehead, curly hair, round glowing eyes and a short nose. Bhim was hardly six years old when his mother Bhima Bai expired.

His early education was at Satara and Bombay. The name given to Ambedkar, who was the last child of his parents at birth was Bhim Rao Ramji Ambavadekar. Bhim from his mother's name Bhima Bai and Ramji from his father's name Ramji Maloji Sakpal. He took his surname 'Ambavadekar' from his native village. A Brahmin teacher at the high school in Satara who was fond of his young pupil changed his name to Ambedkar in the school records and it stuck. In November 1904, when Ambedkar was in class V, he had to leave the school at Satara because the family moved to Bombay and settled down there. Next year in 1905, he at the age of 14, was married to Rami (renamed Ramabai) when Ambedkar was only in fifth standard. At the time of marriage she was 9 years old. She was a sober and good girl. In the year 1908 he passed matriculation from the Elphinstone High School, Bombay and graduated from Elphinstone College, Bombay in 1912.

Ambedkar joined the Baroda State forces as a Lieutenant. He hardly served for 15 days, when he had to return to Bombay in January1913, owing to his father's illness, and he did not go back to Baroda to rejoin the service, as on 2nd February, 1913, his father Ramji Sakpal died. So serious was the outburst of Bhimrao's sorrow that words of consolation failed to soothe his heart and loud lamentations drowned the wails of the members of his family. With the passing of parents the child became orphan and whole responsibility of family fell on Ambedkar's shoulder. Even the destiny was taking examination after examination and testing his courage and patience. The difficulties were making him more courageous and preparing him for future to lead in every aspects of life. His childhood was full of challenges. He overcame all challenges and tides in the life one by one.

Higher Education

In 1913, Ambedkar was awarded a Baroda State Scholarship. He proceeded to the United States of America and joined Columbia University, New York, where two years later he took his M.A. in Economics with a dissertation on 'Ancient Indian Commerce'. He obtained a doctorate from the same University.

In 1916, Ambedkar had moved to prestigious London School of Economics where he prepared for the Bar. A year later, however, he had to discontinue his studies in London due to financial problems. He returned back to India and briefly taught at Sydenham College of Commerce, Bombay, as Lecturer in Political Economy. In 1920, he resumed his studies in London and obtained M.Sc. in 1921 and D.Sc. in 1923. His D.Sc. thesis 'The Problem of the Rupee' was published later on.

Beginning of Public Life

He returned back India after finishing his education in June 1924 and started legal practice at the Bombay High Court. This was the beginning of an active public career where he served as social worker, politician, writer, educationist, reformer and philanthropist. In 1924, he founded *'Bahishkrit Hitkarini Sabha'* (Association for the Welfare of the Depressed Classes) in Bombay for the moral and material progress of untouchables.

In the year 1927, he started a Marathi fortnightly, *Bahishkrit Bharat* and in December 1930, the *Janata,* a weekly. In the same year Dr. Ambedkar founded Samaj Samata Sangh through which he spread social equality among untouchables and caste Hindus. Inter-caste marriages and inter-caste meals were an integral part of Samaj Samata Sangh. The Sangh's organ, the Samata was started in March 1929.

In December 1927, Dr. Ambedkar led a *satyagraha* to ensure the civic right of untouchables to draw water from a public tank "Chavdar Talen" at Mahad, in Kolaba district. Again in 1930, he led another *satyagraha* to establish untouchables' right to enter the famous temple of Kalaram at Nasik.

Besides his leadership of the Depressed Classes, Dr. Ambedkar's eminence as a lawyer began to be widely recognized. In 1928, he was appointed Professor at Government Law College, Bombay and later on became the Principal. In 1935, he was offered the coveted Perry Professorship of Jurisprudence. He was a nominated member of the Bombay Legislative Council (1926-34). This vantage position enabled him to sponsor several bills for the welfare of his community, of which he now emerged as the principal spokesman. He was an official nominee to the three Round Table Conferences (1930-33) and continued to serve on some of their committees till 1934. His appointment, it has been said, marked a milestone in the socio-political struggle of his community.

The British Government's Communal Award, announced on 17th August, 1932, conceded separate electorate for the untouchables. Gandhi went on fast unto death on 20th September, 1932 and on 24th September, 1932 the 'Poona Pact' was made in the Yervada Jail which provided for reservation of seats for the untouchables in the general constituencies. Gandhi believed that the untouchables are an integral part of the Hindu society and called them *Harijans.* Ambedkar was happy with the 'Poona Pact'. He set up an Independent Labour Party in 1936 which captured all the Scheduled Caste seats in Bombay Presidency in the 1936-37 general elections. In April 1942, Dr. Ambedkar organized the All-India Scheduled Caste Federation as a political party. In July 1945, to promote the integrity of his community, he established the People's Education Society. This society was instrumental in starting a number of colleges for scheduled caste students in Bombay Presidency.

From July 1942 to March 1946, Ambedkar served on the Governor General's Executive Council as Labour Member and brought about several changes in the working of the department. The Indian National Congress nominated him to the Constituent Assembly in deliberations of which he was to play a prominent role. His thorough knowledge and understanding of constitutional law marked him out as one of the chief architects of Indian Constitution. In the independent India, he became the Law Minister in Nehru's Cabinet. He was also the Chairman of the Constituent Assembly's Drafting Committee. He resigned from the Cabinet in September 1951. Later, in 1952 and 1953, he lost two successive elections to Parliament.

Dr. Ambedkar who got married at the age of 14 in 1905, lost his wife in 1935. In 1948 at the age of 57 he married for the second time. He was married to Dr. Savita Saraswat, a Brahmin lady. Tall, dark and human from within, all through his life, he had been spurred by difficulties, but never bent and never yielded to pressure. He proved in his career that a man's worth did not depend on riches, high birth and good connections. He was a great patriot who fought for the cause of the downtrodden without sacrificing the wider interests of the nation.

Spiritual Journey

In October 1935, Dr. Ambedkar announced for the first time that his followers would have no faith in Hindu religion altogether for, within it, they would never win social equality.

During 1938-40, he turned to Sikhism, but his efforts to gain a special place for his community within the Sikh fold proved unsuccessful. On 14 October, 1956, Ambedkar embraced Buddhism at a well-attended ceremony at Nagpur, Maharashtra, and advised his followers to accept the new faith and himself gave *deeksha* to hundreds of thousands. In November 1956, he attended the forth Conference of the World Fellowship of Buddhists at Kathmandu, Nepal. This was his last public appearance. He breathed his last in sleep in Delhi. Mrs. Savita Ambedkar at 6.30 a.m. on December 6, 1956, found that Dr. Ambedkar was no more. Thus passed away one of the greatest heroes of the downtrodden people of India. On 7th December, 1956, his mortal remains were cremated on the Dadar sea-shore in Bombay.

PART-II

Dr. Ambedkar was an icon in the past, remains an icon today and will remain an icon for the future generation. What is more remarkable is the fact that his following has not diminished with his demise, rather his influence and acceptability has been increasingly growing with passage of time only because he is one person whose action has been louder than his words. He was an institution and legend in his time. Through his thought, word and deed he has done what he wanted to achieve. Dr. Ambedkar's three word formula—*"educate, agitate and organize"* is a powerful tool of social change even today. According to Ambedkar illiteracy and ignorance is the greatest hurdle in development of humanity. Placing any *dalit* leader at par with Dr. Ambedkar is basically a political gimmick and disrespect to him. Dr. Ambedkar was not a leader of a particular community rather a leader of voiceless and powerless people of India.

The life and work of Dr. Ambedkar, marks one of the most turbulent careers of Indian politics. He was a man of extraordinary qualities. His public career which, for all practical purposes, started in the year 1930, continued with unabated vigour and reached its culmination with the adoption of the

Constitution of free India in the year 1950. Dr. Ambedkar, with his dedication and intelligence, influenced Indian politics and has left his indelible imprint on every aspect of our national life and society as a whole. His pragmatic approach to political, social and economic problems enabled him to become the undisputed leader of not only Scheduled Castes and other backward communities but also the poor, downtrodden people of India as a whole. He was a true democrat. He believed in democratic means. His approach to change the social system was through nonviolent constitutional means.

Since his early childhood he had seen exploitation. As such he was opposed to exploitation of all kinds. He criticized economic exploitation, concentration of wealth and the poverty of the people. According to him, caste itself is an institution for exploitation and domination. It is meant to exploit the weaker sections of the community by the economically and socially dominant classes. His effort was to provide social justice and remove alienation from Indian society. He was a reformer par excellence.

Academic Contribution

Dr. Ambedkar was one of the few politicians who excelled in Academic field. He was a great scholar of economics. He was one of the parliamentarians at that time who could give authoritative statistical information and elucidated explanation on matters relating to India's finance and banking. He studied public finance under Prof. Edwin Seligman and obtained his Ph.D. from the Columbia University for his thesis "National Dividend of India: A Historical and Analytical Study". At the London School of Economics, he prepared the thesis "Provincial Decentralisation of Imperial Finance in India" for which he got the Master of Science Degree. Thus, he got his D.Sc. from the London University for his *magnumopus*, "The Problem of the Rupee". During his stay abroad, Dr. Ambedkar came into close contact with many leading authorities like Prof. Harold J. Laski, Prof. Edwin Cannan, Lord Climent, Richard Attlee and many others. His natural intelligence and acquired knowledge made him a great authority on current economic and political issues of India. He advocated rapid industrialization for economic growth. Along with industrialization he explained that agriculture should not be neglected. He proposed radical measures for the re-organisation of the agricultural sector. Dr. Ambedkar had the farsight to point out that caste is an economic proposition, and, to remove caste system the whole economic structure of the Indian villages should be reorganized. He dedicated his whole life for the eradication of untouchability. In his crusade against untouchability, the most important landmarks were the Mahad Satyagraha of 1927 and Temple Entry Movement of 1930 in Nasik. The epic struggle at Mahad, in March 1927, made him an undisputed All-India leader of depressed class and a national hero. He was one of the first leader to realize that the panacea for all social ills is the spread of education and economic development. The root cause of all evils is ignorance, so he took the first step towards removing illiteracy and ignorance. He founded People's Education Society in 1945. This society established a number of educational institutions in different parts of Maharashtra.

Book Lover

Dr. Ambedkar was a voracious reader. He studied a good deal of literature of so many countries. To Ambedkar love of books was the greatest means of education and self-development and the highest type of recreation and enjoyment. He never read for amusement. "What instruct me", he observed "amuse me". He would read a book on any subject, be it history, economics, law, sociology, literature, philosophy or anthropology. The educational institutions which have been established at Bombay, Aurangabad and other places are the testimony to his great love of learning. He left behind in his house a private collection of books larger than many public libraries. He knew seven languages, and was equally proficient in each one of them. He wrote number of books. Some of his outstanding books are—*Who were the Sudras; Castes in India; Thoughts on Pakistan; Ranade, Gandhi and Jinnah;* and *The Untouchables.*

Dr. Ambedkar was a nationalist, a democrat and a patriot par excellence. He was a great statesman with extraordinarily forthright and was outspoken in his view. His courage of conviction was something astounding, and throughout his life he never compromised his principles even for the sake of his people and motherland. He sought to liberate Indian politics from the crippling effects of parochialism, traditionalism and theology. Being the Chairman of the Drafting Committee of the Constituent Assembly, he hammered out a comprehensive and a workable constitution into which he incorporated some of his views, though not all of them.

Harijans would certainly remember him as their saviour. But Indian nationals cannot but admire his legal acumen, sociological insight, and vast constitutional knowledge. He was a rare combination of these abilities.

Constitutionalist

Gandhi recommended the name of Dr. Ambedkar as Chairman of Drafting Committee. Dr. Ambedkar entered the Constituent Assembly with the only hope of safeguarding the rights of downtrodden. But he was called to play a much wider role. Ambedkar explained this in the following words:

> I came into the Constituent Assembly with no greater aspiration than to safeguard the interests of Scheduled Castes. I had not the remotest idea that I would be called upon to undertake most responsible function. I was, therefore, surprised when the Assembly elected me to the Drafting Committee. I was more than surprised when the Drafting Committee elected me to be its Chairman.

It was Gandhiji who is said to have suggested the name of Dr. Ambedkar for the Drafting Committee. It so happened that Jawaharlal Nehru and Smt. Sarojini Naidu went to Gandhiji to tell him that they are not finding a capable person to prepare the Draft Constitution for India, and they were thinking of inviting a Constitutional expert like Ivor Jennings, who has drafted Constitutions of various countries. On hearing this, Gandhiji instantly suggested the name of Dr. Ambedkar and relieved Nehru from a great worry. It was again Gandhiji who is said to have prevailed upon Nehru to have Dr. Ambedkar in his cabinet. Nehru had frankly told Gandhiji that he would not have Dr. Ambedkar in his cabinet, because he was a blockade in the Freedom struggle. Gandhiji told Nehru that freedom has come to India and not to Nehru and, therefore, Dr. Ambedkar's talent and capability should be utilised for building up modern India. Nehru was, thus, left with no alternative except inducting Dr. Ambedkar as Law Minister.

Dr. Ambedkar will go down in history as one of the greatest Constitutionalists of India. He did a splendid work in piloting the Constitution in the Constituent Assembly. His sharp and trenchant replies to critics, his sound arguments and his perseverance made the passage of the Constitution possible in a comparatively short time. As a man of thought and action, he influenced, immensely, India's political and constitutional development. His outlook on life was essentially practical and realistic. Had he devoted more time to more fundamental issues of politics and society, he would have certainly eclipsed many social and political thinkers of the world. Dr. Ambedkar's loyalty to India was great as his hatred for the traditional values of the orthodox Hindu society. Orthodox values never allow the society to progress. Dr. Ambedkar rightly said in the Constituent Assembly "we must be determined to defend our independence till the last drop of our blood". It will be relevant to note the concluding statement which he made in the Constituent Assembly adopting Free India's Constitution—**"our work is over; but the sun rise tomorrow—New India gets political freedom and liberty; but social liberty and economic liberty are yet to come !".**

Summing Up

After four decades of his death the Government of India recognized his contribution and conferred its highest award 'Bharat Ratna' on him, on 14 April, 1990, as a mark of recognition of his services to the country. In fact by conferring the award to Dr. Ambedkar, the award's prestige was enhanced, not the prestige of Dr. Ambedkar.

The Government of India had done lot to study Gandhi and Nehru and spread their work and deeds. But same is not in the case of Dr. Ambedkar. Even in the universities few researches had been done. Even in the syllabus, proper justice has not been done in the case of Dr. Ambedkar. Even his so called followers have not properly understood the life and the mission of Dr. Ambedkar properly. Dr. Ambedkar's life, thought and action must be understood in context and content. There is a need to study this great man with open mind above ideology and free from any bias. In the era of globalization and economic depression, his words—***'educate, unite and struggle'*** is still relevant. Bharat Ratna Ambedkar wrote his name on the future of this great country and in the history of human freedom and became an icon for present and future generations not only of the downtrodden but of the poor, voiceless and powerless Indians. There is a need to establish *dalit* friendly administration at all levels and to adopt *dalit* friendly policy in and outside government.

One can conclude by quoting P.S. Krishnan: the most fitting tribute to Dr. B.R. Ambedkar's memory will be to follow his teachings and action without any further delay, break the walls of the prison, that the Indian society still remains for the *dalit*, downtrodden, poor and powerless people. The choice for the Indian State, leaders of political parties including industrial houses is between honest time bound completion of the liberation initiated and indicated by Dr. Ambedkar or push the desperate masses of *dalit*, downtrodden, poor and powerless people towards the rapidly expanding cult of violence and thereby hamper the progress and growth of India to its full potential. We have to empower—politically, economically and socially and bring these sections of the people in the mainstream. We can ignore Dr. Ambedkar's works, deeds, thought and path shown by him at the nation's peril. We must learn the lesson from Dr. Ambedkar that he never deceived any people. His motto was success is yours and failure is mine. Think differently. Find purpose. The means will follow. In fact Dr. Ambedkar stood for a human spirit that refuses to be crushed by the 'Leviathan' of modern state and age old oppression, exploitation and suffering. Dr. Ambedkar aspired for a better, more equitable and just society, which is still a dream and is yet to be achieved even after six decades of independence. Whether we accept or not, but the fact remains that Dr. Ambedkar's spoken words, writings, and work done by him will resonate for centuries to come.

3

Political Thinking of Dr. B.R. Ambedkar

RAMASHRAY ROY

The significance of political thinking of B.R. Ambedkar does not rest so much on its distinctive perspective on man and his world as it on its emancipatory power that focused on a group of people in India who exemplified "the wretched of the earth". These people are the untouchables of *Panchamas*, Harijan, Dalits. These epithets apply to those who, condemned for ages, to the most demeaning bottom of Hindu social order, shorn of worldly possessions, and oppressed by obnoxious ritual abasement inspired by considerations of purity and pollution, have endured indignities, humiliations and insulting discrimination. Ambedkar's political thinking has proved for these people a *mantra* of great potency in emancipating them from their abject existential condition; it has served as a greatly efficacious political weapon for them to beat their tormentors with and win for them a foothold in the social universe. This, in turn, can serve as a springboard to gain self-determination, dignity, and self-respect.

It should also be added that political thinking of Ambedkar is by no means a philosophical cogitation of an armchair philosopher; it is the outcome of a close interaction between thought and action that took place over a long conflict-ridden life of a political activist. As such, Ambedkar's thinking is a guide to experience as well as chiselled by experience. Tempered in the fire of political struggle, his thinking forged a political weapon which helped him to emerge as a leader of *dalits* transcending the role of the Messiah of Mahars. As a consequence, his movement that helped Mahars to emancipate themselves unfolded later to embrace the *dalits* at large. It is his thinking that constitutes the impulse of inspiration for the *dalit* movement even today.

Given the significance of Ambedkar's political thinking, we need to ask two questions: One, what constitutes the core of his political thinking and, two, what are the referent points that provide substance to his political ideas. It must be emphasized that for apprehending the essential features of a notable political thinker or leader, it is necessary to locate his ideas in a space defined by the interaction of three major forces acting on him and influencing his thought-ways and work-ways. The thinker receives as a legacy a body of ideas that have appeared from time to time to stir up human imagination and action, ideas that have become an integral part of our intellectual heritage. Apart from this, the thinker/activist lives in a particular age with features that distinguishes it from other ages and is characterized by distinct structural and other properties, both seen and unseen. It is the particular time period with its own specific characteristics that the thinker/activist lives in that moulds, to a considerable extent, what he thinks about problems he confronts that what he does or suggests to do to cope with the encountered problems. What makes these two referent points significant for the thinker/activist is his own life experiences, experiences that he acquires by virtue of simply trying to make a sense of his own existential condition and seeking to give a meaning to his own existence by the kind of interaction he has to go through in life. It is his life experience that impels him to articulate his ideas and determine his action choices for himself and others who he thinks to be similarly situated.

Concerning the intellectual heritage, a thinker/activist confronts a large body of ideas that have occupied men's minds in different times and climes. He is not obliged to accept them all; what he does is to pick and choose. In this, he is guided by what can be called pre-selectivity meaning the standards located in his own psyche. This is true of Ambedkar also. What was immediately germane for his was the ascendance of liberal world view with which he came to be intimately acquainted during his residence in the West. In India, too, the climate of opinion had subtly changed to make the liberal view of man and his world much more palatable. This was facilitated by a process of inversion that the British presence in India contrived. The arrival in India of William Bentinck as Governor-General in 1828. As C.H. Philips reports, Bentinck had assured James Mill before his departure for India that "... I am going to British India but I shall not be Governor-General. It is you that will be Governor-General".[1] Despite his strong preference for reform and with little sympathy for Indian culture and institutions, Bentinck went slowly in the beginning. However, the momentum of change gathered speed when Thomas Macaulay joined him in 1835 as a new Law Member. In the beginning Bentinck:

> though a reformer, was running along with accepted lines of governance. A reforming Mughal, we might say but still a Mughal. It was his other measures which may fairly be said to have introduced the West to the East and to have set in motion that process which has produced the India of today.[2]

The process of inversions initiated by what William Jones calls "the wand of empire"[3] was to completely transform the orientation and attitude of at least the intellectuals belonging to the upper strata of Indian society. This is reflected in their outlook towards their own society and their evaluation of its cultural and institutional characteristics. More than this, these inversions went to a long way in propelling an organic society that India's happened to be for ages towards becoming an atomistic society. It is this movement that has constituted a great dividing line between traditional and modern India. It is also this movement that lends such a significance to different inversions wrought by the British presence in India of almost two centuries. Three of these inversions are relevant for this discussion. These inversions involve release of the individual from the constraining grip of the social group and attainment by him the primacy over society, ascendance of the material dimension of the individual's existence over against the spiritual, and the emergence of politics as the arbiter of the pattern of living as against the social order.

It is not necessary to go into any detail of how these inversions were wrought.[4] However, it is beyond any doubt that it is a consequence of these inversions that some far-reaching changes, including the ascendance of the untouchables, who happened to be the lowest of the low, as a distinct and politically powerful socio-economic interest, pervaded the traditional Indian society. With the loosening of the grip of the old, organic social order, the material concerns of the individual came to occupy the centre-stage of man's existence, and the individual emerges as the self-defining subject who derives his wants and needs from his own nature. As a result, society beats retreat from its position as an authoritative entity that prescribed what man ought to do and how should go about it. Once material concerns assume centrality, competition for access to and control over societal resources assumes a virulent form inviting politics (or the state) to resolve emergent conflicts. As such, the state comes to play a crucial role in maintaining social peace and cooperation and restore it when it has been disturbed.

The perspectival change pointed out earlier constitutes the primary influence which impacted heavily on Ambedkar's thinking about man and his world. This influence represents nothing else than the liberal world-view which places the autonomous individual at the centre of the social universe and is committed to the preservation of individual dignity, self-respect and self-determination. But the individual cannot by himself subsist in a socio-economic condition where economic inequality verging not infrequently on deprivation and destitution for many; deprivation and destitution also imply, exploitation and oppression. Even social cooperation in such a situation can and often does imply exploitation and growing economic distress for those who happen to stand on the lowest rungs of economic hierarchy. It is this situation that leads to the formation of groups informed by the perception of the environment from the same vantage point. This paves the way for political conflicts involving groups that claim to have equitable share in societal resources. It is this phenomenon that links individual well-being with the well-being of larger groups he belongs to by virtue of his birth or his socio-economic condition or his political inclinations and commitments.

Since Ambedkar came from the lowest stratum of the Hindu social order, and had himself to undergo the humiliation, the slights, and the indignition that happened to be the fate of the untouchables in India, he was well aware of the fate of others similarly placed in the social space, being meted out the same, and often even worse treatment from the heads of men from the privileged upper castes. Once the awareness of the degrading socio-economic condition pervades the collective consciousness of a particular group, or leader emerges to perform a dual role of giving a voice to its grievances and of organizing the group politically for action. In so far as the former is concerned, it includes both a reformulation of the actual position and status of the group involved in terms of a historical myth taken as a fact. This reformulation provides the basis of providing the shelter of a commonality under which the diverse elements in the group can define their identity. The leader then can formulate action plans with a view to attaining a socio-economic position commensurate with the "mystified" image of the group. The refurbished image of the group concerned is fashioned after ransacking the store-house of history, of the past, for envisaging a preferred future; this is basically a political act even though such a ransacking yields only "imagined" materials as ingredients for the construction of a new identity. Such a ransacking, it must be emphasized, is intended not only for emotional boarding of the group, but also for laying claims for access to scarce social resources that happen to be unequally distributed.

It is against this background that we can appreciate why Jyotiba Phule should hold that the aboriginals like the Gonds and the Bhils happened to be the masters (rulers) of the land of India. And when the Iranians (Aryans) came to India the Brahmins "desecreted sacrifices here, robbed and opposed the original inhabitants and stigmatized them as *dasyus*."[5] He also contends that *shastras* were compiled by the Brahmins with a view to retaining their hegemony. Thus, for Phule, the subjugation nation of the original inhabitants was originally a political act, an act that led to the subjugation nation of the former masters of India and pushing them down to the position of primitives. The development and observation of rituals were aimed at consolidating and perpetuating the lowly place of the former masters of India. Similarly, Periyar E.V. Ramaswamy, the leader of the Dravidian movement, despised everything that has come to be known as "Hinduism", portraying it as a symbol of the imposition of the Aryan. Each on an indigenous Dravidian population and of defiling and degrading Dravidian rulers and heroes. It is not surprising to find Ramaswamy declaring Ravan a true Dravidian hero who attempted, unsuccessfully though, to save his people from the exploits and tyranny of the invading Aryans.

For Ambedkar, too, the untouchables were not originally the lowliest of the low; they too were Aryans belonging to the Kshatriya *Varna*. As a matter of fact, Ambedkar suggests that there were two Aryan races and not one. He further suggests that the degradation of the Kshatriyas as *shudras* was the result of a violent conflict between the Kshatriyas and the Brahmins as evidenced by the enmity between Vishwamitra and Vashishtha. The enmity involved differences about three main issues: the right to receive gifts, the right to teach the *Veda*, and the right to officiate at the sacrifice.[6] These differences led the Brahmins to refuse to pertorm *samskaras*, especially the Upanayan *samskar*, for the Kashatriyas. The denial of the Upanayan *samskar* proved the most deadly weapon that the Brahmins employed against their adversaries, that is, all those Kshatriyas who were errant in their eyes. It was this weapon that compelled the *shudras* to look up to the three higher castes as their superior and enabled these higher castes to look down upon the Kshatriyas as their inferiors. Thus, the race compared of the Brahmins and the Kshatriyas split into two, the Brahmins and the *shudras*, by the machinations of the former.

Ambedkar holds that the Brahmins believed in two nation theory[7] and relegated the untouchables to the lowest possible position in the Hindu social order. It was Manu who invested the classificatory system of *varnas* with a degree of divinity and infallibility which it did not earlier have.[8] The caste system does not only divide the Hindu society into four unequal hierarchically organized and ritually graded occupational groupings. It also makes these divisions permanent and immutable. As such, it represents a conspiracy on the part of the Brahmins who sought to perpetuate an illegal gain obtained by an unjust wrong reflected on another.[9] This conspiracy deprived the untouchably of the means of subsistence, let alone the necessary means of improving their condition whether social, economic or political. As a result, they have been forced to carry on the burden of poverty and destitution and face the indignities, humiliations and oppression as the necessary concomitant of poverty. And since untouchability has been forced upon them against their will and they have been made to remain poor, they have lost the will to resist and overcome tyranny. They are virtual slaves to those who they have looked up to for succour and sustenance. The overall result is that the Hindu society has denied social justice to a large number of people dubbed as untouchable.

It created the will among the untouchables and to instill in them the confidence to fight tyranny and to acquire the necessary means of improving their earthly condition. But what was the appropriate strategy for obtaining results Ambedkar worked for the untouchables? And here lies the third point of reference of Ambedkar's political thinking. This point concerns his differences with M.K. Gandhi in so far as the proper approach to the solution of the problems of the untouchables was involved. While Gandhi focused mainly on the removal of untouchability within the fold of Hinduism with its emphasis on *varna vyavastha,* Ambedkar was neither satisfied with the mere removal of untouchability nor was he assured of a better treatment of the untouchables at the hands of *savarna* Hindus. It was this mistrust of the good intention of *savarna* Hindus towards untouchables that impelled Ambedkar to embrace Buddhism shortly before his death.

It is the combination of all these diverse sources that moulded Ambedkar's political thinking. Ambedkar embraced wholly and completely the liberal image of man as a self-defining subject, who makes use of his inborn or acquired capabilities to fashion the condition of his own existence through his interaction with the external world, both society and nature. Holding this image of man, Ambedkar would like the untouchables to rise up to conform to this image. And since the essential characteristic of man in the modern times is his autonomy informed by equality, Ambedkar had no hesitation in embracing completely the slogan of the French Revolution of liberty, equality and fraternity. As he puts in, "My social philosophy may be said to be enshrined in three words: liberty, equality and fraternity". He, however, later explained that he did not borrow this philosophy from the French Revolution. He claims to have derived it from religion, not political science, he rather derived it from the teachings of his master, the Buddha.[10]

Liberty and equality as the primary attributes of man in modern times necessary means a *homo economics* (economic man). As an economic man, he must pursue economic activities not simply as a means of ensuring his subsistence by arranging for provisioning. It is also a prerequisite, as Lord Keynes insists, a necessary condition, for the all-round development of man's personality. It is for this reason that Ambedkar considers poverty to be a sin and a crime. "To declare poverty to be a blessed state is to prevent", Ambedkar notes, "religion, to perpetuate vice and crime and to make earth a living hell".[11] If poverty is tolerated, the consequence is that the "poor are made to suffer wants, privation and humiliation not because it was preordained by the sins committed in their previous births, but because of the overhearing tyranny and treachery of those who are above them."[12] And since Indian economy happens to be very backward with agriculture being its mainstay, degrading conditions of the untouchables is also economically reinforced. The liberation of the untouchables from their highly depressed and deprived social and economic conditions requires not only major social reforms but also far-reaching economic and political reforms. In short then, the overhauling of the social, economic and political conditions is necessary for improving the lot of the untouchables. All these reforms are then conjoined and must go in tandem.

If the society that has for ages relegated the untouchables to be a position of deprivation and destitution, and if their existential situation has robbed them of the will to fight to regain their social position which belongs to them as their right, what needs to be done to enable them to enjoy self-determination with self-respect? The creation of such a will in those, who have already accepted defeat in the battle of life and have surrendered their will to power, cannot, Ambedkar believed, be ensured by making available to them the placebo of formal, representative democracy. Ambedkar did not put his faith in democracy as it is practiced everywhere. As he says, "I am no believer in democracy as an ideal to be pursued in all circumstances and in all climes; and having regard to the present day conditions in India, democracy is a most unthinkable system of government. At any rate, for some time India needs the strong hand of an enlightened autocrat."[13]

The reason why Ambedkar does not prefer democracy and calls for an enlightened autocracy lies in his perception and evaluation of the Hindus and their social system. What was very clear to him was that the Hindu social order lacked completely social conscience, the one factor that could have saved the untouchables all the troubles—social, economic, political—that they have had to go through the passage of history. He comes to this conclusion through a logical steps. He rightly considers the Hindu society to be divided into privileged and under- and un-privileged classes. Such a divided factual order breeds prejudice; this, in turn, brings about isolation; isolated socio-economic groups develop hostility towards each other; and this paves the way for the infringement of law. This situation gets greatly aggravated in India since society in India is divided into hierarchically organized rigid caste groups. What is more important, the

Hindu society is marked with an ingrained tendency towards the exploitation and oppression of the weak by the strong. The untouchables, whom Ambedkar calls *bahiskrit samaj* (the boycotted social groups), have been the habitual victims of this tendency.

What is most disturbing to Ambedkar about formal democracy is that its working is bound, especially in India, to perpetuate majority rule signifying the majority not of opinion but of numbers. And the majority of numbers will necessarily favour the *savarna* Hindus who, by inclination and interest, would always oppress the unfortunate untouchables. In view of this, Ambedkar rejects the definition of democracy advanced by Abraham Lincoln and Walter Bagehot. He has no objection to how Lincoln defines democracy as "a government of the people, by the people and for the people", or as Bagehot declares democracy as "a form of government by discussion". However, he enters two caveats pertaining to these definitions. In the first place, democracy, he asserts, is always changing its form; it is not always the same in any particular country. It goes on changing its purpose as the governing elites change place.

In the second place, if democracy changes its purpose with every change in the governing elite, it follows that the purpose of democracy must consist in doing something more than curbing an autocratic King; it should address itself now to new problems that the passage of history has given rise to. And one of the most urgent problems is to bring revolutionary changes in the socio-economic conditions of the people so that they could get leisure to pursue the goal of realizing the good life of modern conception. This, however, is beyond the capacity of formal democracy to attain inasmuch as it is beholden to the regnant public opinion. And the regnant public opinion favours vested interests. This leads Ambedkar to define democracy as "a form of government whereby revolutionary changes in the economic and social life of the people are brought about without bloodshed." And the first thing, among others, essential for the successful functioning of democracy is to see that there are no glaring inequalities and there must not either be oppressed class or a suppressed class.[14]

It is clear, then, that the successful working of democracy in the sense Ambedkar perceives it can be ensured only if political and social reforms of radical kind are carried on in tandem. He makes a sharp distinction between political and social reforms. In his Ranade Memorial lecture Ambedkar referred to two schools of reforms, one of which favoured social reforms and the other opted for political reforms to remove social ills. He specifically mentioned Justice Tailang who, Ambedkar pointed out, held that political reforms were more effective and should have precedence over social reforms.[15] He rejects this on several grounds one of which needs special mention. He calls Tailang's thesis absurd unless "the idea is that the Government should reward those who have vested rights and to penalize those who have none".[16]

Ambedkar's preference for social reform is inspired largely by the sufferings and humiliations experienced by the untouchables because of their lowly social and economic condition. That is why he gave first priority to the cause of the untouchables than anything else. Participating in the Bombay Legislative Council debates on 2 October, 1939, he emphatically observed that his loyalty to the country was not in anyway lesser than anybody else. However, he also unscored the fact that he had another loyalty "to which I am bound and which I can never forsake. That loyalty is the community of untouchables, in which I was born, to which I belong and which I hope never desert."[17] He also made it clear that whenever there was any conflict of interest between the country and that of his community, he would always give preference to the latter. "As between the country and the depressed classes, the depressed classes will have precedence, the country will not have precedence."[18]

In view of Ambedkar's stated preference for his community as compared to his country, it is not at all surprising to find him asserting that "I am not a part of the whole, I am a part apart."[19] Undoubtedly, this signifies a determination on his part to disrupt the links that bound the untouchables to the Hindu social order and seek their emancipation not as a part of the larger community but as a separate group. Even when the untouchables are part of the Hindu social order, they constitute *bahiskrit samaj*, that is, outside the pale of the Hindu society. To treat the untouchables as not a part of the whole but a whole in themselves has two profound ramifications. First, it is symptomatic of the distancing of the untouchables from the larger Hindu social order. This distancing involves two things: one, balancing the Hindu social order squarely for the deplorable existential condition of the untouchables.

Since the untouchables have been exploited and oppressed by the Hindu social order, they do not form a part of the Hindu society because the oppressed is different from the oppressor. As such their interest do not match. Secondly, it must be reorganized that the relationship that obtains between *savarna* Hindu and the untouchables is not god-made but man-made. It has, therefore, no inevitability about it; it can very well be changed. This inevitably calls for opposing and actively resisting and fighting the unjust system the untouchables have been saddled with. It is also in this sense that the untouchables form a whole in and by themselves since it is their identity and its active play in political arena that can ensure their emancipation from the firm grip of the unjust system. Their collective identity can be supported and sustained only by a conscious recognition of the fact that they constitute a whole in and by themselves.

Second, the interest of the untouchables is distinctly apart from the interest of other groups. It is true that the untouchables as a group too can be said to share the primary defining characteristics with other socio-economic interests. This primary defining characteristic is, of course, the primacy of the material aspect of existence that expresses itself in the pursuit largely, even exclusively, of economic well-being. Each of the socio-economic interests comprising Indian society is competitor to others in the game of gaining and retaining privileged access to and control over scarce societal resources. As a result, politics twins out to be a hazardous game of reciprocal resistance. To take part in this game; not to take part in it means to give up the hope of acquiring the necessary ingredients of the good life of modern conception. Thus socio-economic interest finds it absolutely necessary to engage in promoting its interest whether through politics or any other means. However, in contradistinction to other groups the untouchables are hampered in this by one very significant factor, that is, their ritual status of being untouchables along with being impecunious. They are thus doubly handicapped and cannot take part in the game of competition for access to societal resources in any effective way. As a consequence, their socio-economic condition remains highly depressed. It is in this sense that the untouchables can be said to have their own separate interest which they fail to promote because of the jeopardy they suffer from. As such, their effective participation in this game requires that their social condition must be radically revised and changed.

Without stopping to examine here the propriety or implications of Ambedkar's preference for the destiny of the untouchables as against that of the country, we can admit that to state his conviction openly is indeed an act of courage. And this was precisely the point that made him apart from other politicians of his day who saw in this a sign of extreme partisanship, even parochialism varying on separatism of even unreason. It was again this that pitched him against his contemporaries some of whom were very tall political figures and personalities including Mahatma Gandhi. This single minded pursuit of a single point led him to belittle both Gandhi and Jinnah as "selfish leaders who fought for their own self-conceived notions of what was good for the people without budging from it." In contradistinction to them, he was all praise for Ranade, who despite being a judge, earned Ambedkar's praise because he, as Ambedkar saw him, transcended the sharp division that was so evident between those who gave primary importance to political reforms and those who treated social reforms to have primary importance.[20]

It is against this background that we can appreciate why Ambedkar defines democracy in a way that includes both political and social action for radically changing the Hindu society. He was quite aware of the fact that political action is something that frequently favours those who have power and, therefore, have a stake in the preservation of the system that has made possible for them to capture or control power apparatus of the society. But then Ambedkar realizes that since social reform is neither effective nor capable of speedily solving the problems of the untouchables, he turns around and exalts political action as the only means which could come to the rescue of the untouchables who have nothing else to rely on in getting adequate relief from the inequities, humiliations and insufferable indignities heaped upon by them by the *savarna* Hindus. Arguing in the Round Table Conference in support of installing representative government in India, he observed:

> We are often reminded that the problem of the Depressed Classes is a social problem and that its solution lies elsewhere than in politics. We take strong exception to this view, he hold that the problem of the Depressed Classes will never be solved unless they get political power in their own hands. If this is true… the problem must be treated as such.[21]

Again, he argued further that the coming of Swaraj, as a result of the devolution of British power meant the tyranny of the majority community. However, he was willing to take the risk in the hope that "we shall be installed in adequate proportion as the sovereign of the country along with our countrymen".[22] This is the rational behind separate electorate for the untouchables in reserved constituencies voting for the untouchable candidates. Again, this is harping back to the idea of the untouchables being not a part but a whole in themselves. This is also indicative of Ambedkar's shift towards a position signifying greater dependence on the state to initiate action for safeguarding and promoting the interest of minority groups.[23] This underlines the realization that no minority group can on its own mobilize the necessary resources to successfully launch political struggle for forcing the powers that is to grant the demands that it might ask for fulfilment, if the result of the political battle is to be determined by the arithmetic of numbers.

Dependence on the state becomes necessary in a situation where structural inequalities are so deeply ingrained and highly valued that any political battle launched by a minority group is sure to invite resistance by groups with vested interest in the preservation *status quo*. If the interest of these groups is vitally affected, they will certainly seek to defeat the minority group in the political battle. Representative democracy means majority rule tending to place political power in the hands of a sub-coalition of vested interests, which, in the case of India, means *savarna* Hindus. It is for this reason that Ambedkar insists that representative of parliamentary democracy must be beefed up by firm commitment to pursue certain substantive concerns. This commitment must be informed by principles derived from socialistic vision of society and affirmed in constitutionally sanctioned and guaranteed provisions. Such provisions should have the triple objectives of safeguarding socialism, parliamentary democracy and of ensuring good life with ample leisure for all.[24] He insists that a democratic policy committed to the ideal of state socialism must guarantee to all the life of reason. This is possible if everybody has enough leisure to seek the attainment of culture and refinement. This is possible only when physical appetites of the individual are amply satisfied. For this to happen, the use of machines and technologically induced economic growth, that is, industrialization, become inevitable.[25] But industrialization alone would fail to solve the economic problem facing India. What is also needed is to make large inputs of capital and heavy mechanization of agriculture. Thus, intensive development of the country's industry and agriculture must take place side by side.[26]

The ideal society that Ambedkar envisages must be equipped with a proper political institutional arrangement since it alone is capable of achieving the triple objectives of establishing socialism, operating parliamentary democracy, and preventing dictatorship. However, if democracy is to prove salubrious and beneficial for every citizen and if it meant one person, one value, it must have not only political equality but also economic equality. Ambedkar took socialists to task for their erroneous belief in the equalization of property as the most efficacious means of safeguarding life, liberty and equality. He argues that property to be the source of power in India, as it still continues to be the case in Europe. However, along with, religion, social status, socio-economic divisions constitute the source of the power too in India. As such, the more equalization of property will fail to ensure equalization of power resources. On this view, political power is the function of socio-economic differentiation. To have political democracy without its counterpart in social and economic spheres is to allow the government "to protect those who have vested right and to penalize those who have none".[27] Unequal access to power resource is, Ambedkar underlines the result of inequality in the distribution of social resources.

It is quite clear, then, that Ambedkar was fully aware of the dangers that the full functioning of representative democracy can engender for the untouchables. He was convinced that the government would, in such a democracy, be controlled by those who happen to be the *causa prima* of the sufferings and existential troubles of the untouchables. He was also certain that such a government could be in no position either to end their sufferings or to make their life any better. His realization that political system based on representative democracy is quite deficient in discharging its responsibility the depressed and the deprived led him to opt for a democracy that could instill the feeling of respect for the dignity of others. That is why Ambedkar equates democracy with fraternity. As he says:

> An ideal society should be mobile, should be full of channels for covering carrying over a change taking place in one part to other parts. In an ideal society there should be many interests consciously communicated and shared. There should be varied and free points of contact with other modes of association. In other words, there must be social osmosis. This is fraternity that is the only other name of democracy. Democracy is not merely a form of government. It is primarily a mode of

> associated living, of conjoint communicated experience. It is essential an attitude of respect and reverence towards fellowmen.[28]

Since this type of democracy is nowhere in sight, Ambedkar settles for representative democratic government with certain features added on to it, so that it would prove effective in protecting and promoting the interests of the untouchables. His insistence on reservation with weightage in the representation of the minorities. But these special features would protect them only against tyranny and safeguard their rights and interests. They would not in and by themselves remove economic and social inequalities that lie at the root of unequal access to societal resources. It is, therefore, necessary to simultaneously work for radical changes in social and economic fields with a view to striking a balance between liberty and equality.

NOTES

1. C.H. Philips, ed. *The Correspondence of Lord William Cavendish Bentinck*, 2 Vols. (Oxford University Press, 1977), I, Introduction, p. xv.
2. Perceival Spears, *A History of India* (Hammondsworth: Penguin Books Ltd., 1986), p. 120.
3. Sir William Jones, "The Hymn to Lakshmi", *The Works of Sir William Jones*, ed. A.M. Jones, 6 Vols. (London: G.G. and J. Robinson, R.H. Evans, 1799), VI, p. 365.
4. For details, see Ramashray Roy, *Gandhi and Ambedkar: A Study in Contrast* (Delhi: Shipra Publications, 2006, Chap.6).
5. *Collected Works of Jyotiba Phule*, trans. P.G. Patil (Bombay: Education Department, Government of Maharashtra, 1991), p. 131.
6. B.R. Ambedkar, *Who Were The Shudras?* (Bombay: Thacker & Co., 1937), p. 76.
7. *Ibid.*
8. B.R. Ambedkar, *Annihilation of Caste* (Bombay: Thacker & Co., 1936), p. 6.
9. Who were the Shudras, *op. cit.*, p. 76.
10. Ambedkar's claim, it must be noted, suffers from a bout of anachronism since his first explicit reference to the slogan of the

French Revolution goes back to 1927. Since then he used the slogan as a *mantra* repeating them frequently. For example, he advocates these values with a greater force in his chapter "Annihilation of Caste".

11. Quoted in S.R. Bakhshi, ed. *Social Ideology of B.R. Ambedkar* (New Delhi: Deep and Deep Publications, 2001), p. 34.
12. He expressed this view on 4 January, 1938 in Sholapur in reply to the address presented to him by the Sholapur Municipality, Quoted in Dhanjay Keer, *Dr. Ambedkar: Life and Mission* (Bombay: Popular Prakashan, 1954), p. 297.
13. *Dr. Baba Saheb Ambedkar: Writings and Speeches* (Bombay: Education Department, Government of Maharashtra, 1982), II, pp. 222-23.
14. *Ibid*, I, p. 221.
15. *Ibid*, I, pp. 221-22.
16. *Ibid*, II, p. 258.
17. *Ibid*.
18. *Ibid*, II, pp. 503-504.
19. *Ibid*, I, p. 222.
20. *Ibid*, I, p. 508.
21. *Op. cit*.
22. *Loc. cit*.
23. Long back Alexis de Tocqueville pointed to the phenomenon of dependence on the state as a basic feature of modern times that put so much accent on liberty and freedom.
24. Ambedkar had preferred in March 1947 a memorandum for the consideration of the Constituent Assembly. The Memorandum was later published under the title of States and Minorities. In this monograph he details out his own personal preference for an ideal social life and the requisite politico-administrative and social system for achieving this ideal. See Keer, *op. cit*, pp. 389-90.
25. H.V. Desai, *My Interviews with Eminent Personalities*, p. 26. Quoted in Keer, p. 389.
26. Ambedkar, *Collected Writings*, I, pp. 221-22.
27. *Ibid*, I, p. 506.
28. *Writings and Speeches*, II, p. 261.

4

Political Thought of B. R. Ambedkar

The Constitutional Structure of State in India

M.P. SINGH

Political Mobilizational Background

The 1980s may be regarded as the phase of Indian electoral democracy that witnessed two major developments: the fruition of the process of federalization of a predominantly parliamentary regime and the political arrival of the *dalit* citizens. It is not my argument that these two trends are entirely new in Indian politics. The antecedents of both may well be traced back to earlier post-Independence decades. However, it was by the 1980s and later that these two processes crossed the thresholds of new moments of efficacy in the politics of the Indian nation. Ambedkar is a posthumous *purodha* of the *dalit* political assertion and arrival.

There have been two models of political mobilization and participation of the section of the Hindu society variously called the *panchmang* (the fifth class beyond the four *varnas* of Brahmans, Kshatriyas, Vaishyas, Shudras); most depressed classes, scheduled castes, *harijans* (by Mahatma Gandhi), and *dalits* (by Ambedkarites) through the ages. We may dub these as the Harijan model of political mobilization and the Dalit model of political participation. If the Harijan identity formation and Jagjivan Ram in Congress politics in Bihar/India since the mid-1930s represented the first model, Bahujan-Dalit identity formation and Bhimrao Ramji Ambedkar since the late 1920s represented the second model.[1]

With minor variations, both Ambedkar and Jagjivan Ram initially conformed to sanskritization-*cum*-westernization model of social change and political participation. Ram began as a liberal and Gandhian brand of Congressman who believed in a secular and modern Hindu identity and never wavered from the Congress way of national freedom struggle against the British colonial rule. Ambedkar also began with a secular and modern Hindu identity, but subsequently graduated to a more radical assertion of *dalit* political identity, and after much soul-searching embraced Buddhism in 1956. Apparently, under the belief that in the context of the Indian society, especially the Hindu society, social reform with a focus on the emancipation of untouchables must precede political independence, Ambedkar took his political plunge in organizations and activities of radical Hindu social reform. In his submission to the Simon Commission in the late 1920s and during his participation in the First Round Table Conference on Indian constitutional reforms in January 1931 (boycotted by the Congress and Gandhi), Ambedkar supported separate electorate for untouchables (like the one for the Muslims). Ambedkar changed this stance only in face of a fast unto death by Gandhi and settled for reserved reservation in the general electorate meant for Hindus.

Ambedkar has written intensively and extensively on the basic structure of the Hindu society as well as the basic structure of the Indian state. Since the recent spurt in Ambedkar and *dalit* studies has already produced tomes on the first dimension, this paper purports to discuss Ambedkar's contributions to the making of the Indian Constitution and the praxis of the Indian state.

Constituent Assembly Entrée

The Constituent Assembly of India was elected in July 1946 under the British Cabinet Mission Statement of May 16, 1946. The desire of the Congress nationalists for a directly elected Constituent Assembly was rejected in favour of an indirect election by the Provincial Legislative Assemblies elected on the basis of a franchise restricted by educational and property qualifications that gave voting right to about 25 per cent of Indians under the Government of India Act, 1935. Elections were held for 296 seats from British Indian provinces under the direct rule of the Crown. The remaining 93 seats were allotted to the Indian princely states holding suzereignty under the paramountcy of the British Crown. By agreement between elected part of the Constituent Assembly and its prospective princely part at least 50 per cent of the latter's representatives were to be elected by assemblies in princely states wherever they existed and the remainder could be nominated by the rulers.

It was such a Constituent Assembly that Ambedkar entered as the leader of the All India Scheduled Castes Federalism, a party founded by himself in 1930. This party could elect only two representatives to the Constituent Assembly, one from Central Provinces and one, Ambedkar himself, from Bengal. There were four independent scheduled caste members from Bengal besides Ambedkar. I could not ascertain how many scheduled caste members were elected on Congress ticket, except the fact Jagjivan Ram, President of the All-India Depressed Classes League, was there as a nominee of the Indian National Congress. Congress as a party commanded the overwhelming majority in the Indian part of the Constituent Assembly, especially following the partition of India under the Mountbatten Plan of June 3, 1947. In addition to a party leader, Ambedkar's eminence at that time also rested on the fact that he was an ex-member of the Governor-General's Executive Council.[2]

Work in Various Preparatory Committees

In pursuance of paragraph 20 of the Cabinet Mission's Statement of May 16, 1946, the Constituent Assembly resolved to constitute an Advisory Committee consisting of not more than 72 members who might include persons who were not members of the Assembly on a resolution moved by Govind Ballabh Pant (the Premier of the United Provinces and elected on a general seat) on January 24, 1947. Ambedkar was a member of this all-important committee of the Assembly chaired by the President, Rajendra Prasad himself, to determine fundamental rights and minority rights of citizens and appoint sub-committees to prepare for the administration of the north-eastern (and north-western) tribal areas and the excluded and partially excluded areas from both British India and Indian states. Besides Ambedkar, the Congress Harijan Jagjivan Ram was also a member of this committee.

Besides this advisory committee of overriding importance, there were over eighteen committees or sub-committees of standing and *ad hoc* character. Among other substantive committees were the following with the names of their chairs:

1. States Committee: Jawaharlal Nehru,
2. Advisory Committee on Fundamental Rights, Minorities and Tribal and Excluded Areas: Ballabhbhai Patel,
3. Union Powers Committee: Jawaharlal Nehru,
4. Union Constitution Committee: Jawaharlal Nehru,
5. Provincial Constitution Committee: Ballabhbhai Patel, and
6. Drafting Committee: B.R. Ambedkar.

Overview notes and questionnaire were first prepared by Benegal Narasimha Rao, who had served earlier as a member of the famed Indian Civil Service (ICS) and a high court judge and finally ended up the legal adviser to the Assembly and its President. Partial drafts were produced by the myriad committees and sub-committees. Those were then passed on to the drafting committee for scrutiny, settlement, and presentation for clause-by-clause debate in the Assembly. Besides Ambedkar, other members of the drafting committee included Alladi Krishnaswami Ayyar, N. Gopalaswami Ayyangar, K.M. Munshi, Saiyed Mohd. Sadulla, B.L. Mitter, and D.P. Khaitan. Ambedkar had occasionally participated in the debate on the reports of the committees and sub-committees. His main task was to present the draft Constitution once it was crafted by the drafting committee for debate in the

Assembly, defend it, and finally to reply to the debate spanning over 13 months.

Piloting the Draft Constitution

Ambedkar presented the draft constitution for debate in the Assembly on the 4th of November, 1948 and rose to reply to the deliberations on the 24th of November, 1949. I will take the texts of these two memorable addresses as the basic of my explication of Ambedkar's understanding and interpretation of the philosophy and basic structure of the Constitution[3]. He began by explaining its "salient and special features". He drew attention to the fact that even before its formal tabling in the Constituent Assembly, the draft constitution had already been in the public domain, and its "friends, critics and adversaries have had more than sufficient time to express their reactions to the provisions contained in it."[4] Ambedkar went on in his masterly and magisterial exposition to make the point that the form of government preferred was parliamentary rather than that of executive presidency. Said he:

> "Under the draft constitution the President occupies the same position as the King under the English Constitution. He is the head of the state but not of the Executive. He represents the Nation but does not rule the Nation. He is the symbol of the Nation. His place in the administration is that of a ceremonial device on a seal by which the nation's decisions are made known."[5]

Despite this clear-cut postulation, Ambedkar did leave a few ambiguous loose ties. Consider, for example, the pregnant sentences in this address such as the following:

> "The President of the Indian Union will be *generally* bound by the advice of his Ministers." (emphasis mine)[6]

> "He can do nothing contrary to their advice nor can do anything without their advice. The President of the

> United States can dismiss any secretary at any time. The President of the Indian Union has no power to do so long as his Ministers command a majority in Parliament."[7]

Ambedkar proceeded to say that a democratic executive must satisfy two requirements: it must be *stable*, and it must be *responsible*. Stability is the hallmark of the U.S. and Swiss executive, whereas the responsibility is characteristic of the British executive. "Draft constitution is recommending the Parliamentary system or has preferred more responsibility to more stability."[8]

Having explained the "form of government" under the draft constitution, Ambedkar went on to discuss the "form of constitution" in the draft making a distinction between unitary and federal constitutions exemplified classically by the United Kingdom and the United States respectively, Ambedkar made the perceptive point that even though the USA and India had both adopted the federal form of constitution, the two were very different. To quote him, "The differences that distinguish them are more fundamental and glaring than the similarities between the two."[9] The fundamental differences between the two federations that Ambedkar specified boiled down to dual citizenships and dual constitutions that the US federation and the federating states maintained unlike India.[10]

"Why did Ambedkar not bring it here the obvious and patent difference between the presidential-federal system and the parliamentary-federal system? Was it deliberate? I am raising this question with the benefit of hindsight as with the advent of a multi-party system with federal coalition governments in New Delhi and rise of strong regional parties that are tending to make the Indian political system confederal in its dynamics."[11] By now it is becoming dimly evident that due to phenomenon of divided governments in a fragmented society, parliamentary federal system is showing signs of a separation of powers political configuration.[12] Ambedkar next tries to draw attention to "some other special features of the proposed Indian Federation which mark it off not only from the American Federation but from all other Federations."[13] In his opinion, the American and other federal systems "are placed in a tight mould of Federalism" that can never be broken. Contrariwise, the draft Constitution was a two-in-one framework of government, which "can be both unitary as well as federal according to the requirements of time and circumstances." In times of constitutionally contemplated emergencies, the same constitution gets transformed into a unitary one.[14]

Ambedkar then took up two typical weaknesses of federal constitutions, especially the American, namely, rigidity and legalism, and scores a debating point how the draft constitution had intendedly tried to avoid both. Like the Australian constitution (Ambedkar here could have also easily added the Canadian Constitution), the draft constitution had kept rigidity under check by giving the Parliament wide powers of concurrent legislation. Moreover, the draft constitution also sought to escape rigidity and legalism by keeping the amending procedure fairly easy. On this point, it must be added, Ambedkar did not visualize the present political scenario when due to the phenomenon of divided government and differentiated party systems in the two chambers of the Parliament and at the Union and State levels, the task of constitutional amendment has become extremely difficult, if not impossible.

A third way to reduce rigidity and legalism in the draft constitution was, according to Ambedkar, to avoid the American practice of having dual citizenship and dual constitutions, one for the state and one for the nation/ federation. In addition, the draft constitution also preferred an integrated single hierarchy of courts, uniformity in fundamental laws of the land (civil and criminal—it was intended to have a common civil code as well), and a common All India Services system to man the highest posts in both orders of governments.[15]

Reading this long presentation speech of Ambedkar in the Constituent Assembly, it is difficult not to be amply convinced of Ambedkar's abiding conviction in nationalism, strong state, democracy, and minority rights. His defence of the draft constitution, the values it stood for, and state apparatus it intended to establish is absolutely unambiguous and unexceptionable.

Ambedkar finally rose to reply to the debate on the draft constitution on November 24, 1949. He meticulously took up the criticisms made by ideologues—communists, socialists, Gandhians—as well as those made by legal experts and political activists about specific details in the constitution. He stood by the liberal-democratic credentials of the constitution, pointing out that India did not need either communist dictatorship of the prolitariat or socialist collectivism or Gandhian traditionalist village society because all these were undemocratic and unjust. An important point of constitutional import in the critique to the constitution that Ambedkar chose to reply related to the too much of centralization reducing the states to Municipalities. He argued the crux of federalism lies in the demarcation of legislative and executive powers between the Union and States umpired by a judiciary. And this was, in his opinion, the constitutional order envisaged by the draft constitution in normal times, barring constitutional emergencies.

Finally, he philosophically reflected on the paradox that India under the constitution would come to have procedural democracy without a substantive democracy. He laid down three conditions to actualize this goal. First, India must "hold fast to constitutional methods of achieving our social and economic objectives." [16] Secondly, he stressed that "Bhakti in religion may be a road to the salvation of the soul. But in politics, Bhakti or hero-worship is a sure road to degradation and eventual dictatorship."[17] Thirdly, he emphasized that "We must make our political democracy a social democracy as well. Political democracy cannot last unless there lies at the base of it social democracy." [18]

On Safeguards for Scheduled Castes

The problems of the scheduled castes were always uppermost in the thought and action of Ambedkar, especially prior to his deep involvement in the making of the constitution for India. Since he was born an untouchable, he had been a victim of untouchability himself. This remained unchanged even after his elitist higher education and his marriage to a Brahman lady, Savita Ambedkar.

His views on what the Constituent Assembly could do to better their lot could be gleaned from a memorandum he prepared on this question to be submitted to the Constituent Assembly on behalf of the Scheduled Castes Federation. It was subsequently published in 1947 (Preface date) for wider readership. He countered the view that the scheduled castes were not minorities; in fact, he also referred to Gandhi's editorial in the *Harijan* (21 October, 1939, "The Fiction of Majority") saying that in India the scheduled castes were the real minority among minorities.[19] The religious affiliation is not the only criterion of a minority; the correct test is social discrimination, Ambedkar argued.[20] He deplored the tendency of dubbing any demand on the part of minorities for power sharing as "communal". In his opinion the scheduled castes were in a worse condition than any other minority. He made out a case for constitutionally entrenched rights for the scheduled castes and reservations for them in legislatures, executives, and civil services in proportion to their population in the country. He also pleaded for constitutional provisions casting special responsibility on the Union and State governments for state-funded higher education for the scheduled castes.[21]

On Linguistic States

The Constituent Assembly left the task of the reorganization of internal boundaries of the federating states unresolved. The matter was forced upon the post-independence Nehru government by linguistic agitations in several states in western and southern India. A reluctant Nehru government first appointed a States Reorganization Commission in the early 1950s, and on the basis of the Commission's report (1955) enacted the States Reorganization Act (1956). The approach of the Commission as well as the Nehru government was to maintain, wherever possible, multi-lingual composite states, and concede the demand for a linguistic states only in face of a strong mass pressure.

During the parliamentary debate on the 1956 Reorganization Act, Ambedkar was incapacitated by illness. Yet he took pains to write a critique of the States Reorganization Commission Report (SRCR) in a pamphlet, *Thoughts on Linguistic States* (Prefact date 23 December 1955).[22]

In the booklet, Ambedkar candidly admits what other Indian nationalists fought shy of, even those who agreed with the arrangement which the British settled on the eve of their departure:

> "I was glad that India was separated from Pakistan. I advocated partition because I felt that it was only by partition that Hindus would not only be independent but free. If India and Pakistan had remained united in one State, Hindus, though independent, would have been at the mercy of the Muslims.... A merely independent India would not have been a free India from the point of view of the Hindus. It would have been a Government of one country by two nations, and of these two the Muslims without question would have been the ruling race..."[23]

Interestingly, while Ambedkar perceptively welcomed the partition based on religion in 1947, he lamented the divisiveness of the linguistic states and their penchant to make regional languages as their official languages. To Ambedkar, it "will be a death knell to the idea of united India."[24]

Ambedkar's main criticisms of the SRCR may now be briefly enumerated:

1. It regarded apparently that vastly varying sizes of various states is federally irrelevant. This is "the most terrible error. He refers approvingly to the dissenting note to the Report given by K.M. Pannikar that the federating units are left very asymmetrical and the

undermining effect of this factor on the federal structure is left unmitigated by the failure of the constitution to give them equal representation *qua* state in the Rajya Sabha. Ambedkar adds failure of the constitution in this respect is not making the federal second chamber equal in power with the popular parliamentary chamber.[25]

Ambedkar's solution to this problem was a thorough going reorganization of states in India to make them comparable in size in terms of population and territory.

2. SRCR willy-nilly contained the effect of consolidating the North and balkanizing the South inasmuch as the former region would have smaller linguistic states, while big states in the North like Bombay, U.P., Bihar, Madhya Pradesh would remain intact. He asked: "How can the rule of the North be tolerated by the South? Already there are signs of the South wanting to break away from the North."[26] Ambedkar also narrated that C. Rajagopalachari once told him: "You are committing a great mistake. One federation for the whole of India... will not work ... you should have two Federations, one Federation of the North and one Federation of the South, and a Confederation of the North and the South with three [common] subjects for the Confederation to legislate upon and equal representation for both the Federations." [27]

   Ambedkar's solution to this problem was a trifurcation of the old Bombay state into Western, Central, and Eastern Maharashtra. Uttar Pradesh was to be similarly divided into three parts, Bihar into two parts, and Madhya Pradesh into two parts.
3. The SRCR in Ambedkar's opinion had ignored the fact, or failed to realize it, that smaller states were a safeguard to the minorities. With the safeguards of separate electorate gone in the constitution of post-colonial India, "The lambs are shorn of the wool," and "They are feeling the intensity of the cold."[28]

The solution to this problem was offered as follows: "It would be [simple] enough to have plural-member constituencies (of two or three) with cumulative voting in place of the system of single-member constituency embodied in the present constitution. This will allay the fears which the minorities have about Linguistic States."[29]

4. Ambedkar alleged that SRCR conceded in agitating states that all people speaking one language should be brought within one state. Ambedkar's preference was that "people speaking one language may be grouped under many states, provided each state has under its jurisdiction people who are speaking one language."[30] To quote Ambedkar again: "The formula one state, one language, must not be confused with the formula of one language, one state."[31]
5. Climatic conditions, feeling of the people of the South, and considerations of defence prompted Ambedkar to suggest two capitals for India, Delhi and Hyderabad.[32]

Conclusion

Ambedkar's political thought may well be the gateway to the constitutional architecture of the state in India. Those who have surveyed the entire spectrum of his social and political thought would probably find it difficult to determine whether he can be said to be primarily a theorist of the Hindu social structure with special reference to the formerly untouchable castes and their emancipation or primarily a comparative political theorist of constitutional engineering and constitutional government. In my opinion, he was, on the balance, a statist in both the social and political domains. The overriding role of the state looms large in his political thought not only in the realm of the internal structure or governments in India's parliamentary-federal democracy but also in the spheres of the civil society and economy. Consider, for example, his proposal at one stage to reform the temple establishments by instituting the system of recruitment of priests across the caste divisions and their training and appointment under a positive law.[33] Moreover, his memorandum on rights of and safeguards for scheduled castes to the Constituent Assembly that were largely incorporated in the constitution also banks upon state law and action. The same memorandum also proposed collective farming under state ownership in agriculture and state socialism in the industrial sector. Neither tenant ownership nor consolidation of land holdings would, he was sure, benefit the scheduled castes. State socialism to his mind was essential for rapid industrialization of India.[34] These arrangements were not to be instituted by parliamentary enactment or executive action, as Jawaharlal Nehru unsuccessfully pleaded for the agricultural sector at the Awadi session of the Indian National Congress in 1955 and successfully introduced through the process of planning since the early 1950s in the public industrial sector in the framework of mixed economy. Ambedkar advocated state socialism with constitutional entrenchment that could not be undone by legislative or executive action.[35]

NOTES

1. See Mahendra Prasad Singh, "Political Arrival" in *Seminar,* New Delhi, No. 243, November 1979: 12-18, a special issue on Harijans guest-edited by MPS.
2. See B. Shiva Rao *et al.* (eds.), *The Framing of India's Constitution: Select Documents,* Vol. I, New Delhi: Indian Institute of Public Administration, 1966: 287-310.
3. I must clarify that I use the term "basic structure of the constitution" in a general sense, not in the sense of the judicially constructed constitutional theory of the basic structure of the Indian Constitution since the Supreme Court judgement in Keshavananda Bharati *v.* State of Kerala in 1973 and further elaborated in various other judgements since then.
4. *Constituent Assembly Debates: Official Report,* New Delhi: Lok Sabha Secretariat, 1999, 3rd reprint by Jainco Art, New Delhi, Book No. 2:31.
5. *Ibid.,* 32.
6. *Ibid.*
7. *Ibid.*
8. *Ibid.,* 33.

9. *Ibid.*
10. *Ibid.*, 34.
11. Douglas V. Verney, "From Quasi-Federation to Quasi-Confederacy Transformation of India's Party System", *Publius: The Journal of Federalism*, Vol. 33, No. 4, Fall 2003.
12. M.P. Singh, "Foreword", Rekha Saxena, *Situating Federalism: Mechanisms of Intergovernmental Relations in Canada and India* (New Delhi, Manohar, 2006: 9-10.
13. *CAD, op. cit.*, 34.
14. *Ibid.*, 34-35.
15. *Ibid.*, 36-37
16. *CAD*, Book No. 5, *op. cit.*, 978.
17. *Ibid.*, 979.
18. *Ibid.*
19. Shyam Singh Shashi, (ed.), *Babasaheb Ambedkar: Sampoorna Vangamay, Khand 2* (Trans. From English), New Delhi: Ministry of Welfare, Government of India, 208.
20. *Ibid.*
21. *Ibid.*, 185-87.
22. B.R. Ambedkar, *Thoughts on Linguistic States* (Aligarh: Anand Sahitya Sadan, 1989, reprinted).
23. *Ibid.*, 16-17.
24. *Ibid.*, 17.
25. *Ibid.*, 10 and 18-19.
26. *Ibid.*, 12 and 22.
27. *Ibid.*, 22
28. *Ibid.*, 52.
29. *Ibid.*, 52.
30. *Ibid.*, 18.
31. *Ibid.*, 44.
32. *Ibid.*, 53-55.
33. From my memory of reading Ambedakarana but cannot readily cite the source here.
34. Shyam Singh Shashi (ed.), *Babasaheb Ambedkar, Sampurna Vangamay, Khand 2, op. cit.*, 194.
35. *Ibid.*

5

Dr. Ambedkar's Contribution in the Framing of India's Constitution

JAYTILAK GUHA ROY

Dr. B.R. Ambedkar (1891-1956) dazzled like the brightest star on the Indian firmament during the span of about four decades of his truly extraordinary public life from 1918 to 1956. He had amazingly surpassed many of his great countrymen of his generation, despite his humble family background of the untouchable Mahar community in Maharashtra, as a brilliant scholar, a philosopher, a professor, a jurist, a legislator, a constitutionalist, a social reformer, a statesman, a cabinet minister, and above all, a rebel *dalit* leader. He was the most revered crusader of the twentieth century against India's irrational caste system and obnoxious practice of untouchability. He held a unique place among the builders of modern India. His most notable contribution could be traced to the framing of independent India's Constitution which laid the foundation of resurgent modern India.

Although the Constituent Assembly was adorned with a galaxy of jurists, scholars, statesmen, social activists and political leaders, yet it had the privilege to have Ambedkar as one of its members who played a leading and historic role in the framing of India's Constitution. He entered this august body like a belligerent 'Protestant', but was soon destined to hold a key position—the Chairman of the Drafting Committee. Ambedkar's unique idea of social justice, his dynamic political thought, his liberal views on constitutionalism, his progressive concept of rights of the people, his vision of an ideal society, and above all, his concern for the welfare and development of the *poor, little Indians*, the dumb millions, or the *dalits*, were not only echoed during his illustrious deliberations in the Constituent Assembly but also reflected in each and every part of the Constitution of India.

Ambedkar's Idea of Social Justice

Ambedkar's unique idea of social justice emanated from his vision of an ideal society or *samata samaj*, based on a social order of equality, unity and justice. In fact, the root of his concept of social justice could be traced to his own sufferings as well as those unfortunate millions who were born in the families of lowly castes in the hierarchy of caste based Hindu society. As a true social humanist and activist, he fought throughout his life for the abolition of all kinds of discrimination in society as well as the caste system which was an institutional mechanism for pampering and perpetuating discrimination between man and man for centuries. He, therefore, advocated for time bound protective discrimination for the vulnerable sections of society as an affirmative state action.

As an activist social thinker, Ambedkar emphasized forthrightly the need of the *samatagrahis*, the crusaders of "secular and humanistic nature for equality and social justice." In other words, the idea of social justice has to be pursued in both spirit and action, and for that, there is need fo nurture the spirit of unity and fraternity. In short, the essence of Ambedkar's concept of social justice, illustrates Jatav very aptly, consists of such humanitarian ingredients as "the unity and equality of all human beings, the equal worth of men and women, the respect for the weak and the lowly, the regard for human rights, the feeling of benevolence and mutual love, the abundance of social sympathy, the religious tolerance and charity, the sense of fellowship with others, the humane treatment in all cases, the dignity of all citizens, the abolition of caste distinctions, the education and property for all, the goodwill and gentleness..."[1] In order to achieve the goal of social justice, Ambedkar laid emphasis on the evolutionary process of social change through legal and constitutional means. He was a strong proponent for the common civil code for all citizens of India in order to ensure social harmony and spirit of fraternity without which social justice would remain a distant dream rather than a reality.

Constitutional Mandate for Social Justice

Dr. Ambedkar, as the Chairman of the Drafting Committee, played a leading role in mandating the State to create a new social order in independent India through incorporation of several provisions in the form of Fundamental Rights, Directive Principles of State Policy and affirmative state action. The Preamble itself, which specifies the objectives containing the unalterable basic structure of our Constitution, promises to secure to all its citizens:

> *JUSTICE, social, economic and political;*
> *LIBERTY of thought, expression, belief, faith and worship;*
> *EQUALITY of status and of opportunity and to promote among them all;*
> *FRATERNITY assuring the dignity of the individual and the unity and integrity of the Nation...*

These resonant words of the Preamble lucidly highlight the long-cherished desire of the people of India to be a part of an ideal society based on justice, liberty, equality and fraternity. In its quest for such an ideal society, the Constitution, through its Preamble, has authorised the state and its three principal organs—legislature, executive and judiciary—to take all necessary measures to create a sustainable social order in which every citizen could be assured of all inclusive justice without any discrimination on grounds of religion, race, caste, sex, descent, place of birth and residence. Article 38, for instance, says, "The state shall strive to promote the welfare of the people by securing and protecting as effectively as it may a social order in which justice, social, economic and political, shall inform all the institutions of the national life." Likewise, Article 46 stipulates, "The state shall promote with special care the educational and economic interests of the weaker sections of the people, and in particular, of the Scheduled Castes and the Scheduled Tribes, and shall protect them from social injustice and all forms of exploitation." Again, Article 44 provides, "The State shall endeavour to secure for the citizens a uniform civil code throughout the territory of India." These three Articles are part of the Directive Principles of State Policy under Part IV of the Constitution.

Constituent Assembly Debate on Issues related to Social Justice

The proposal relating to the incorporation of social and economic rights as non-justiciable rights in the Constitution did not initially find favour with some members of the Sub-Committee on Fundamental Rights. At the first meeting of the sub-committee held on February 27,1947, Alladi Krishnaswami Ayyar saw no use in laying down in the Constitution precepts which would remain unenforceable or ineffective. A similar view was expressed by K.M. Munshi, M.R. Masani and Dr. Ambedkar.[2] The opposition to the proposal did not, however, remain formidable for long, and gradually, most of the members of the sub-committee including Ambedkar, realized that it was not practicable in the context of the then socio-economic conditions of the Indian society after about 200 years of the British colonial exploitation to categorize declarations of social and economic policies as justiciable rights. However, while including them as the Directive Principles of State Policy, our Constitution makers gave a mandate *vide* Article 37 that these principles, though not enforceable by any court, "are nevertheless fundamental in the governance of the country and it shall be the duty of the State to apply these principles in making laws". Introducing the Draft Constitution in the Constituent Assembly on November 4, 1948, Ambedkar said very forthrightly that though the directive principles had no legal force behind them, he was not prepared to admit that they had no sort of binding force, nor was he prepared to concede that they were "useless" simply because they had no binding force in law.[3] On the whole, this event highlights that Dr. Ambedkar, though being an undisputed national leader of the *dalits,* was indeed a rational and pragmatic social and political thinker who was guided more by rational and practical considerations rather than emotion while taking part in the historic deliberations of the Constituent Assembly.

Another controversial issue that was deliberated intensively in the Constituent Assembly related to the proposal of the Sub-Committee on Fundamental Rights for a uniform civil code. Three eminent members of this committee, namely, M.R. Masani, Mrs. Hansa Mehta and Rajkumari Amrit Kaur, contended that one of the factors keeping India back from advancing to nationhood was the existence of personal laws based on religion. They suggested, therefore, the transfer of the clause regarding a uniform civil code to the part dealing with justiciable rights.[4] The Minorities Sub-Committee, on the other side, agreed that a uniform civil code was desirable, but felt that the application of such a code could be made on an entirely voluntary basis, and recommended in its interim report that the clause regarding a uniform civil code be suitably redrafted.[5]

Taking cue from these deliberations, Dr. Ambedkar, while introducing the Draft Constitution in the Assembly pointed out very poignantly:

> We have in this country a uniform code of laws covering almost every aspect of human relationship. We have a uniform and complete criminal code... We have the law of transfer of property which deals with property relations and which is operative throughout the country...I can cite innumerable enactments which would prove that this country has practically a civil code, uniform in its content and applicable to the whole of the country.

Dealing with the apprehension that a uniform civil code might be forcibly imposed on unwilling minorities or groups, Ambedkar said very emphatically that there was nothing in the draft article to warrant the view that the state would enforce a uniform civil code upon all citizens merely because they were citizens, and it was possible that a future Parliament might make a provision that, to begin with, the code would apply only to those who declared that they were prepared to be bound by it.[6]

As for the fundamental rights and affirmative state action, which together constitute the most effective instrument of social justice and harmony, Dr. Ambedkar, being the Chairman of the Drafting Committee as well as a member of the Sub-Committee on Human Rights, played a significant role in their formulation. India being the motherland of one of the oldest civilizations of the world and the birth place of diverse cultures and religions has been blessed with a very rich heritage of human rights, ideals and values. Ironically, despite such a rich heritage, there had been barbaric societal violence against women, children and the so-called untouchables in our society since ancient times, and that too, in the name of religion or *dharma*. However, the late eighteenth and early nineteenth centuries witnessed vibrant social reform movements in Bengal, Maharashtra, Andhra and other parts of India against such societal violence. Later on, in the twentieth century, when the nationalist movement became a mass movement under Gandhiji's leadership, social reform for preservation of human rights of the *harijans* and other vulnerable groups became an integral part of India's freedom struggle.[7]

Dr. B.R. Ambedkar who was one of the main architects of the Constitution of Republic India also cherished the ideals of human dignity and human development for all without any discrimination whatsoever. It was a significant historical coincidence that around the time the Constituent Assembly of independent India was deliberating upon the Draft Constitution prepared by its Drafting Committee under the Chairmanship of Dr. Ambedkar, the newly constituted world body, the United Nations General Assembly, with wider representation of the newly independent Afro-Asian nations including India, was also engaged in intensive discourse on the draft Universal Declaration of Human Rights in the backdrop of unprecedented human losses, devastation and destruction of the Second World War. It was, therefore, quite natural that the ethos of our national liberation movement and the world community's concern for human rights and dignity were manifested in the framing of our Constitution. Apart from the incorporation of socio-economic rights as Directive Principles of State Policy, other ingredients of human rights such as civil and political rights and the rights of vulnerable sections found expression in the forms of justiciable fundamental rights as well as affirmative state action. Constitutional provisions relating to right to equality (Article 14), prohibition of discrimination on grounds of religion, race, caste, sex or place of birth (Article 15), abolition of the practice of untouchability (Article 17), prohibition of employment of children in factory or mine or in any other hazardous employment (Article 24), are examples of notable fundamental rights. Likewise, provisions authorizing the state to make any special provision for women and children [Article 15(3)], and appoint a Commission to investigate the conditions of socially and educationally backward classes (Article 340) are examples of affirmative state action. In pursuance with these constitutional provisions a number of legislations were enacted by the Union and State governments from time to time.

Ambedkar's Views on Constitutionalism

Constitutionalism denotes a kind of political order with certain political objectives like protection of individual's rights and limitation on powers of the government, while constitution is a necessary means for achieving such objectives.[8] This close relationship between constitution and constitutionalism is evident since a constitution defines political institutions, prescribes restrains upon political power and guarantees individual's rights. However, the fundamental difference between them lies in the fact that while constitutionalism is based on ideology, the basis of legitimacy of a constitution is law. Yet, the two are closely related since the constitution is the means and constitutionalism the end.[9]

Ambedkar, like other great national leaders of his generation, was influenced by the western liberal ideas. During his stay in America (1913-16), England (1920-21) and Germany (1922-23) for higher studies in Political Economy and Law, he was exposed to the western liberal thoughts on constitution and constitutionalism. His advocacy for parliamentary democracy, federal constitution, supremacy of the constitution as a fundamental document, fundamental rights with necessary restrictions, safeguards for minorities and provisions relating to amendment of the Constitution, emanating from his exposures to the western liberal ideas as well as his own ideas as a distinguished social and political thinker and a jurist, had been manifested in the framing of India's Constitution.

Justifying the merits of the Parliamentary system *vis-à-vis* a non-Parliamentary system, Dr. Ambedkar, the Chairman of the Drafting Committee, in his speech.[10] While moving the Draft Constitution in the Constituent Assembly on November 4, 1948 argued:

> ...The Parliamentary system differs from a non-Parliamentary system inasmuch as the former is more responsible than the latter but they also differ as to the time and agency for assessment of their responsibility. Under the non-Parliamentary system, such as the one that exists in the U.S.A., the assessment of the responsibility of the Executive is periodic. It takes place once in two years. It is done by the electorate. In England, where the Parliamentary system prevails, the assessment of the responsibility of the Executive is both daily and periodic. The daily assessment is done by members of Parliament, through questions, resolutions, no-confidence motions, adjournment motions and debates on addresses. Periodic assessment is done by the electorate at the time of the election which may take place every five years or earlier. The daily assessment

> of responsibility which is not available under the American system is, it is felt, far more effective than the periodic assessment and far more necessary in a country like India. The Draft Constitution in recommending the Parliamentary system of Executive has preferred more responsibility to more stability.

As regards the form of the Constitution, the Draft Constitution proposed a federal constitution inasmuch as it sought to establish a dual polity consisting of the Union at the Centre and the States at the periphery, each endowed with sovereign powers to be exercised in the field assigned to them respectively by the Constitution. Pointing out the differences between the proposed Indian Federation and other federations, Dr. Ambedkar observed eloquently in his historic speech:

> ...There are two weaknesses from which federation is alleged to suffer. One is rigidity and the other is legalism. That these faults are inherent in federalism; there can be no dispute. A federal constitution cannot but be a written constitution and a written constitution must necessarily be a rigid constitution. A federal constitution means division of sovereignty by no less a sanction than that of the law of the constitution between the federal Government and the States, with two necessary consequences (1) that any invasion by the federal Government in the field assigned to the States and *vice versa* is a breach of the constitution; and (2) such breach is a justiciable matter to be determined by the judiciary only. This being the nature of federalism, a federal constitution cannot escape the charge of legalism. These faults of a federal constitution have been found in a pronounced form in the Constitution of the United States of America.

"In assuaging the rigour of rigidity and legalism", observed Ambedkar, "the Draft Constitution follows the Australian plan on a far more extensive scale than has been done in Australia. Like the Australian Constitution, it has a long list of subjects for concurrent powers of legislation." Yet, as he noted further:

> ...The biggest advance made by the Draft Constitution over the Australian Constitution is in the matter of exclusive powers of legislation vested in Parliament. While the exclusive authority of the Australian Parliament to legislate extends only to about three matters, the authority of the Indian Parliament as proposed in the Draft Constitution will extend to 91 matters. In this way the Draft constitution has secured the greatest possible elasticity in its federalism which is supposed to be rigid by nature.

Pointing out another ingenuity of the proposed Indian Federation *vis-à-vis* other federations, Ambedkar said:

> The Draft Constitution has sought to forge means and methods whereby India will have a federation and at the same time will have uniformity in all basic matters which are essential to maintain the unity of the country. The means adopted by the Draft Constitution are three:
>
> (1) a single judiciary;
> (2) uniformity in fundamental laws, civil and criminal; and
> (3) a common all-India civil service to man important posts.

Responding to the accusation that the Draft Constitution has produced a good part of the provisions of the Government of India Act, 1935, Dr. Ambedkar made a very frank and fair submission as he said, "I make no apologies. There is nothing to be ashamed of in borrowing. It involves no plagiarism. Nobody hold any patent rights in the fundamental ideas of a constitution. What I am sorry about is that the provisions taken from the Government of India Act, 1935 relate mostly to the details of administration."

Replying to the objection of some critics to the description of India in Article 1 of the Draft Constitution as a *Union of States* instead of a *Federation of States,* Ambedkar made the following enlightening observations:

> It is true that South Africa which is a unitary State is described as a Union. But Canada which is a Federation is also called a Union. Thus the description of India as a Union, though its Constitution is federal, does no violence to usage. But what is important is that the use of the word "Union" is deliberate. I do not know why the word 'Union' was used in the Canadian Constitution. But I can tell you why the Drafting Committee has used it. The Drafting Committee wanted to make it clear that though India was to be a Federation, the Federation was not the result of an agreement by the States to join in a Federation and that the Federation not being the result of an agreement no State has the right to secede from it. The Federation is a Union because it is indestructible. Though the country and the people may be divided into different States for convenience of administration the country is one integral whole, its people a single people living under a single imperium derived from a single source. The Americans had to wage a civil war to establish that the States have no right of secession and that their Federation was indestructible. The Drafting Committee thought that it was better to make it clear at the outset rather than to leave it to speculation or to dispute.

The provisions relating to amendment of the Constitution also came in for a "virulent attack" from the critics of the Draft Constitution on the ground that the provisions contained in the Draft made amendment difficult. It was proposed that the Constitution should be amendable by a simple majority at least for some years, and to justify this proposal, the critics argued ingeniously and subtly that this Constituent Assembly was not elected on adult suffrage while the future Parliament would be elected on adult suffrage and yet the former had been given the right to pass the Constitution by a simple majority while the latter had been denied the same right. They contended this flaw as "one of the absurdities of the Draft Constitution". Dr. Ambedkar, while responding to this criticism, used his expertise in constitutional jurisprudence to argue vigorously:

> I must repudiate the charge because it is without foundation. To know how simple are the provisions of the Draft Constitution in respect of amending the Constitution one has only to study the provisions for amendment contained in the American and Australian Constitutions. Compared to them those contained in the Draft Constitution will be found to be simplest. The Draft Constitution has eliminated the elaborate and difficult procedures such as a decision by a convention or a referendum. The powers of amendment are left with the Legislatures, Central and Provincial. It is only for amendments of specific matters and they are only a few that the ratification of the State Legislatures is required. All other articles of the Constitution are left to be amended by Parliament. The only limitation is that it shall be done by a majority of not less than two-thirds of the members of each House present and voting and a majority of the total membership of each House. It is difficult to conceive simpler method of amending the Constitution.

Refuting the critics' misconceived contention in regard to the absurdity of the amending provisions, Dr. Ambedkar being a great visionary, clarified the position of the Constituent Assembly and the future Parliament very lucidly in the following words:

> The Constituent Assembly, in making a Constitution has no partisan motive. Beyond securing a good and workable constitution it has no axe to grind. In considering the articles of the Constitution it has no eye on getting through a particular measure. If the future Parliament met as a Constituent Assembly, its

> members will be acting as partisans seeking to carry out amendments to the Constitution to facilitate the passing of party measures which they have failed to get through Parliament by reason of some article of the Constitution which has acted as an obstacle in their way. Parliament will have an axe to grind while the Constituent Assembly has none. That is the difference, between the Constituent Assembly and the future Parliament. That explains why the Constituent Assembly though elected on limited franchise can be trusted to pass the Constitution by simple majority and why the Parliament though elected on adult suffrage cannot be trusted with the same power to amend it.

Concluding his historic speech moving the Draft Constitution in the Constituent Assembly, Dr. Ambedkar once again demonstrated his brilliance as a great thinker and a visionary in the following observations:

> No Constitution is perfect and the Drafting Committee itself is suggesting certain amendments to improve the Draft Constitution. But the debates in the Provincial Assemblies give me courage to say that the Constitution as settled by the Drafting Committee is good enough to make in this country a start with. I feel that it is workable, it is flexible and it is strong enough to hold the country together both in peace time and in war time. Indeed, if I may say so, if things go wrong under the new Constitution, the reason will not be that we had a bad Constitution. What we will have to say is, that Man was vile.

Concluding Observations

Our foregoing discourse presents a glimpse of Dr. B.R. Ambedkar's unparalleled contribution in the framing of India's Constitution after the advent of freedom. Even his stern critics in the Constituent Assembly were ultimately convinced with his unique idea of social justice, his liberal views on constitutionalism, his progressive concept of rights of the people, his vision of an ideal society and his enlightening deliberations on the Draft Constitution. The Constituent Assembly took up the third reading of the Constitution on November 17, 1949, on a motion by Ambedkar "that the Constitution as settled by the Assembly be passed." The discussion on the motion concluded on November 26 and the motion was put to vote and adopted amidst prolonged cheers. On the same day the President of the Constituent Assembly, Dr. Rajendra Prasad, authenticated the new Constitution of India, which came into effect on January 26, 1950.

Paying a tribute to Dr. Ambedkar and also acknowledging his contribution as one of the main architects of India's Constitution, Dr. Rajendra Prasad observed, "Sitting in the chair and watching the proceedings (in the Constituent Assembly) from day-to-day, I have realized, as nobody else could have, with what zeal and devotion the members of the Drafting Committee, and specially its Chairman, Dr. Ambedkar, in spite of his indifferent health have worked. We could now make a decision which was or could even be so right as when we put him on the Drafting Committee and made him its Chairman. He has not only justified his selection but has added luster to the work he has done."[11]

NOTES

1. Jatava, D.R.; *B.R. Ambedkar: Study in Society and Politics*, Jaipur/ Delhi, National Publishing House, 1998, p.118.
2. Rao, B. Shiva, *The Framing of India's Constitution: A Study*, Delhi, IIPA, 1968, Vol.V, p. 321. In India, the idea of the division of rights to be incorporated in the Constitution into justiciable and non-justiciable rights was for the first time envisaged in the report of the Sapru Committee in 1944-45. This Committee was formed with the approval of Mahatma Gandhi. Its object was to understand the point of view of each political party and act as a conciliation board by establishing contact with leaders of all parties and to recommend on its own responsibility solution of India's political problems. The members of the committee were eminent persons in Indian public life but not belonging to any of the organized political parties. Its Chairman was Tej Bahadur Sapru.

3. *Ibid.*, Vol. IV, p. 432.
4. Report of the sub-committee, Minutes of Dissent, *Select Documents* II, 4(ix), p. 177.
5. *Select Documents* II, 5(ii), p. 209.
6. *Constituent Assembly Debate,* Vol. VII, pp. 540-52.
7. Guha Roy, Jaytilak, *Human Rights for the Twentyfirst Century,* Delhi, IIPA, 2004, pp. 6-7.
8. Friedrich, Carl J., "Constitution and Constitutionalism," *Encyclopedia of Social Sciences,* Vol. 3, p. 319.
9. Tiwary, Shailendra K., *Dr. Ambedkar and Indian Constitution,* Gurgaon, Haryana, Shubhi, 2008, p. 27.
10. For full text of Ambedkar's speech, see *Constituent Assembly Debate,* Vol.VII, pp. 31-34.
11. *Supra.* n. 9, p. 58.

6

Ambedkar on Economic Development

Visioning and Reasoning

P.K. CHAUBEY

Introduction

It is well recognized that Ambedkar was one of the great intellectual giants who contributed to making of the nation that India is today through intellectual discourse and social activism, to an extent through a kind of crusade, besides leading the drafting committee of the Constitution—which later in life he might have loved to repudiate. Much research has been carried out on his work and contribution to the much desired social causes but, in my estimate, enough attention has not been paid to his contributions in the economic domain.

Undoubtedly, he always used his understanding of economics, western as it was in its orientation, to improve the economics of India. If one cares to classify his economics contributions he would find that they were mainly in three areas: (i) monetary system and monetary policy, the role they are supposed to play in furthering welfare of people, (ii) fiscal federalism, the manner in which revenue be collected from the social economy, as he calls it, for fiscal operations and the manner and principles on which should base the relationship between provincial governments and the central government so that a kind of co-ordinate relationship is established, and (iii) economic transformation of the Indian economy from its exclusively agrarian character to substantially industrial one in order to create productive employment to idling masses on the one hand to raise productivity of agriculture on the other, and ultimately to end crushing poverty.

I propose to pursue the third theme outlined above, primarily perusing his work published full ninety years ago in 1918, basically because this aspect of his work is in my view the most neglected one. It is here that he says industrialisation of India is the soundest remedy for the agricultural problems of India, which was no ordinary thing to say in those days, where the stalwarts of the day were moving in circular grooves and actually remedies suggested by them could only aggravate rather than resolve the problems of the Indian economy. In fact Ambedkar could clearly anticipate development economists (like Fisher, Clark, Nurske, and Lewis) to come decades after and could articulate the argument in general equilibrium framework in a concrete situation. But I would like to develop the theme by incorporating his views on the nature of industrialisation as well as on the role of the State to bring about it.

However, I am tempted to devote some space to his own progression in life albeit briefly and his intellectual journey particularly in relation to his deliberations in matters economique. In the following section I shall touch upon his progression from Bhim to Bharat Ratna Babasaheb Dr. Bhimrao Ramji Ambedkar. Thereafter, I shall again be devoting some space to his academic achievements and contributions. Though there shall be some overlap with other contributions in the volume in this respect yet it will pay, I hope, the reader who picks up to exclusively read this particular chapter. Thereafter, I shall devote a section to evolution of his economic vision of India, which is an industrialised India and another on what kind of industrialisation he visualised and whom was it meant for and how it woud be brought about. I shall also be providing an annexure, though a bit of digression, which shows incisiveness of analytical acumen of a theoretician.

Affection, Admiration and Veneration

Born in Mhow on 14th of April, 1891 as fourteenth child of Ramji Maloji Sakpal from Mahar caste, a sepoy in the British army—actually a trainee teacher in the military school to serve as headmaster with the rank of Subedar Major, and Bhimabai Murbadkar, Bhim chose for his surname Ambavadekar after the name of his ancestral village Ambavade, following the Maharashtrian tradition, though the family had long left the village for better fortunes. However, his surname got changed in the school records from Ambavadekar to Ambedkar due to his teacher Mahadev, a Deshastha Brahmin, who was himself an Ambedkar and loved Bhim so much for his brilliance and often gave him his food in recess. A respectful suffix Rao got added to his first name, it seems, after he brilliantly passed his High School and joined the University of Bombay at Elphinstone College in 1907. He received, from a Maratha scholar Krishnaji Arjun Keluskar who was his father's friend in a function organized on his success, a book on Buddha penned by him for Sayaji Oriental Series.

It was quite early in age, may be in his late twenties, that he started being addressed as Babasaheb by his followers who found in him a steadfast, an unparalleled, intellectual crusader against untouchability from which suffered a big section of society for a good number of centuries. He was the one to tell his followers: Educate, Agitate and Organise.

He was posthumously awarded with highest national civilian award Bharat Ratna in 1990 in recognition to his services to the nation. Though bitter critic of the positions taken by many national heroes of his times and particularly of Gandhi, he was adopting only non-violent means in his agitations and would not mind seeking, if necessary, the State support for reforms, so badly needed, in the manner Raja Rammohun Roy and Mahadev Govind Ranade did before.

There is no doubt that he also had his lot of brickbats as any activist of his level would have. He was called a bourgeois reformer as well as a believer in state socialism, a rank patriot as well as a stooge of British imperialism, and a sectarian thinker as well as a great modern secularist.

Academic Achievements and Contributions

With a financial assistance from the State of Baroda, Bhimrao, as he was known now, could continue his studies and passed B.A. in 1912 with Economics and Politics as special subjects. Again with a scholarship of £ 11.5 per month for three years from the State of Baroda (Sayaji Rao III) yet again, he proceeded to join the University of Columbia at New York in July 1913. Majoring in Economics in his graduation in 1915 by opting 29 out of 60 courses in Economics, History, Sociology, Philosophy, Anthropology, Politics, French and German and writing two M.A. level theses in Economics, viz. *Ancient Indian Commerce* (1915) [and there is a reference to his thesis on *Administration and Finance of the East India Company* (1915)] and *National Dividend of India: A Historic and Analytical Study* (1916), but he had also written a piece on *Castes in India: Their Mechanism, Genesis and Development* for an anthropology seminar, which was subsequently published in the *Indian Antiquary* (1917)—twenty years later to be developed into the monograph *Annihilation of Castes* (1936). He was formally awarded his Ph.D. degree by Columbia University on 8th June in 1927, presumably for his work on *The Stabilization of Indian Exchange* submitted by him in 1922 (as appears from his letter to his teacher R.A. Seligman). This University chose to award him with an *honoris causa* in 1952 and to honour him by a Bronze bust on the Campus in1995 and again in a function organized in the celebration of its 250th birth anniversary which was attended by his widow Savita Ambedkar.

Back in India *via* England, where he stayed for a while and enrolled in London School of Economics and Grey's Inn, on expiry of his scholarship given by the State of Baroda, he opted to become Professor of Political Economy in Sydenham College of Commerce and Economics in 1918 when he failed to carry on well in Baroda State as Military Secretary and in Bombay as investment consultant and accountant, all on account of caste prejudices then prevailing in the society. Incidentally this was the time the Indian National Congress had adopted a resolution in its Calcutta session under presidentship of Annie Besant, whom Ambedkar met little before, to do away with disabilities imposed by custom on the Depressed Classes.

During the small period he was in Sydenham College he contributed to the journals of newly established Indian Economic Association and Indian Economic Society one of which was on *Small Holdings in India and their Remedies,* which was published in the Journal of Indian Economic Society in 1918 alongside deposing testimony and arguing in writing for a separate electorate for Untouchable Hindus in addition to those for Muslims, Christians, Parsees and Jews. He started publishing a weekly *Mooknayak* in 1920 where he wrote about emancipation of Depressed Classes from perpetual slavery, poverty and ignorance, and participated or organized Depressed Classes conferences—all with the support of Shahuji, the Maharaja of Kolhapur. In a way he was pursuing two somewhat unconnected lines during this time: one of an academic and analytical professional and the other of a social, political activist, a bit of crusader, for securing an honourable position for the people of the Depressed Classes to which he belonged to by birth. It seems the second line quite justifiably overtook him in his subsequent career.

However, he chose to resign from Sydenham College in July 1920 to go to London, with financial support from quarters like State of Kolhapur, and completed his M.Sc. in Economics in 1922 in London School of Economics by writing a thesis on *The Evolution of Provincial Finance in British India: A Study in the Provincial Decentralisation of Imperial Finance,* which was published a few years later in 1925 by P.S. King & Son. He was allowed to submit a thesis for D.Sc. degree to the University of London (1923). He was most probably the first Indian to receive a doctorate in Economics. His D.Sc. thesis on *The Problem of the Rupee* was challenged on political grounds (for being allegedly subversive and having anti-British implications), and had to be resubmitted but was finally accepted. It was immediately published by P. S. King & Son. During his stay in London he had joined Grey's Inn and was admitted to the British Bar as a Barrister at Law. He spent a few months in Germany also. Back in India he was nominated to Bombay Legislative Council in 1926. In 1928 he was appointed Principal of Government Law College at Bombay.

Ambirajan feels that (unfortunately) he left the pursuit of academic professional economics very soon after coming to India having served for a brief period as professor of political economy at the Sydenham College of Commerce and Economics, Bombay. Without controverting Ambirajan, one can assert that Ambedkar continued doing Economics from 1913 when he joined the University of Columbia till at least 1925 when his D.Sc. work was published while he was in Sydenham College only during 1918-20. Moreover he did his B.A. with Economics and Political Science from the University of Bombay.

Besides deposing on economic questions before committees and commissions or submitting memoranda and intervening in Bombay Presidency Legislative Council/ Assembly, he delivered some important memorial lectures. He was invited to deliver R. R. Kale Memorial Lecture on *Federation versus Freedom* in Gokhale Institute of Politics and Economics in 1939. He delivered Presidential address on the occasion of 101 anniversary of Justice Mahadev Govind Ranade which he published in 1943 with the title *Ranade, Gandhi, and Jinnah.*

In July 1942, when Congress had boycotted the Government, Ambedkar was inducted as Labour Member of the Viceroy's Executive Council, a little before Congress launched Quit India Movement, where his portfolio also included the subjects of irrigation and power, all subjects being part of the provincial list under Government of India Act, 1935. During this period as the Minister in charge of Labour, Irrigation and Power, he had chance to pick up, articulate and develop economics of development in a planning framework. Even though his role was somewhat limited he chose to formulate strategies in a wider perspective. However, he resigned from his position in 1946 when the interim government, with Jawaharlal Nehru as premier, was formed.

After Independence Ambedkar, a member of Constituent Assembly elected from Bengal, was invited by Nehru to join his Cabinet as Law Minister in late August 1947 and was appointed Chairman of Drafting Committee of the Constitution of India, which was to envision a polity incorporating aspirations and accommodating interests—a job which he did remarkably well with the assistance of B.N. Rau. However, when he found that the Hindu Code Bill, drafted and presented by him in the Parliament, did not have full support of Nehru (who swore to swim or sink with it) and the Congress, despite the fact it contained provisions of expanded rights for women, he chose to resign as Minister in September 1951 only to become the Leader of the Opposition. However, he was defeated in Lok Sabha in 1952 elections but was however got elected to Rajya Sabha in March 1952.

It is reported that Ambedkar was denied the Deputy Chairmanship of the Planning Commission, which he very much desired and was tipped for. It is also reported when he was made Law Minister while he was expecting the Ministry of Finance, Home, or Industries—which he took as a humiliation. In view of Gopal Guru, Ambedkar demonstrated by pushing forward the Hindu Code Bill and resigned on matters of principle.

A little before *nirvana* on 6th December, 1956, he had embraced Buddhism (14th October), which he had in mind since 1935 when he declared he was born a Hindu but he would not die as one.

Evolution of Economic Vision

It was clear right from the beginning that Ambedkar used his scholastic understanding, western as it was, to study the problems of India—her society, economy, and polity—was facing, much in the fashion classical economists were doing in the eighteenth and nineteenth centuries in Europe. He made many contributions, as a budding economist, in his twenties but the one which gives glimpse of his vision of Indian economy was contained in his paper titled as *Small Holdings in India and their Remedies* and published in the very first volume of the *Journal of the Indian Economic Society*—the learned body which came up along with the Indian Economic Association but did not survive for long. The paper engages in a debate about a problem that involved many a great mind of the day as well as the governments—both British Indian and princely States. Underlying the importance of agriculture, as everybody else does, Ambedkar says that its importance cannot be exaggerated particularly when a country entirely depends on farming. But he further says out of many problems the agriculture economy suffers from he chooses to deal with the problem of the size of holdings as it affects the productivity of agriculture. Undoubtedly, he does much more as he examines many concepts and propositions as academic exercises. Nevertheless, he was trying to repudiate the economists and officials who all seemed to be echoing, in Ambedkar's words:

> Enlarge and consolidate the holdings, it is confidently argued, and the increase in agricultural productivity will follow in its wake !

It is here that Ambedkar comes with the conclusion that industrialisation of India is the soundest remedy for the agricultural problems of India but he was careful to preface this conclusion with words 'strange though it may seem'. Only authorities he quotes for support were Robert Griffen and Henry Cotton. Robert Griffen had studied the economic tendencies in various countries and had found that as the wants of men increase with resources, the proportion of people engaged in primary activities (agriculture and mining and analogous pursuits) is destined to decline and that of the people engaged in (miscellaneous) industry to increase (AGB Fisher and Colin Clark were to say so much after). Henry Cotton—an officer of Bengal Civil Service serving for long in Assam and the President of Indian National Congress in 1904, whom he quotes to end his paper, held that there was a danger of too much agriculture in India. Ambedkar seems to agree with them but gives solid reasoning for adoption of the policy of industrialisation.

Context

Beginning of the twentieth century most Indian thinkers, Ambedkar being one of the firsts, were worried about superfluous and idle labour and what to do about their productive engagement. We may note that terms such as unemployment and at that disguised unemployment or surplus labour had yet to assume technical meaning.

Most had noted the long continuing process of de-urbanisation and blamed the British rule for it, few thought about the possibility of industrialisation in the fashion of the USA, which started out as an agricultural country. Ranade whom he admired a great deal was one of the exceptions who wanted the State to promote and protect industries, arguing in the fashion of List and questioning the universalism of economic theories. He naturally thought of stemming the tide of swelling rural population beyond need. He was not contemplating some extra engagement for rural population by reviving handicrafts. We may recall that by then the kind of Swadeshi Gandhi advocated a little later had not been articulated and Gandhi was still wearing coarse mill cloth rather than khadi.

Ambedkar was not the first to take note of low productivity of agriculture, or of idleness of labour, nor was he the first to advocate for industrialisation but, it is important to underline, he was probably the first to interconnect the three in a general interdependence framework. He was not questioning universalism of economic theories as Ranade was doing but was finding instead the Indian case as an aberration; he was not seeking protection for Indian industries from foreign competition but was seeking industrialisation to relieve agriculture of excess labour and to provide alternative source of livelihood to those who hardly had anything to do.

Perspective

Around the time of the First World War, economists and other thinkers as well as various provincial governments were grappling with the issue of low productivity of agriculture in

India, on which depended a lot of its labour—particularly because of deurbanisation and deindustrialisation of India, rare phenomena wrought by industrialisation in Britain and thus reversing the trade flows in the later half of the rule under East India Company which came to import calicos and condiments from India. This overdependence of labour, often erroneously imputed to rise in population (a view shared by Ambedkar), on agriculture work resulted in subdivision and fragmentation of agricultural holdings, permitted under inheritance laws—both Hindu and Muslim. The suggestions that were being made in those days were to disallow fragmentation, to restrain subdivision, to consolidate holdings, and, if possible, to enlarge holding size—all through administrative and legal measures, and at times to go for capitalist farming. Ambedkar chose to intensively examine the problem and the solutions offered by various economists and came to conclude, to repeat, industrialisation of India is the soundest remedy for the agricultural problems of India.

The prominent academics involved in the debate included H.S. Jevons of the University of Allahabad and Gilbert Slater of the University of Madras. Ambedkar seems to have interacted, at least through correspondence, with them. Jevons has either published or presented the following: *Capitalist Development of Agriculture* (1915) and *The Consolidation of Agricultural Holdings in the United Provinces* (1918). Slater had published *The Village in the Melting Pot* in the very first issue of the *Journal of the Indian Economic Society* to which Ambedkar contributed subsequently in the third issue, the very same year. The documents he seems to have gone over and examine the recommendations and arguments were Report of the Committee to make proposals on the Consolidation of Small and Scattered Holdings in the Baroda State (1917) and a draft bill prepared for introduction in the Legislature of Bombay Presidency by G.F. Keatinge (Director Agriculture), particularly its Statement of Objects and Reasons. There is a reference to Dr. H.S. Mann and his colleagues who carried out a survey of holdings in a village near Poona. He also consults Report on the Enquiry into the Rise of Prices in India (K.L. Datta, 1914), Indian Industries (Elliot James), Survey Settlement Manual,

Bombay Presidency (1888), Report on the Agricultural Indebtedness in the Baroda State (M.B. Nanawati, 1913) and an authoritative work on India by James Caird (1884), viz., *India, the Land and the People.* There are references to (then) latest issue of *American Economic Review* (1919), besides standard texts by Richard T. Ely, N.G. Piersson and J. Davenport, besides Adam Smith's *Wealth of Nations.* He uses measures (mean and mode) of so-called central tendency (a little imprecisely) and frequency distribution—quite a feat in those days as Lorenz curve had hardly arrived and was not within the grips of social scientists—but not measures of dispersion.

Capitalist Development of Agriculture

It was in December 1915 in Indian Industrial Conference that Jevons read a paper with the title *Capitalist Development of Agriculture* where he argued against industrialisation to which Ambedkar reacted in a footnote of his *small holding* paper that capitalist development of agriculture is possible only through industrialisation and makes reference to Griffen's work. In fact Ambedkar finds much of reasoning that Jevons employed as basically flawed. For example, Jevons wanted capitalist development of agriculture and surplus population of villages to migrate to towns while opposing industrialisation !

Jevons was mechanically transporting the British economic history to the case of Indian economy without adequately appreciating the difference between the economics of India *vis-à-vis* those of Britain. Ambedkar till this time was employing standard tools of capitalist enterprise, looking into factors of production, their costs, produce and implicitly revenue therefrom though his farmers, it seems, were self-employed and were employing their resources in agricultural (farming) operations.

Fact of Subdivision and Fragmentation

Quoting Adam Smith as to how the law of primogeniture came into being in the succession of landed estate in England (though not in France, Holland and Denmark) in troubled times, that is, in order to preserve large holdings and save it from ruin due to subdivision, Ambedkar shells out statistics from four provinces, districts in the State of Baroda and a village in Poona to show that (average) size of the holding varied from 26 acres to 1 acre. He further quotes statistics for typical cases of fragmentation, collected by G.F. Keatinge from different villages from different talukas of different districts to show that a holding of as small size as one acre had as many as 14 plots and another of little over ½ acre with 9 plots while a holding of about 48 acres had as many as 53 plots. There is only one case, that is, of a large holding of 220 acres, having only one plot (though the copy of the paper I could catch hold of shows a holding with zero area !) He shares the worry and anxiety of everybody about small and scattered holdings. How did it come about? In each successive generation, (male) children will get a share not only in the holding but may get a share in each of the plots in that holding with a man howsoever he acquires—through inheritance or purchase. Total agriculture land of a person in a village constitutes his holding.

Ambedkar adds two comparative international statistics (without quoting source): one about occupation statistics in terms of percentage agricultural population (labour force), and the other about yield (produce per acre) in pounds. Of the fourteen countries, India had 71.5 population engaged in agriculture whereas England (and Wales) had only 15.3 per cent and USA, 33.3 per cent so engaged. Only Hungary was close to Indian scene and perhaps Denmark exceeded. From eleven countries and five provinces, one can find that in terms of yield UP, the best in India, had yield less than half of that in the UK in wheat and less than one-third of what Canada had in maize. In fact, every country quoted was doing better than UP which in turn had been doing better than every other province in the country. These painful truths made many people to inquire into the causes of this low productivity. The answer that seemed obvious to most was that it was so because of excessive subdivision and fragmentation of agricultural holdings and solution that seemed obvious to most was consolidation of the holdings and, if possible, enlargement thereof and they thought all will be well in terms of the increase in agricultural productivity (in terms of per acre yield). And since subdivision and fragments of holdings was permitted by law, law had to be changed to consolidate fragments and to prevent subdivision and fragmentation below a certain level (floor).

Solutions of Consolidation

Deliberating on the issue of consolidating fragmented holding into and holding on to it perpetually, Ambedkar points out that fragmentation is not a necessary corollary of subdivision of a holding but sadly it happens and efficiency is pitted against some kind of distributive justice and it results in a variety of wastage of land in hedges/boundary, of manure and cattle power, and of labour as well as renders capital improvement in land through roads, water channels. This affects yield and raises cost of production.

Ambedkar scrutinizes three proposals on consolidation of fragmented holdings, which were advocated by Baroda Committee for Consolidation (1917), by G.F. Keatinge in his draft bill for consolidation in Bombay Presidency (1918 ?), and by H.S. Jevons in *The Consolidation of Holdings in the United Provinces* (1918). There are two issues in the exercise—one of consolidating fragmented holdings, that is, uniting all plots of a holding into one and the other of keeping it united in future. Given the empirical reality, desire of one account holder will not be sufficient condition for any consolidation, a good number of them have to come forward. A measure of compulsion may be needed. Baroda Committee favours compulsory consolidation of holdings in a village if two-thirds of account holders, occupying more than half the land opted for consolidation while Jevons would be happy if holders of half the area desired so irrespective of their number. While Jevons does not bother about subdivision in future whether through succession or sale of a part of a holding Baroda Committee wants that subdivision should not go below a floor—economic unit—whether given to a family or cultivated in common. Keatinge is happy with preventing further fragmentation. Law of succession may permit inheritance of land to one child only, in case there are many children, if the size of land on division is below a certain floor. In these proposals, it may be noted, consolidation and preservation of consolidated holdings are all to be achieved through administrative actions and legislative means.

This idea of economic holding is discussed in the Baroda Committee Report (though not advocated at consolidation stage) as well as in Statement of Objects and Reasons in the bill drafted by Keatinge (Director, Agriculture, Presidency of Bombay). If it is said that Indian agriculture suffers from small and scattered holdings we must not only consolidate, as Ambedkar words it, but also enlarge them. It must be borne in mind that consolidation may obviate the evils of scattered holdings, he points out, it will not obviate the evils of small holdings unless the consolidated holding is an economic, i.e. an enlarged holding. (It should however be noted that most of the discussion, if not all, is being discussed in the context of self-employed pursuit.)

Malady of Social Economy

On the issue of economic holding there is a good amount of digression in the paper (*See* Annexure) where he comes to conclude that existing holdings, small in acreage, are too big when considered in relation to the instruments of production other than land (and, we may add, labour !). So the solution, argues Ambedkar, lies not in enlargement of holdings but in increasing capital and capital goods, which requires savings and savings are where surplus is !

How to bring about surplus in agricultural economy, that is, how to turn a deficit agricultural economy into a surplus one? Here he says he agrees/approves (in a way comes back to the view of others) that consolidation and enlargement of holdings is the answer but he demurs with the method of realizing it. Here he points out that evil of small holding is not fundamental but one derived from the parent evil of maladjustment in her social economy and holds that permanent cure of the evil lies in treating the parent malady.

This enormous pressure of population, as exemplified by population density in general and that over cultivable land, is the chief cause of subdivision. The failure to grasp this fact makes scholars question the law of inheritance, which is to invert the real problem. When one has to choose between a small piece of land and nothing, one has to the former. That is why there is so much premium on land. Not law of inheritance but high pressure of population is the real cause (or non-availability of other avenue). So the issue is to enlarge the choice set.

Estimate of Idle Labour

Despite the fact that India is largely an agricultural economy, Ambedkar points out, per capita land available in 1895 (collected from Mullhall) was only one acre, too small as compared to 5.6 acres to the Russians, 3.3 acres to the Irish, 2.9 acres to the Spaniards and Portuguese, 2.3 to the French, 2.0 acres to Austrians, 1.7 to Italians and Germans whereas Uncle Sam is big with 9 acres. Only John Bull had a little lower. For British India it came down gradually from a little over one acre in 1881 to less than 0.9 acre in 1911—varying between 0.75 acre in UP and 1.8 acre in CP. Using (i) Caird's observation on the estimate of idle labour that '(A) square mile of land in England cultivated highly gives employment to 50 persons, in the proportion 25 men, young and old, and 25 women and boys. If four times that number, or 200, were allowed for each square mile of cultivated land in India, it would take up only one-third of the population', and (ii) census returns of 1881 that two-thirds people were engaged in agriculture, Ambedkar infers that one-third of population (read labour) was 'lying idle instead of performing any sort of productive labour'.

Agriculture population as returned by 1911 census at 71.5 per cent, when compared to 64.4 per cent in 1891, suggests increasing ruralisation and perceptibly is noticed by Ambedkar.

With decreasing land under cultivation, volume of idle labour must have increased to an enormous extent.

Idle Capital and Idle Labour

Ambedkar makes an important distinction between idle capital and idle labour, making it evident that there might have occurred cases of idling capital before the Great Depression of 1930s. He paraphrases the difference between capital and labour: Capital exists, but labour lives. Capital when idle does not earn, but does not also consume much to maintain itself while labour, whether earning or not, consumes in order to live. He goes on telling:

> Idle labour is, therefore, a calamity; for if it cannot live by production as it should, it will live by predation as it must. This idle labour has been the canker of India gnawing at its vitals. Instead of contributing to our national dividend it is eating up what little there is of it.

Since the income of a society, as of an individual, is derived from the efforts made and from possessions used, the aggregate income of any individual or society must be derived either from the proceeds of the current labour or from productive possession already acquired. Actual dividend is much less than the potential because of idleness of labour for want of capital. Capital is, he says as was said in those days, but crystallized surplus and surplus depends upon the proceeds of effort. But where there is no effort there is no earning, no surplus, and no capital.

Small Holding or Large Population

Ambedkar says those who see the fact of small holding as the fundamental evil will definitely advocate enlargement but those who view pressure of population on agriculture as the fundamental evil will try to seek solution outside agriculture.

Even if we enlarged the holdings and bring in somehow capital and capital goods and made their operation economic, he argues, we will only aggravate the evil by increasing our stock of idle labour as economic operation would require far less labour.

Real Status of Forced Consolidation

Consolidation of holdings would prove no more than a legal eyewash and bring no relief. In order to establish this conclusion Ambedkar points out preservation of a compact holding will mean blocking the subdivision, which may be necessitated by various reasons—including reduction in one's stocks, which will further mean causing a serious depreciation of the value of land. Further, if economic circumstances would require subdivision, holdings will be divided in actual practice, even if not permitted on paper. Thus, records will not reflect the real scene. It will prove a work of Sisyphus—rolling a heavy stone uphill which rolls down just before it reaches the top. To those who still want consolidation, Ambedkar says yes but not the way they want.

Industrialisation and Legislation

Concentrating on the efforts to put idle labour to sensible use, he argues if somehow we can sponge off this idle labour in non-agricultural channels, we will be able to accomplish:

1. lessening the pressure on land and destroy the premium it enjoys,
2. ceasing the living of idle labour on predation, and
3. getting surplus from the idle labour after maintaining its keep.

Once the process of industrialisation gathers momentum the pressure on land will lessen and an increasing amount of capital and capital goods will be available for agriculture, which will necessitate, by economic forces, enlargement of the holdings. Since it will destroy the premium on land there will be few occasions for its subdivision and fragmentation of the holdings. Industrialisation is thus, holds Ambedkar, a natural and powerful remedy and is to be preferred to the other suggested schemes, which he found ill-conceived. To quote Ambedkar:

> By legislation we will get a sham economic holding at the cost of many social ills. But by industrialisation a large economic holding will force itself upon us as a pure gain.

In other words, legislation is an idle remedy whereas industrialisation is the ideal remedy for doing away with small holdings and creating large holdings which consolidation proposals aim to carry out.

In fact, the very same was articulated, as reported in Krishnamurthy (2008), in the Report of the Indian Famine Commission (1880):

> ...at the root of much of the poverty of the people of India, and of the risks to which they are exposed in seasons of scarcity lies in the unfortunate circumstance that agriculture forms almost the sole occupation of the mass of the population and that no remedy for present evils can be complete which does not include the introduction of a diversity of occupations, through which the surplus population may be drawn from agricultural pursuits and led to find the means of subsistence in manufactures or some such employments.

So it is clear that the idea of industrialisation as the ultimate solution of the fundamental problem of the Indian economy is not entirely Ambedkar's brain child. But the articulation he made almost, four decades after, along with marshalling of facts and figures from a variety of sources was quite an art perfected by him.

Industrialisation: Type and Strategy

Industrialisation of Indian economy could be conceived in those days basically on two lines—one by reviving her traditional village industries and crafts, operation of which is usually small in scale and the other by establishing modern manufactories, involving large scale operation, to produce both consumer and producer goods, the latter to be ploughed back in production process. By then in India some of the traditional industries had vanished and some were vanishing and their replacement by modern counterparts was slow and tardy. Except a steel mill in Jamshedpur and few textile mills in Bombay and Ahmedabad and jute mills in Calcutta there was little of modern European variety. Ambedkar had exposure of modern industry in the USA and Great Britain and the textbooks of the day had the background of the kind of economies those countries were. Modern industrialisation was what was advocated by the economists of the previous generation, like Ranade. By then Gandhi had not arrived on the scene with his economic agenda either. It was but natural for Ambedkar to think of modern variety of industrialisation for India. There could be other reasons as well like his disdain for discriminatory practices prevalent in rural locales and better likelihood of emancipation of the downtrodden through urbanization and industrialisation.

It is also true that British arrival coincided with the particular era when societies world-over were emancipating themselves from the medieval social systems. The emergence of urban civilizations was a great phenomenon, which made medieval institutions redundant world-wise. Emergence of urban civilizations was intrinsically inter-woven with inventions of modern tools, scientific discoveries, spread of modern education, in other words, industrial revolution, with which were associated the notions of liberty, freedom and democracy. This is what Ambedkar was exposed to and believed in.

His 1918 paper which advocates industrialisation as the soundest remedy for evils of small holdings does not say anything on this except a quotation from *London Times* which discusses diversification of activities in the USA across space and its implications for employment and land value and so on in order to impress upon that his solution is not a utopia (visionary is the word used by him) but quite workable. He also quotes Griffin on the economic tendencies that countries seemed to have been following and cotton on the place of agriculture in Indian economy. He could not go much beyond in this paper as the start of the paper, which was to deal with the problem of small holdings, would logically conclude where he concluded.

We can now perhaps delineate his views on what, whom and how as we have already discussed why industrialisation is needed.

Nature of Industrialisation

It appears that he could develop his views further on the issue of industrialisation when, during 1942-46, he was Labour Member of the Viceroy's Council and had also charge of Irrigation and Power. Besides his direct contribution to erection of long lasting projects and direction to policy orientation, he picked up the thread again and developed the industrialisation theme further. It appears that in his article in the *Times of India* on 26th October, 1943, he argued:

> India was caught between sides of a pincer...increase of population on land...and...increase in deterioration of the soil...leaving India with the inheritance of poverty, more poverty and chronic poverty. This process could be stopped when agriculture was made profitable. Nothing could open possibilities of making agriculture profitable except a serious derive in favour of industrialisation. For it is industrialisation alone which could drain away the excess of population, which was exerting such enormous pressure on land, into gainful employment other than agriculture.

In fact it was becoming clear that after the cessation of the War, while India may gain Independence, plans would be needed for rehabilitation and reconstruction of the economies involved. A Reconstruction Committee of the Viceroy's Council, of which Ambedkar was an important member was constituted with a number of policy committees couple of which were also associated with the Department under the charge of Ambedkar. Ambedkar is quoted from the records of a meeting, on 23 September, 1943, of the Policy Committee on Public Works and Electrical Power of the Reconstruction Committee (Thorat, 1998), where he makes a distinction between the problems of reconstruction in India and elsewhere:

> In other countries the problem of reconstruction is a problem of rehabilitation of industry, which had been in existence. The problem of reconstruction in India, as I see it, is a problem mainly of the industrialisation of India as distinguished from the rehabilitation of industry and industrialisation.

Ambedkar is quite obsessed with the issue of industrialisation. Even when he is referring to water issues, he is keeping in mind that water would be needed for industrial use. When he is talking of need for electrical development, he is again very categorical (Thorat, 1998):

> Why do we want cheap and abundant electricity in India? The answer is that without cheap and abundant electricity no efforts for the industrialisation of India can succeed ...

If the issue of industrialisation is being discussed in the context of electricity development, it is abundantly clear that one is talking about modern type of industrialisation where electricity is a critical input. But on why, Ambedkar makes it clear that industrialisation is needed to rescue people from the morass of poverty.

It is important to remember that most of the national leaders of the time were clear that India needed a modern type of industrialisation that existed in the West and was being pursued in the Soviet Russia. They included Nehru and Bose, industrialists and scientists, and capitalists and communists as is clear from the documents of the National Planning Committee, Bombay Plan and People's Plan. Gandhi was an exception. In fact, the difference between Gandhi and others was much deeper. While the former was for the agraria—the agricultural civilisation and the latter were for the industria—the industrial civilisation.

Industrialisation for Whom

In the address referred to above he further asked the question as to why industrialisation is necessary and answered it in the following words:

> And you will have the full significance made clear to you at once, for the answer to the question is, we want industrialisation of India as the surest means to rescue the people from the eternal cycle of poverty in which they are caught. Industrialisation of India must, therefore, be grappled with immediately.

Further, in his address to an Indian Labour Conference in 1943, he makes it ample clear (Thorat, 1998):

> We must be prepared for the revaluation of the value. It will not be enough to make industrial development of India as a goal. We shall have to agree that any such industrial development shall be maintained at a socially desirable level. It will not be enough to bend our energies for the production of more wealth in India. We shall have to agree, not merely recognize, the basic right of all Indians to share in that wealth as a means for a decent and dignified existence, but devise ways and means to ensure him against insecurity.

From the very start of his work, one may see that his plea for industrialisation comes from the deliverance of labour, peasant, workers and farmers from acute poverty as agriculture, the sole industry of India, could not employ productively so many hands. He did not seek industrialisation for its own sake or for propertied class, businessmen and traders, to prosper further, nor to cater to foreign demands. He is very clear on removal of poverty and makes a suggestion about reduction in inequality through sharing in growth—as would be clear from another quotation below.

How to Go About Industrialisation

It is only in 1947 that Ambedkar clearly delineates his views on the role of the State in economic life though he had been giving his views, with corroboration from Jevons, on the ownership of public enterprises like those of power generation. In his monograph titled *States and Minorities*, prepared by him in March 1947—which is actually an alternative draft constitution—on behalf of All-India Scheduled Castes Federation (founded by him), Article II, Section II, Clause 4 (Protection against Economic Exploitation) provides that the United States of India would be governed by the following:

1. Key industries would be owned and run by the State.
2. Basic industries would be run by the State or corporations established by the State.
3. Insurance would be a State monopoly. Every adult citizen would have a life insurance policy.
4. Agriculture would be organized under the State cooperative sector with compensation to the owners. The cooperatives would be organized with no regard to the caste of members.

Explaining the reasons behind the clause quoted above, the monograph holds:

> The main purpose behind the clause is to put an obligation on the State to plan the economic life of the people on the lines which would lead to highest point

> of productivity without closing every avenue to private enterprise, and also to provide for equal distribution of wealth. The plan set out in the clause proposes state ownership of agriculture with a collectivized method of cultivation and a modified form of state socialism in the field of industry. It places squarely on the shoulders of the state the obligation to supply the capital necessary for agriculture as well as for industry.

State socialism is needed for rapid industrialisation of India. Private enterprise cannot do it, said Ambedkar at some other place, and if it did it would produce those inequalities of wealth which private capitalism has produced in Europe and which would be a warning to Indians. It is another matter when K.T. Shah, a Professor of Economics and Member-Secretary of the National Planning Committee (1938), moved a resolution in the Constituent Assembly to characterize India as a socialist state, Ambedkar opposed it holding that it was not proper to introduce in the Constitution a concept as vague as socialism. Therefore, some scholars have called it 'four anna socialism'. We shall not however delve any further in this direction.

However, the weakest part of this analysis, actually a little retrogression, is that puts the obligation on the state to provide capital for both the sectors of agriculture and industry, ignoring the issue where the surplus is likely to generate. Resources do not come from heaven they have expropriated from economic activities which were either agricultural or industrial (no third sector was articulated in those days). In 1918, he is talking of surplus and saving when Bukharin-Praeobrezhensky debate had not taken place. However in 1947, when the strategy is being formulated it had become place to find wherefrom to mobilize resources and to devise mechanism to mobilize them.

Conclusion

Babasaheb Dr. Bhimrao Ramji Ambedkar did all his degrees—M.A., M.Sc., Ph.D. and D.Sc.—in Economics and wrote brilliant pieces—practically all published immediately yet he chose to change over, and for good, from economics to law and politics, and assured his readers in the Preface to the Indian edition of *The Problem of the Rupee*, in 1947, a little before independence that 'they will not have to wait long for volume two', where he would tell the story of Rupee after 1923—which was not to happen as he had to shoulder a major responsibility of drafting the Constitution as Chairman of the Drafting Committee.

While in India between his two spans of studies abroad, Ambedkar wrote an analytically incisive paper which breaks a ground by considering the whole economy as an interwoven system and seeks the solution for excess labour forced on agriculture in the absence of doing anything better. When most scholars and government committees were seeking to improve agricultural productivity through means of consolidation of fragmented holdings and, if possible, through enlargement, and suggesting to carry them out through legal, legislative and administrative recourse, here was a young scholar to examine each of the proposals with keen analytical angle and empirical eye to claim that the industrialisation of India was the soundest remedy for the ills of small holdings. But he goes beyond and anticipates economics of development that was articulated only in the late 1930s and thereafter.

In any grand proposal we should ignore minor glitches and if we do so we find Ambedkar had profitably used all his understanding of economics learnt in the portals of Columbia University and empirical facts about various developed countries for which relevant data were available and could convincingly impress that the problem of small holdings, as it appears, is actually a problem of maladjustment in the social economy. But he also collects as many relevant reports from various parts of the country and the reports of Indian censuses to establish various relationships as well as changes over time.

Ambedkar was not the first to suggest the dire need of industrialisation of India. Ranade was advocating industrialisation and was seeking protection of infant industries from foreign competition. Ambedkar was also not the first to fathom the problem of idle labour in agriculture sector of the Indian economy. For example, James Caird was there in 1884 to make the estimates, which Ambedkar has profitably used in his paper. One may also find the same suggestion of industrialisation in the Report of the Indian Finance Commission (1880) in a crude form. Ambedkar's articulation and reasoning is definitely remarkable.

Though Ambedkar continued working in economics and on economics of India, it seems, till 1925 he did not pursue the theme of industrialisation. It is possible he had occasions to depose before committees and commissions on the issues. But after he became Labour Member in Viceroy's Council in 1942, he again picked up the thread and developed it further till the making of Constitution. In numerous meetings of the ministries and reconstruction committees, he did not forget to point out water for industrial use and power for industries. In equally numerous addresses in different forum and writings in the form of monographs, he made it clear that industrialisation is a means to improve the lot of the poor and to do that active state invention is the need of the hour.

[The author is grateful to Prof. S.N. Misra and Prof. Sushma Yadav who were kind enough to go through the first draft and offer their valuable comments for improvement. However, the author alone is responsible for the lapses that may be there in the paper.]

REFERENCES

Ambedkar, B.R. (1918), Small Holdings in India and Their Remedies, *Journal of the Indian Economic Society*, Vol.1, No.3, from internet.

Ambedkar, B.R. (1947), *States and Minorities*, from internet.

Krishnamurthy, J. (2008), Indian Antecedents of Disguised Unemployment and Surplus Labour, *The Indian Journal of Labour Economics*, Vol. 51, No.1.

Thorat, Sukhdeo and Aryama (2007, ed.), *Ambedkar in Retrospect: Economics, Politics and Society*, Indian Institute of Dalit Studies, New Delhi and Rawat Publications, Jaipur.

Thorat, Sukhdeo (2006), *Ambedkar's Role in Economic Planning, Water and Power Policy*, Shipra Publications, Delhi, Second Edition.

ANNEXURE

Discourse on Economic Holding

While Ambedkar finally made a case for enlarging holdings so that they could operate as economic units, he indulges in examining what constitutes an economic holding. There were three main proposals:

1. Baroda Committee gives a plurality of definitions. At couple of places it defines economic holding in terms of a minimum size in one plot which is necessary for full engagement of a family and provide support for it. At another place, it says an ideal economic holding would consist of 30 to 50 bighas of fair land in one block with at least one good irrigation well and a house situated in the holding. At yet another place, the (average) holding in a compact field, belonging to a *Khatedar* was, the situation would be an ideal one and would not leave much to be desired. This led Ambedkar to comment that 'the Report of the Committee is a model of confused reasoning though it is a valuable repository of facts bearing on the subject'.
2. Keatinge writes in *The Rural Economy in Bombay Deccan* an economic holding is a 'holding which allows a man chance of producing sufficient to support himself and his family in reasonable comfort, after paying his necessary expenses'.
3. According to Jevons, in the consolidated village the mode should be between 29 and 30 acres to which Ambedkar retorts by asking why not 100 or 200 acres. But Jevons is found by Ambedkar to relate the size of holding with improved standard of living through higher quantum of production and in fact Jevons keeps on harping on the issue of raising the standard of living.

We leave statistical weaknesses and inner-logic inconsistency but concentrate on Ambedkar's theoretical contribution in the form of an issue which economists dealing with problems of Indian agriculture were ignoring.

Ambedkar is dismayed with non-availability of a scientific definition of economic holding but gathers an impression that a large holding is somehow considered an economic holding. But question he raises is how could anyone judge an economic production unit from the consumption of the owning family; he asks if the rate of return on each of the input is highest but produce is not enough to support a family (which is, suppose, large for reason of customs), could this unit be called uneconomic in any sense. He says such an accounting practice could declare any successful business enterprise as a failure but the fact is that no entrepreneur is going to close his concern so long the outturn is paying well for his investment irrespective whether it supports the family well or not. Contrary-wise, size of any economic unit is not to be reduced because family which owns it is small and, therefore, produce far exceeds the consumption requirements of the family. Thus, Ambedkar takes a scientific view of farming as an economic enterprise.

Ambedkar holds the view that industrial facts do not support the classification (of investments) in terms factors of production traditionally accepted as wages/labour, rent/land, interest/capital and profits, and that there are many more factors which share in the derivative process and, therefore, should have contributed. He is not quite correct but he chooses to ignore it as he finds the matter inconsequential.

But he raises a pertinent question which involves the law of (variable) proportion. In any given technology it is understood that there is an ideal or efficient combination of factors, owing to the fact of interdependence, an excess or deficiency of one factor will impact the efficiency of all. Here he makes reference to a book by Davenport and two papers in a (then) recent issue of the *American Economic Review* by Taylor and Young. He agrees that there exists a possibility of substitution between factors, which is brought about by changes in factor prices, but he asserts that law of substitution is too limited in application to invalidate the law of proportion (until technology of production itself changes). Adopting a modern outlook on agriculture he remarks 'if agriculture is to be treated as an economic enterprise, then, by itself, there could be no such thing as a large or a small holding' or 'mere size of holding is empty of all economic connotations'. Elaborating on it, he further says that economics language does not permit one to assert that a large holding is economic or a small holding is uneconomic. It is a question of right or wrong proportion of factors that renders cultivation of a piece of land as economic or uneconomic. For efficient production the farmer has to have other factors of production in order to maintain due proportion but uses equipment, not labour, as illustration for other factors. He goes on further to suggest if one's equipment enlarges, land should enlarge and if his equipment shrinks, by logic, his land should also shrink. [Obviously the above observation holds only when starts out from a position of right proportion.] However, he concentrates finally on the proportion between equipment and land.

The theory was actually applied in India when settlement was effected in Presidency of Bombay through survey. He digs out Survey *Settlement Manual of Bombay Presidency* (1882) prepared on the basis of Joint Report (1840) whose officers faced the challenge of levying the assessment of land revenue—from the lands of village as a whole or from individuals or co-parceners, whether proprietors or occupants. The Report reported that individuals chose to enlarge or contract his farm, according to agricultural capital (like bullocks) at his disposal, which was of incalculable importance to farmers possessing so limited resources as those of cultivating classes throughout India. Without having the privilege of contracting the farm, say on loss of a few bullocks, a farmer would ruin his fortune as his liabilities would remain undiminished whereas his produce would diminish. He quotes in support of his arguments, Richard T. Ely from his book, *Outlines of Economics* (1913):

> Obviously no simple answer can be given to the question [as to what should be the size of a farm]. The value of land or the rent it will bring is perhaps the most important factor... In addition to the factor of rent the amount of capital that he can command, the kind of farming in which he is most skilled, the character of the labour he can secure, the proximity of markets, and the adequacy of transportation facilities, all must be taken into account by the farmer in determining how large a farm he will attempt to manage and how intensively he will farm it...This question is primarily one of private profit which the individual must decide for himself, but the legislator and the scientific student can be of some assistance in helping to develop that most difficult branch of commercial science—farm accounting—and in keeping the farmer alive to those changes in prices, wages, and transportation charges into which the farm organization must adjust itself.

He concludes that in spite of good intentions vicarious mission of those who try to fix size of holding will end in disaster for none other than the cultivator can decide what should be the size of his holding; and that the size of his holdings will vary in time because of technology and resources in command.

There are basically two proposals, one of enlargement and the other of consolidation, which were critically examined by Ambedkar, in that order. Under the assumption that proportions between different factors of production, primarily two, viz., land and stocks (equipment such as ploughs and bullocks), Ambedkar holds that there is case for enlarging size of land holding can be entertained provided it can be shown that stocks with farmers have grown. Observations of K.L. Datta based on his survey into the rise of prices are quoted by Ambedkar to show that decrease in supply of agriculture produce owes to the inefficient tillage of land, which in turn owes to the scarcity and dearness of plough, cattle and labour (this is only reference to hired or wage labour). This all causes reduced number of ploughings of land and of irrigatings, and less of manuring and weedings. In good number of circles it was found that the number of plough cattle was less in 1908-09 than fifteen years ago in 1893-94, triggered by famine—even if good reliance could be placed on figures there is ample evidence of dearth of plough cattle. In the State of Baroda, figures, which are more definitive, definitely show that there is a plough between two holders and a pair of bullocks for 36 acres instead of 25 acres for healthy ones and 20 acres for those poor in health. This leads Ambedkar to conclude that existing holdings, small in acreage, are too big when considered in relation to instruments of production other than land (and, we may add, labour).

7

Economic Ideas of Dr. Ambedkar

JAI NARAIN SHARMA

An important aspect of Dr. Ambedkar's versatile personality does not, however, seem to have attracted enough attention especially in the light of his achievements in the field of social justice and drafting of the Constitution that, he was an eminent economist. This was also due to the fact that Dr. Ambedkar himself perhaps chose to underplay his role as a professional economist, as he was mostly preoccupied with vital issues of social justice and in the drafting of the Constitution. Yet it would be grossly unfair to relegate his economic ideas to a secondary status.

As a Gaekwar scholar, young Ambedkar at the age of 24 years emerged as a learned student of economics, when he was studying at Columbia University, U.S.A. Within a period of three years stay in America he completed two dissertations on economic disciplines. The first dissertation was "Ancient Indian Commerce", which he submitted in 1915 for the award of Master in Arts degree. The another thesis was on "National Dividend in India: A Historical and Analytical Study", which he submitted in 1916 for his Ph.D. degree in economics. As his thirst for knowledge was unquenched, he left America and joined Gray's Inn for Bar-at-Law and the London School of Economics and Politics for academic research, simultaneously, in 1916. But he came back in 1917 as the Maharaja of Baroda did not extend his fellowship for further studies under a Bond, executed earlier. Under compulsion he joined Baroda State as

Military Secretary to Maharaja, with a view to being ground for the post of the State's Finance Minister.

In 1921, he got his M.Sc. (Economics) degree on his thesis, "The Evolution of Provincial Finance in British India" from the London School of Economics. This dissertation was published by P.S. King & Son Ltd, Westminster, Great Britain in 1925, with a foreword by Professor Edwin R.A. Seligman of the Columbia University. In its Preface, Ambedkar wrote, "For long time to come students will be saved the conventional humiliation of making an apology for presenting a study of Indian Finance or Economics. Even when the treatment of a subject is analytical, a good analytical study of ten requires an historical setting. Unfortunately no spade work has been done in the field of Indian Finance".[1] Professor Seligman in his foreword wrote, "The problem discussed by Mr. Ambedkar in his excellent dissertation is arousing a growing interest in all parts of the world. What Mr. Ambedkar call assignments, assigned revenue and share revenue, is symptomatic of the choice of methods in all countries."[2] This study in the provincial decentralization of Imperial Finance was well received and welcomed in the academic world.

The Problem of the Rupee

Writing the Preface of the *Problem of the Rupee: Its Origin and its Solution,* published in 1923 in London, Dr. Ambedkar said, "Not only have other writers begun abruptly the story of the exchange standard, but they have popularized the notion that the exchange standard is the standard originally contemplated by the Government of India. I find that this is a gross error. Indeed the most interesting point about Indian currency is the way in which the gold standard came to be transformed into a gold exchange standard. Some old, but by now forgotten, facts had, therefore, to be recounted to expose this error".[3]

In the same preface Dr. Ambedkar said that he has sharp conflict with the opinion of Professor J.M. Keynes, the noted British Economist as follows, "On the theoretical side, there is no book but that of Professor Keynes which makes any attempt to examine its scientific basis. But the conclusions he has arrived at are in sharp conflict with those of mine. Our differences extended to almost every proposition he has advanced in favour of the exchange standard. This difference proceeds from the fundamental fact, which seems to be quite overlooked by Professor Keynes, that nothing will stabilize the rupee unless we stabilize its general purchasing power. That the exchange standard does not do. That standard concerns itself only with symptoms and does not go to the disease indeed, on my showing, if anything, it aggravates the disease".[4]

Ambedkar further suggests, "I think, a far better way would be to have an inconvertible rupee with a fixed limit of issue. Indeed, if I had any say in the matter, I would propose, that the Government of India should melt the rupee, sell them as bullion and use the proceeds for revenue purposes and fill the void by an inconvertible paper. But that may be too radical a proposal, and I do not, therefore, press for it, although I regard it as essentially sound".[5] Joining issues with an economist of the stature of Lord J.M. Keynes at that time really required great courage and knowledge which Dr. Ambedkar undoubtedly held in abundance.

Professor Edwin Cannon writing the foreword said, "In 1893, I was one of the few economists, who believed that the rupee could be kept at a fixed ratio with gold by the method then proposed. I do not share Mr. Ambedkar's hostility to the system, nor accept most of his arguments against it and its advocates; but he hits some nails very squarely on the head, and even when I have thought him quite wrong, I have found a stimulating freshness in his views and reasons".[6] Cannon further writes, "In his practical conclusion, I am inclined to think, he is right. The single advantage offered to a country by the adoption of the gold-exchange system instead of the simple gold standard is that it is cheaper, in the sense of requisiting a little less value in the shape of metallic currency than the gold standard".[7]

The Indian rupee until 1893 was linked to silver standard meaning that the Indian rupee was based on the value of the silver contained in it. Due to enormous silver discoveries subsequently, the price of silver fell and hence the price of rupee slipped also in terms of gold. From 1872 to 1893, the decline in price of silver led to automatic devaluation of the rupee. While devaluation helped Indian exports, it was bad for the country's economy as we had to pay in gold, which was the currency in England (Gold Sterling). Subsequently, the gold standard was established in 1906 in England. However, the system broke down in 1916 with the enormous rise in the price of silver and the system effectively became the silver standard. Dr. Ambedkar argued for a proper gold standard with gold currency, as he was highly critical of the gold exchange standard. Dr. Ambedkar argued that this system vested the government with enormous power to increase the money supply. The excessive importance, given to maintain the stability of exchange as against internal stability of the value of currency was not a proper policy for India. He effectively argued that the low exchange rate increased exports and boosted internal prices, which benefited the trading classes at the expense of the poor people at home. Dr. Ambedkar emphasized "what really concerns those who use money is not how much gold that money is worth, but how much of things in general that money is worth. Everywhere, therefore, the attempt is to keep money stable in terms of commodities in general, and what matters to the welfare of people is not so much the precious metals as commodities and services of more direct utility".[8] His commitment obviously was for internal stability of prices. In short, his conclusion is clearly towards price stability through conservative and automatic monetary management.

Dr. Ambedkar's views are extremely relevant, in these days of massive budget deficits and their automatic monetization. It would appear that we could do with an effective restraint on liquidity creation through an automatic mechanism. Today we have no gold or gold exchange standard. The whole perspective has undergone a sea-change. However, we can still take lessons from his economic philosophy. For instance, during later years of 1980s, 1990s and even in early

2000s, the rupee has depreciated in relation to major currencies, so much so it seriously affected the credit rating of India. This is also the period of high prices. Thus, we find that currency was issued in excess, resulting in fall in the purchasing power of rupee locally and the depreciation of the rupee internationally. This is exactly the situation visualized by Baba Saheb. A strict control on issue of currency was what he advised in those days, which is exactly what we need today.

Administration and Finance of the East India Company

Dr. Ambedkar dealt with the finances of East India Company in his work 'Administration and Finance of the East India Company' and disagreed with the entire fiscal system under the regime of the East India Company. He believed that the finances of a country are to be judged from the point of view of developmental expenditure and among the developmental expenditure, the public works benefiting the entire community take an important place. He observed, that the surplus generated by East India Company, were not used to undertake irrigation and other works of improvement and were used to pay dividends to the East India Company's shareholders and as the flow of money from India was not sufficient to pay the dividends, the East India Company was resorting to heavy public debt. Dr. Ambedkar felt that this large size of the debt was the result of mismanagement and extravagance by the Company. He also opined that while heavy land tax levied by East India Company prevented the prosperity of the agricultural sector, the customs taxes and heavy export duties hampered the growth of trade and industry, the goods produced in the country were unable to meet the external competition.[9] He came down very heavily on the taxation policy of the Government by stating that:

> "The landlords who passed their lives in conspicuous consumption and vicarious leisure on the earnings of the poor tenants, and the many European civil servants were supremely exempted from any contribution

> towards the maintenance of the government. On the other hand, the salt tax and tax on trades and occupations embracing weavers, carpenters, all workers in metals, all salesmen or vendors by the road side, etc., extending to the most trifling articles of trade and the cheapest tools, mechanics can employ, and other oppressive taxes continued to harass the industrious poor."[10]

Dr. Ambedkar also examined how the revenues raised through such taxes were spent. He observed that education formed no part of the expenditure and useful public works were lamentably few. He found that during 1809—1857, the military expenditure accounted for more than half of the total revenues, without benefiting the general public of India. He concluded that collapse of imperial system was due to a faulty fiscal system marked by indiscriminate taxes and unproductive and extravagant expenditure.

Taxation

Baba Saheb knew clearly the problems in levy of taxes. He pointed out that it is very difficult to have proper taxation, policies, as the Governments which depend on the people's vote to govern, would always be hesitant to mobilize the needed resources through requisite taxation and at the same time the Government cannot take measures to reduce public expenditure by enforcing administrative economies. Dr. Ambedkar has effectively summarized the position by stating, if however, the "seat is a gift of the elector, a candidate to the Legislature who proposes to touch his pocket has a small chance of success, even though the new taxes are to result in more than proportionate benefit". In any case a political party which "has won power from a bureaucracy by accusing it of heavy taxation cannot easily disgrace itself by continuing the same policy". The result was that "the chances of an early equilibrium in Provincial finance are very small".[11] Though Dr. Ambedkar expressed these views in 1939, one wonders whether he was talking of the present status of state finances in India.

Dr. Ambedkar having analysed the evaluation of public finances in provinces never missed any opportunity to comment on the taxation policy and suggest an alternative tax policy. His views on taxation were included in the election manifesto of his Independent Labour Party (1936). Dr. Ambedkar had criticised the Government of Bombay in a public meeting held in Ahmedabad in 1938 for not reducing the land tax rates and for not taxing the rich people. The following are the important components of the taxation policy advocated by him:

(a) A personal tax should be based on taxable capacity of the individual and not on his gross income;
(b) Tax rates should be progressive, meaning the rich should be taxed more and the poor less;
(c) There should be exemptions subject to a limit of income tax for tax payers.[12]

Dr. Ambedkar had shown considerable concern about using taxation policy for reducing income inequalities between different people. According to him, taxes should help to achieve equity between different sections of people. He has also argued that "no taxation system should be all to lower the standard of living of the people."[13]

Power to States to Levy Taxes

Dr. Ambedkar has identified that the provinces had come to rely on grant-in-aid from the central government in British India. He considered it a fiscal imbalance. Dr. Ambedkar argued in favour of provincial governments retaining the power of sales tax, since it is an important source of their revenue. He had argued in the Constituent Assembly that:

> "If we permit the sales tax to be levied by the provinces, then the provinces must be free to adjust the rate of

> the sales tax to the changing situation of the provinces, and therefore a ceiling from the centre would be great handicap in the working of the sales tax. The sales tax in its fundamental character must be a tax on consumption".[14]

Baba Saheb was in favour of imposing an estate tax. He suggested it as a measure of achieving economic equity. A similar proposal was made by Nicholas Kaldor, a famous British economist in his Integrated Tax structure for India. This recommendation was accepted by the Government of India in 1956 and implemented. However, Government of India had abolished it subsequently.

One of the criticism of Dr. Ambedkar about the provincial finances was that the allocation for social services by the provincial governments was inadequate, which criticism still perhaps holds good, looking at the level of poverty in the country.

Principles Governing Expenditure of Government

Dr. Ambedkar, during the discussion on the functions of the Comptroller and Auditor General, at the time of framing the Constitution in 1949 has enunciated that governments should spend the resources mobilized from the public not only as per rules and regulations, but also to ensure that "faithfulness, wisdom and economy" have gone into the acts of expenditure by public authorities. It is necessary for the Government to recognize that the main reason for the existence of public finance is to utilize these funds on creating common facilities and services used by the society like roads etc. As the cost and benefit analyses of such items cannot easily be worked out, it will not be possible for the private sector to provide such facilities. It is the duty of the Government to provide such facilities for the common man. The Government is expected to take judicious decisions in taking up such works, which would give maximum benefit for maximum number of people. Care should also be taken, not only in allocating funds for common facilities, but also in spending such funds objectively, without frittering away on wasteful expenditure. Hence, it becomes all the more necessary for the government to be faithful to the original intentions. The expenditure must be committed with circumspection and understanding of the deeper issues involved in public expenditure. It does not simply mean a low level of public spending, but it is the intelligent use of funds so that every paisa fetches the maximum benefit. Those in charge of public funds must strive to evaluate alternative methods of achieving the objectives and see to it that leakages do not occur. The Government should ensure that the expenditure decisions are closely related to the specified objectives and the available resources besides ensuring economy, efficiency and effectiveness in the implementation of government decisions. In the present context of high fiscal deficits, a rigorous application of the principles enunciated by Dr. Ambedkar can help moderate the quantum of public expenditure and utilization of limited resources in a need based and judicious manner.

Economic Reforms

Several of his economic writings bear an eloquent testimony to his concern for the common man. According to him, the well-being of the common man could be secured, among other things, through the state planning the economic life of the society and not leaving it to the whims of the market alone; by ensuring domestic price stability as inflation hits the poor the most; the poor are not adversely affected through incidence of taxation and the expenditure policy of the Government being so framed that the quantum of productive expenditure is enhanced and the unproductive expenditure is curtailed to the barest minimum.

Dr. Ambedkar wanted the expenditure policy of the state to be guided, among other things, by the principle of providing more public utility services as also generating more employment.

Small Holdings in India and their Remedies

Dr. Ambedkar felt that the agricultural farming is by far the most among the primary industries. India depends almost wholly upon the agricultural farming. The problems of agricultural economy dealing directly with agricultural production are what to produce, the proper proportion of the factors for production, the size of holdings, the tenures of land and other related issues. In spite of various reforms ushered in the country, which are implemented in varying degree in different states, agriculture continues to suffer from the problems, which Dr. Ambedkar envisaged in his Article on "Small holdings in India and their remedies" nearly a century ago. In his Article published in 1918, Dr. Ambedkar takes on a problem that is still haunting Indian agrarian system of small land holdings and low productivity of lands. He made a critical examination of the prevailing situation and was of the view that there can be no such thing as a correct size of agricultural holdings.[15] As Dr. Ambedkar argued, land was only one of the other factors of production and the productivity of one factor of production is dependent upon the proportion in which the other factors of production are combined. In his words: "the chief object of an efficient production consists in making every factor in the concern contribute its highest". He further stated that if agriculture is to be treated as an economic enterprise, there could be no such thing as a large or small holding and certainly it is not due to want of efficiency in utilizing whatever the peasant has. Dr. Ambedkar's answer rests on the inadequacy of other factors of production. The insufficiency of capital which for acquiring "agricultural stock and implements" arises from lack of savings. But as he remarks "that saving is possible where there is surplus, is a commonplace of political economy."[16] "A large agricultural population with the lowest proportion of land in actual cultivation means that a large part of the agricultural population is superfluous and idle."[17] A consolidated holding should also be an enlarged holding. He advised to keep in mind that the consolidation may obviate the evils of scattered holdings, but it would not obviate the evils of holdings, unless the consolidated holding is an economic holding, i.e. an enlarged holding. Dr. Ambedkar further adds even if the lands are consolidated and enlarged and cultivated through capitalistic enterprise, it will not solve the problem as it will only aggravate "the evils by adding to our stock of idle labour". According to him, mere size of land small or large does not determine the land to be economic or uneconomic and the economic holding depended on all the factors of production including land. Consequently, the remedy for the ills of agriculture in India did not lie primarily in the matter of enlarging holdings but in the matter of increasing capital as capital goods. The only way out of this impasse was to take people away from land. This would automatically "lessen and destroy the premium that at present weighs heavily on land in India" and large "economic holding, will force itself upon us as a pure gain". He advised for sponging off this surplus labour for non-agricultural areas, to lessen pressure on land. He concludes that "industrialization of India is the soundest remedy for the agricultural problems of India".[18] This can generate adequate surplus that will also eventually benefit the agricultural sector. Indeed a shift from primary industry to secondary industry is vital and it must be attempted seriously to prevent the present enlargement of the rural population that was being witnessed and remedies based on what he calls "faulty political economy" were being advocated. It is seen that in spite of best efforts of the Government, it is apparent the rural people still largely depend on agriculture as industrialization is still lagging behind.

State Socialism

Dr. Ambedkar advocated State Socialism in the field of industry and also state ownership in agriculture with a collectivised method or cultivation, he was one of the few Indians who demanded nationalization of Insurance. He was of the firm opinion that the plight of 60 million untouchables who were landless labourers cannot be ameliorated through consolidation of lands or by tenancy legislation. Only collective farms can solve the problems of the landless labourer. Therefore, Dr. Ambedkar writes, "The plan has two special features. One is that it proposes state socialism in important fields of economic life, the second special feature of the plan is, that it does not leave establishment of state socialism to the will of the legislature. It establishes state socialism by the law of the constitution and thus makes it unalterable by any act of the legislature and the executive."[19]

Thus Dr. Ambedkar wanted to include the provisions of state ownership of agriculture in the fundamental rights as these provisions are unalterable by any act of Legislature and the Executive. The purpose is to protect the liberty of the individual from invasion by other individuals. The connection between individual liberty and the shape and form of the economic structure of society becomes real only when state socialism has been established through political democracy. State socialism and political democracy are not incompatible. Therefore, Dr. Ambedkar wanted to establish state socialism not through dictatorship but through political democracy. He writes, "the problem, therefore, is to have state socialism without dictatorship, to have state socialism with parliamentary democracy. The way out seems to be to retain parliamentary democracy and to prescribe state socialism by the law of the constitution so that it will be beyond the reach of parliamentary majority to suspend, amend or abrogate it. It is only by this that one can achieve the triple object, namely, to establish socialism, to retain parliamentary democracy and avoid dictatorship."[20]

His views on state socialism are similar to that of collectivism. Following are the essential features of Dr. Ambedkar's socialism:

(i) A condemnation of the existing social, political and economic order as unjust;

(ii) An advocacy of a new order based on one man, one value, one vote;

(iii) A belief that this ideal is realizable in state socialism and parliamentary democracy;
(iv) The conviction that immorality of established order is traceable to corrupt social institutions;
(v) A programme of actions leading to the ideal to be achieved through constitutional means only; and
(vi) A revolutionary will for establishing social democracy to carry out the programme of social solidarity.[21]

Ambedkar had no fascination for fashionable ideologies. His sole concern was the all-round prosperity and well-being of the downtrodden masses. His unambiguous commitment to democratic values and equally forthright despisal and denunciation of dictatorship made him suspect in the eyes of the guardian angels of world revolution.

When Dr. Ambedkar came to know that the Cabinet Mission, 1946, did not consider the separate entity of the Depressed Classes, he sought for a compromise with the majority political party, i.e. the Indian National Congress. The sole reason was to safeguard the interests of the downtrodden. Even though Dr. Ambedkar was against the formation of the Constituent Assembly up to 1946, he did not challenge the legality of the Objectives Resolution of Jawaharlal Nehru. It may appear strange that Ambedkar, who never hesitated to criticize towering personalities like Mahatma Gandhi and Jinnah failed to denounce the Objectives Resolution in spite of his unconcealed disagreement with the contents of the Resolution. The reason was that he desired to get the safeguards to the weaker sections incorporated in the constitution. N.V. Gadgil appropriately remarked about the change of attitude of Ambedkar in the following lines:

> "The London conference had convinced Dr. Ambedkar that partition was inevitable and he was preoccupied with its possible effects on the position of the Harijans. In an interview after his return from the London Conference, he had said that the promises given by the British to the Harijans would prove futile, 'The sand is

> crumbling under my feet'. He was far-sighted and willing enough to sacrifice his self-esteem for the love of his people. He spoke in the Constituent Assembly a day after the meeting in my house. His speech was so statesmanlike, so devoid of bitterness and so earnestly challenging that the whole Assembly listened to it in abrupt silence. His main points were that the Constitution must be framed in the interest of the nation as a whole and that it should be acceptable to the generations to come and should unify the country. The speech was greeted with a tremendous ovation and he was smothered with congratulations in the lobby."[22]

An impression has gained currency that Dr. Ambedkar's energy and enthusiasm were directed towards securing conditions for the fulfilment of the bare necessities of the weaker sections. Far from it, satisfying the bare necessities, according to him, was only a pre-condition for the cultivation of the finer aspects of life. Therefore, he fervently advocated the restructuring of Indian economy in the following words:

"It is true that man shares the constitution and functions, of animals, nutritive, reproductive, etc. But these are not distinctively human functions. The distinctively human function is reason, the purpose of which is to enable man to observe, meditate, cogitate, study and discover the beauties of the universe and enrich his life and control the animal elements in his life. Man thus occupies the highest place in the scheme of animate existence. If this is true then what is the conclusion that follows? The conclusion that follows is that while the ultimate goal of a brute's life is reached once his physical appetites are satisfied, the ultimate goal of man is culture. Culture is not possible for the brute, but it is essential for man. That being so the aim of human society must be to enable every person to lead a life of culture, which means the cultivation of mind as distinguished from the satisfaction of mere physical wants. How can this happen?

"Both for society as well as for individual there is always a gulf between mere living and living worthily. In order that one may live worthily one must first live. The time and energy spent upon mere life, upon gaining of subsistence detracts from that available for activities of a distinctively human nature and which go to make up a life of culture. How then can a life of culture be made possible? It is not possible unless there is sufficient leisure. For, it is only when there is leisure that a person is free to devote himself to a life of culture. The problem of all problems, which human society has to face, is how to provide leisure to every individual. What does leisure mean? Leisure means the lessening of the toil and effort necessary for satisfying the physical wants of life. How can leisure be made possible? Leisure is quite impossible unless some means are found whereby the toil required for producing goods necessary to satisfy human needs is lessened. What can lessen such toil? Only when machine takes the place of man. There is no other means of producing leisure. Machinery and modern civilization are thus indispensable for emancipating man from leading the life of a brute, and for providing him with leisure and for making a life of culture possible. The man who condemns machinery and modem civilization simply does not understand their purpose and the ultimate aim which human society must strive to achieve."[23]

Ambedkar was conscious of the intimate connection between individual liberty and the shape and structure of the economic aspect of social life. Therefore, in order to make the principle of one man, one value, real and operative, he wanted political democracy to be reinforced by economic democracy.

In his memorandum submitted to the Advisory Committee of the Constituent Assembly which was later christened, 'States and Minorities'. What are their Rights and How to Secure these in the Constitution of Free India, he included (i) the fundamental rights of the citizen, and, (ii) the remedies against invasion of the fundamental rights, wherein he has not only provided a fertile field for the efflorescence of individual freedom and cultural faculties but also the essential ingredients of economic democracy which would afford sustenance and support for the unhindered realization of the former. He repeatedly asserted that it should be the aim and purpose of any rational scheme of social reconstruction to provide for the economic security and political liberty of every single individual. His condemnation of arbitrary power and tyranny in any form was forthright and categorical.

"I see that there is a great deal of misunderstanding as to the real provisions in the Constitution in the minds of those members of the House who are interested in this kind of directive principles. It is quite possible that the misunderstanding is due to the fact that I myself in my opening speech in support of the motion that I made, did not refer to this aspect of the question. As it is stated, our Constitution as a piece of mechanism lays down what is called parliamentary democracy. By parliamentary democracy we mean one man, one vote ! We also mean that every Government shall be on the anvil, both in its daily affairs and also at the end of a certain period when the voters and the electorate will be given an opportunity to assess the work done by the Government. The reason why we have established in this Constitution a political democracy is because we do not want to install by any means whatsoever a perpetual dictatorship of any particular body of people. While we have established political democracy, it is also the desire that we should lay down as our ideal economic democracy. We do not want merely to lay down a mechanism to enable people to come and capture power. The Constitution also wishes to lay down an ideal before those who would be forming the Government. That ideal is economic democracy, whereby, so far as I am concerned, I understand to mean, one man, one value. The question is : Have we got any fixed idea as to how we should bring about economic democracy? There are various ways in which people believe that economic democracy can be brought about; there are those who believe in individualism as the best form of economic democracy; there are those who believe in having a socialistic state as the best form of economic democracy; there are those who believe in the communistic idea as the most perfect form of economic democracy.

"Now, having regard to the fact that there are various ways by which economic democracy may be brought about, we have deliberately introduced in the language that we have used, in the directive principles, something, which is not fixed or rigid. We have left enough room for people of different ways of thinking, with regard to the reaching of the ideal of economic democracy, to strive in their own way, to persuade the electorate that it is the best way of reaching economic democracy, the fullest opportunity to acting the way in which they want to act.

"Sir, that is the reason why the language of the articles in Part IV is left in the manner in which this Drafting Committee thought it best to leave it. It is no use giving a fixed, rigid form to something which is not rigid, which is fundamentally changing and must, having regard to the circumstances and the times, keep on changing. It is, therefore, no use saying that the directive principles have no value, for they lay down that our ideal is economic democracy. Because we did not want merely a parliamentary form of government to be instituted through the various mechanisms provided in the Constitution, without any direction as to our economic ideal, as to what our social order ought to be, we deliberately included the Directive Principles in our Constitution. I think, if the friends who are agitated over this question bear in mind what I have said just now that our object in framing this Constitution is really two-fold: (1) to lay down that our ideal is political democracy, and (2) to lay down that our ideal is economic democracy and also to prescribe that every Government whatever it is in power, shall strive to bring about economic democracy, much of the misunderstanding under which most members are labouring will disappear".[24]

Thus he wanted that the plan of state socialism must become a part of the Constitutional law of the land so that the legislature would not be in a position to suspend or abandon it at its will. He said that the essential condition for the success of a planned economy is that it must not be liable to suspension or abandonment. He visualised that political democracy taken singly would be unsuited to establish state socialism because the majority in the legislature might suspend or abandon it if it were not incorporated in the law of the land. At the same time he had an abhorrence towards dictatorship, not because it would not achieve state socialism but because it would certainly come in the way of individual freedom.

Dr. Ambedkar's economic views, however, should be seen in the context that nearly one-third of population of the country, if not more, still live below poverty line and substantial number of people are landless and the state must, therefore, continue to play dominant role to bring in economic equality. Dr. Ambedkar's economic thought stood for the progressive transformation of society, removing glaring social and economic equalities.

He extensively contributed to various economic issues covering concrete economic problems. Further, what is creditable is that though most of his economic writings related to the pre-independence period, they reflect not only unique freshness but also his deep insights into the problems. He approached and examined the economic issues with such foresight that his analysis and treatment of some of them is very much relevant even today.

NOTES

1. Ambedkar, B.R., *The Evolution of Public Finance in British India*, London, P.S. King & Sons, 1925. Preface.
2. *Ibid.* Foreword.
3. Ambedkar, B.R., *Problem of Rupee—Its Origin and Solution*, London, P.S. King & Sons, 1923. Preface.
4. *Ibid.*
5. *Ibid.*
6. *Ibid.*, Foreword.
7. *Ibid.*
8. *Ibid.*, p. 60.
9. Ambedkar, B.R., *Writing and Speeches*, Bombay, Education Department, Government of Maharashtra, 1986, Vol. 6, p. 78.
10. *Ibid.*
11. *Ibid.* Vol. 2., pp. 95-103.
12. *Ibid.*
13. *Ibid.*
14. *Constituent Assembly Debate*, Vol. 10, p. 3400.
15. Ambedkar, B.R., *Writing and Speeches*, Vol. 1, *op. cit.*
16. *Ibid.*

17. *Ibid.*
18. *Ibid.*
19. Nim, Hotilal (ed.), *Thoughts of Ambedkar,* Agra, Phoenix Publishing Company, 1971, p. 91.
20. *Ibid.*
21. *Ibid.*, p. 92.
22. Gadgil, N.V., *Government from Inside,* Meerut, Meenakshi Prakashan, 1968, p. 21.
23. Ambedkar, B.R., *What Congress and Gandhi have done to the Untouchable,* Bombay, Thacker & Co. Ltd. , 1945, pp. 294-95
24. Markadan, K.C., *Directive Principles in the Indian Constitution,* Bombay, Allied Publishers, 1966, pp. 137-38.

8

Ambedkar's Contributions to the Study of Indian Economy

RUCHI TYAGI

Ambedkar was among the first set of Indians who were trained in economics systematically and practised it professionally. India had a hoary tradition of economic studies in ancient times as classics like *Arthasastra*, *Sukraniti*, and *Tirukkural* will attest. However, the study of economics untainted by these texts and receiving its inspiration from the largely western (Judeo-Grecian-enlightenment) tradition for analytic study began in the middle of the nineteenth century. Those who studied economics and wrote economic treatises were not strictly speaking professional economists. They used economics as a political tool. Thus, the distinct contributions of Dadabhai Naoroji, Mahadev Govind Ranade, G.V. Joshi and numerous other thinker-activists remain polemical writings notwithstanding solid and substantial analytical content. With the twentieth century dawning, and universities coming to be established, a professional academic economic community began to evolve. A number of Indians went abroad during the first quarter of twentieth century to get advanced training in the discipline of economics to become professional economists, and they set the tone of economics studies in India until the 1960s. In this first group of foreign trained professional economists we can name C.N. Vakil, P.N. Banerjea, Jehangir Coyajee, Gyan Chand, D.R. Gadgil, P.S. Lokanathan, J.P. Niyogi, P.J. Thomas, P.P. Pillai, John Mathai, Radhakamal Mukherjea to name a few.

Ambedkar belonged to this group that received education abroad under some of the most eminent economists of the time. Ambedkar's contribution as an economist has by and large remained unnoticed. Various memorenda and statements that he submitted to the government (under the British rule as well as in the independent India) are indicative of his deep insights into India's economic problems. He was probably the first thinker to analyse economic dimensions of social maladies in India. Ambedkar's contribution as an economist may be characterised by two distinct phases:

The first one up to 1923, which led to several scholarly contributions in the form of dissertations for various advanced degrees that he earned in universities of repute. He was awarded the degrees of M.A. and Ph.D. in Economics by the Columbia University, U.S.A., in 1915 and 1917 respectively. Again, the degree of Doctor of Science (D.Sc.) conferred by the London School of Economics was also for his research in Economics.

The second phase covered the period since his return to India until his demise in 1956, during which he addressed economic problems and economic affairs of the country.

Ambedkar's main academic works include:

- *Administration and Finance of the East India Company* (unpublished MA dissertation, Columbia University, 1915);
- *National Dividend of India—A Historical and Analytical Study*, (Ph.D. Thesis, Columbia University, 1916);
- *The Evolution of Provincial Finance in British India—A Study in the Provincial Decentralisation of Imperial Finance* (D.Sc. Dessertation, London School of Economics, 1921, later published by P.S. King & Son Ltd., London, 1925);
- *The Problem of the Rupee: Its Origin and Its Solution* (P.S. King & Son Ltd., London, 1923);
- "Small Holding in India and their Remedies", *Journal of Indian Economic Society*, Vol. I, 1918;
- *State and Minorities: What are their Rights and How to Secure them in the Constitution of Free India* in 1947

submitted to the Constituent Assembly (Bombay: Thacker, 1947).

These works include finances of the East India Company; evolution of the Centre-State financial relationships in British India; analysis of monetray economics, while examining the evolution of the Indian currency as a medium of exchange and the choice of appropriate currency system for India; examination of Indian agricultural holdings; and the issue of state socialism in India.

Apart from these academic economic writings, there are his Memoranda and evidence given to various government commissions, speeches in the different legislative bodies, and book reviews all of which contain some economic content. All of these have been brought together by the government of Maharashtra in a multi-volumed complete edition, *Dr. Babasaheb Ambedkar: Writings and Speeches.*[1]

Acquaintance with Contemporary Economic Theories

Though Ambedkar's main purpose in the pursuit of the discipline was normative, he hoped that his study of economics will lead to useful policy conclusions. Thus, policy oriented welfare issues interested him more than studying the technical aspects of the discipline to demonstrate economic theorems. This, however, does not mean that he did not show any regard for theoretical conclusions derived by others. Indeed, it is significant that his knowledge of economic theory was amazingly up-to-date. Not only was his reading of contemporary economic literature wide and deep, he applied whatever that was in the cutting edge of the discipline to concrete situations, very imaginatively. For example, in a paper written in 1918, he referred to the contributions that appeared in the *American Economic Review* issued a few months earlier. Likewise, while reviewing Bertrand Russell's book *Principles of Social Reconstruction* in 1918, Ambedkar took him on the question of the 'Love of money' leading to human beings to "mutilate their own nature from a mistaken theory of what constitutes success" with the consequence of promoting a dead uniformity of "character and purpose, a diminution in the joy of life, and a stress and strain which leaves whole communities weary, discouraged and disillusioned". Ambedkar tears into this argument of the 'moralists' against 'love of money' showing that this philosophy is connected to a particular economic circumstances, and not of universal validity. In any case, money is required for something, and it is the purpose for which money is loved "will endow it with credit or cover it with shame".[2] He brings the heavy artillery of neo-classical theory of marginal utility developed by "Cournot, Gossen, Walras, Menger and Jevons" to counter Russell's position that it is all due to individual preference, and that people will give up things as soon as they have too much of anything. His books and papers are full of appropriate citations from the great contemporary economists, Irving Fisher, Alfred Marshall, Richard Ely, Alfred Kemmerer, Allyn Young, and John Maynard Keynes to name a few.

Indian Economic History

Ambedkar was not content with the current corpus of thought, because he had a tremendous historical sense and was fully aware that existing situations wear the scars of the past. In almost all his academic works, he employed the historical method. Whether it is the currency conundrums or public finance, Ambedkar dug deep in the bowels of history to understand the significance of events he was analysing. It was analytical rather than the dialectical method he used though occasionally one does find a dialectical approach in his writings. Thus, dealing with the need for legal solutions to social problems, he said: "Society is always conservative. It does not change unless it is compelled to and that too very slowly. When change begins, there is always a struggle between the old and the new, and the new is always in danger of being eliminated in the struggle for survival unless it is supported".[3] However, dialectics as a method of approaching any subject is absent in Ambedkar's work.

In many areas of Indian economic history, he was truly a pioneer and he faced all the problems that a pioneer faces as he pointed out in the preface of his *The Evolution of Provincial Finance*. Like Karl Marx some decades earlier, Ambedkar too pored over voluminous government reports and blue books to arrive at firm conclusions. Arising from his conscious use of history, was his use of statistical data. Notwithstanding the various lacunae of the official data, he skilfully marshalled the available data and used whatever statistical techniques that were available at that time. The value of his conclusions are substantial precisely because his analysis was based on sound empirical and historical foundations.

Due to Ambedkar's study under eminent economists, like R.A. Seligman and Edwin Cannan at the Columbia University and at the University of London respectively, he thoroughly studied the history of economic thought. Furthermore, he was widely read in history, jurisprudence, literature and classics. All this shows remarkable clarity and a wide range from disquisition on ancient Indian commerce to the current problems faced by the Indian rural population.

Broad themes may be identified in Ambedkar's professional writings as under:

The Evolution of Monetary Standards

The policies examined by Ambedkar in his *The Problem of the Rupee* mainly, and elsewhere, deal with monetary standards as they had evolved during the previous few decades. The basic Indian currency unit, the Rupee, had a long history. Until 1893, it was based on a silver standard which means that the Indian rupee was based on the value of the silver content in it. From 1841 onwards gold coins also became legal tender at one mohur as equal to 15 silver rupees. Owing to vast gold discoveries in Australia and US, gold value fell, and from 1853 onwards gold coins ceased to be legal tender. 1873 onwards, due to enormous silver discoveries, the price of silver fell. Subsequently, the price of rupee slipped in terms of gold. From 1872 to 1893, this acted as a continued devaluation of the Indian currency. It was good for Indian exports but not for the Indian economy, it had to produce more rupees to remit expenses undertaken in England by India which were in sterling (i.e. gold) terms. In 1893, the government stopped coining silver rupees though agreed to coin rupees in exchange of gold at a ratio of one pound four pence per rupee. The idea was to introduce eventually a gold standard with gold currency replacing the existing silver standard. **The pure gold standard** comprises use of gold in some form, especially coins, as a medium of exchange. In its variant called gold-convertible standard, paper money is also issued in addition to gold coins and is pledged to be redeemable in gold.

In 1899, at the suggestion of the currency committee headed by H.H. Fowler, Indian mints were thrown open to issue gold coins. Gold was sought to be used widely, but it also recommended the silver rupee to remain unlimited legal tender. This was mistaken because under gold currency, rupee should have been token coin. From now on, many events took place till the gold exchange standard came to be established in 1906. Under the **gold-exchange standard**, the medium of exchange comprises only paper money, which is kept exchangeable at fixed rates with gold and authorities back it up with foreign currency reserve of such countries as are on the gold standard.

According to this system, silver rupee was guaranteed convertibility into sterling pounds (based on gold value) at a fixed price, and make it available without any limit. The accumulated gold in India, instead of supporting a gold standard with gold currency in India, was kept in London to maintain the stability of the rate of exchange. However, the system broke down in 1916 with the enormous rise in the value of the silver. Silver rupee more or less ceased to be merely token, and the system effectively became silver standard.

For the reform of the Indian currency Ambedkar suggested:[4]

1. Stop coinage of rupees by absolutely closing the units to the Government as they are to be public;

2. Open a gold mint for the coinage of a suitable gold coin;
3. Fix a ratio between the gold coin and the rupee;
4. Rupee not to be convertible in gold and *vice versa*, but both to circulate as unlimited legal tender at the ratio fixed by law.

The items 1 and 4 were intended to impart elasticity into Indian currency system. The problem of suitable denominations and stability of value of Indian currency were sought to be achieved through recommendations 2 and 3.

Further, Ambedkar addressed the issue of effective utilization of gold reserves with the government. He provided a detailed and critical account of various proposals submitted for the reform of Indian currency system, the Temple Plan (1872), the Smith Plan (1876), the Government of India Scheme (1886), Herschell Committee (1892), Fowler Committee (1898) and so on. Moreover, Ambedkar provided an insightful discussion of relative merits and demerits of the gold standard *vis-à-vis* the gold exchange standard.

Ambedkar's writings took all this and argued stridently for a proper gold standard with gold currency as he was highly critical of the gold exchange standard though the latter received powerful theoretical support from all the then leading authorities including John Maynard Keynes. Ambedkar's main thrust was to criticise the "reckless issue of rupee currency" made possible by the gold exchange standard. He highlighted the perversity of the system because gold reserves which were supposed to guard a run on the currency, depend actually upon adding to the currency stock. In general, by removing the automaticity of the currency supply within the country, this system vests the government enormous power to bloat the money supply. The excessive importance given to maintain the stability of exchange as against internal stability of the value of currency was not a proper policy for India, he contended. Neither was Ambedkar a votary of deliberate lowering of the exchange rate whether planned or unplanned. Low exchange rate increases exports and boosts internal prices. This benefits the trading classes at the expense of the poorer people at home.

In a gold exchange standard, the coinage is manipulated by the government to keep it at par with the value of gold. Ambedkar asked: Was the job of currency management only important for the amount of gold it will procure in the external market? Obviously not, because "what really concerns those who use money is not how much gold that money is worth, but how much of things in general (of which gold is an infinitesimal part) that money is worth. Everywhere, therefore, the attempt is to keep money stable in terms of commodities in general, and that is but proper, for what ministers to the welfare of people is not so much the precious metals as commodities and services of more direct utility."[5]

Ambedkar's commitment was internal stability, and he was convinced that only an automatic system based on gold standard with gold currency could achieve this desirable end. Like every economist of his generation, he was a believer in the quantity theory of money and was afraid that governments will tend to artificially increase money in circulation. In his memorandum given to the Hilton Young Commission in 1925, he pointed out: "a managed currency is to be altogether avoided when the management is to be in the hands of the government". While there is less risk with monetary management by a private bank because "the penalty for imprudent issue, or mismanagement is visited by disaster directly upon the property of the issuer". In the case of the government "the chance of mismanagement is greater" because the issue of money "is authorised and conducted by men who are never under any present responsibility for private loss in case of bad judgement or mismanagement."[6]

In short, Ambedkar's conclusion is clearly towards price stability through conservative and automatic monetary management. This is of such current relevance that in these days of burgeoning budget deficits and their automatic monetisation, it would appear that we could do with an effective restraint on liquidity creation through an automatic mechanism.

The Evolution of Provincial Finance

According to Ambedkar, the provincial financial system in British India (upto 1921) evolved through three distinct phases, each with its own characteristic arrangement of the Centre's financial support to provinces:[7]

(a) Budget by Assignments

The inauguration of provincial finance was made through the scheme of 'budget by assignments' that prevailed for the initial six-year period, 1871-72 to 1876-77. The main objective of provincial finance was inculcation of a judicious and economic management of the finance, certain services (police, education, printing, roads, medical services, registration, jails, civil buildings and miscellaneous public improvements) were delegated to provincial budgets under the scheme. Receipts accrued from these services were handed over by the Imperial Government to the respective provinces. Since the receipts were only a small proportion of the total funds necessary to meet the provincialised expenditure, lump sum assignments were provided by the Imperial Government with a view to bring about an equilibrium in provincial budgets. According to Ambedkar, while the scheme made a good beginning, circumstances led to higher taxes as well as more iniquitous taxation. With a part of the financial burden passed on to the provinces, the Imperial Government decided to reduce the rate of income tax to pacify the richer classes. Further, to meet the additional deficit that was expected to arise from the income-tax reduction, assignments to the provinces were curtailed. Consequently, the provinces resorted to higher taxation on already over-burdened class of tax payers.

(b) Budget by Assigned Revenues

This scheme was operational during the five-year period of 1877-78 to 1881-82. Under this scheme certain revenues (besides the receipts from the delegated services) were assigned to the provinces and a special arrangement for 'adjusting assignments' were made. The total resources of the provinces comprised: (i) receipts accrued from the services incorporated in the budget; (ii) yield of the revenues assigned to the province concerned; and (iii) an adjusting assignment. Under the scheme, assignments were computed on the basis of the 'normal yield' from various sources, by averaging yields over a number of years. In order to make allowance for errors of estimating, an ingenious technique was introduced. It was agreed that if the actual results deviated from the estimated normal yield, the difference would be equally divided between the Imperial Government and the provincial government concerned. In other words, if the actual yield turned out to be higher than the normal yield, the corresponding imperial assignment was reduced by half of the excess and if it were less than the normal yield, the assignment would be increased by half of the shortfall. Ambedkar argues that the "prospect of gaining half the excess over the normal gave a more direct stimulus to the provinces to develop their resources beyond the normal, than it would have been the case if the total excess had been entirely appropriated by the Imperial Government."[8] On the other hand, the "consent secured from the provinces to bear half the burden of a possible deficit in the normal estimate directly put a premium on economical and judicial administration of the ceded revenues."

(c) Budget by Shared Revenues

The scheme of 'budget by shared revenue' was introduced in 1882-83 and lasted for nearly four decades until major fiscal reforms were introduced in 1921. Under this scheme, the heads of account under revenue and expenditure were grouped in three categories: (i) wholly imperial, (ii) wholly provincial and (iii) jointly imperial and provincial. In the third category, revenues and expenditure were shared between the Imperial Government and provinces in some definitely fixed proportion. Replacement of assignments by shares in the Imperial revenues had the effect of reducing rigidity and making revenues more elastic for the provincial governments.

While earlier settlements used to be generally on annual basis, subject to repeated renewals; wheras under this scheme of 'budget by shared revenues' five-yearly contracts were adopted. A review of the successive five-yearly settlements up to the settlement of 1902-03 convinced Ambedkar that under this system, the provincial governments "were parsimonious in the first few years lest their expenditure should prove too much for their revenues, and extravagant in the last few years lest their expenditure should shrink below the standard and leave large margins to be cancelled by the Government of India".[9] In order to obviate these evils of parsimony and extravagance, the principle of five yearly revision was abondoned in 1903-04.

A **quasi-permanent revision** was made in 1904-05, wherein the revenues between the Imperial and provincial governments were to be shared on the basis of the total expenditure they controlled. In addition, selective grants were given to provinces.

Soon after the series of quasi-permanent settlements had been concluded with different provinces, the subject of provincial and central finance was investigated into by the Royal Commission on Decentralization. The Commission endorsed the then existing arrangements. With some minor adjustment, a permanent settlement was made operational in 1912. The provincial finance in British India entered a new phase in 1921 under the **major fiscal reform of 1920-21;** under which following principles for equitable distribution of the burden among provinces were adopted:

(i) The total contribution of each province to the Government of India should be proportionate to its capacity to contribute.
(ii) The total contribution of a province would consist of its direct contribution as well as indirect contribution through customs, income tax, salt duties, etc.
(iii) The capacity of a province to contribute would be its taxable capacity, which is the sum of the incomes of its taxpayers, or the average income of its taxpayers multiplied by their number.

Ambedkar provided a perceptive critique of the new arrangement by saying that under the new arrangement, the Government had not been able to marshal properly the land revenue and the custom revenue. According to Ambedkar, the only remedy for placing provincial finance on a sound footing was reduction of expenditure and increase of taxation. As, 'without a sound finance no sound government is possible and without sound government no sound finance is possible.'

Thus, Ambedkar draws his main conclusions from his study of the Indian system[10] which are probably even more relevant now than it was at the time he wrote. What arrangements can be made in a public fiscal system that will enable it to be "administratively workable"? The main objective according to him was: "To make administrative policies independent by requiring them to finance themselves entirely out of their own respective resources without having to depend upon one another must always be regarded as a very important end to be kept in view in devising a new financial arrangement". This is not always possible because of "several concurrent or overlapping tax jurisdiction". The two methods to solve the problem, i.e., 'system of divided heads' and 'contributions' both have advantages and disadvantages.

Ambedkar looked at some of the consequences of the Montague-Chelmsford Reforms in provincial finances. What he cites from the despatch of the Secretary of State could have been written now: "If the financial stability of the Provinces is not to be undermined, with ultimate jeopardy to the Government of India itself, it is impossible to contemplate the continuance of a series of Provincial deficits financed by borrowing either direct from the public or from the Central Government". The similarity does not end. The provinces proposed an increase in their resources by revising the financial arrangements enunciated in the Act. What the Secretary of State said in 1922, might have been said by the Finance Minister today: "Equilibrium can only be achieved by reduction of expenditure and the adoption of measures which will lead to an increase in revenue".

Ambedkar, of course, is scathing towards what he calls the "very unreasonable attitude" of the provinces, and points out how they have all failed their duty. Years later in 1939, he remarked that "patriotism vanishes when you touch a man's pocket and I am sure that the state's representatives will prefer their own financial interest to the necessities of a common front."[11] He squarely blamed the governments for lacking political will to achieve efficient and equitable economic administration: "National prosperity may be great and growing and the increase of national wealth may be proceeding unchecked. If under such circumstances enough revenue is not obtained, the fault does not lie with the social income. Rather it is a fault of the government which must be said to have failed to organise and marshal the national resources for fiscal purposes. The same is to some extent true of the Indian government.

As for the base of taxation, Ambedkar considered income from land as the most likely source to augment state revenue, but he was vehemently opposed to the "pernicious effect of the system which bases the tax on a unit land held".[12] Ambedkar knew the problem clearly of tax proposals. Under the diarchy, when the government is run by a ministry recruited from the elected members of the provincial legislature, it would be futile to expect tax increases. More generally he said that if "nomination was the general mode of obtaining a seat in the Legislature", it was not necessary to "mind the prejudices of the electors". If however, the "seat is in the gift of the elector, a candidate to the Legislature who proposes to touch his pocket has a small chance of success, even though the new taxes are to result in more than proportionate benefit". In any case a political party which "has won power from a bureaucracy by accusing it of heavy taxation cannot easily disgrace itself by continuing the same policy". But can they reduce public expenditure by enforcing administrative economies? Not likely because under diarchy, the governor in council would not allow retrenchment as he has no particular interest in effecting economies in public expenditure. The result was that "the chances of an early equilibrium in Provincial finance are very small". One wonders whether Ambedkar was talking of state finances in democratic India?

Ambedkar's criticism of diarchy has a modern ring to it. Again in Ambedkar's words: "if there is no sound finance in the Provinces it is because diarchy is not a good form of government. Now, why is diarchy not a good form of government apart from its basic undemocratic character? The answer...is very simple...it is opposed to the principle of collective responsibility." If an administration has to work smoothly, "it must recognise the principle of impartibility of governmental work and a collective responsibility of the administrators in the execution thereof". It is not easily understood that government work by nature is invisible because in practice "the functions of government can be and commonly are partitioned, as they are between local bodies and between departments".[13] This does not mean that there is no "common thread that runs through them all: that no function of government acts in vacuole; that each reacts on some other function, and that the various functions cannot act at all produce orderly progress unless there is some force to harmonise them". Collective responsibility is this harmonising force. The conclusion is unmistakable: "Hybrid executives, divided responsibility, division of functions, reservation of powers, cannot make for a good system of government, and where there is no good system of government, there can be little hope for a sound system of finance".[14]

Utilization of Public Finances

In 1949, while discussing the functions of the Comptroller and Auditor General during the framing of our Constitution, Ambedkar said that governments should spend the resources garnered from the public not only as per rules, laws and regulations, but also to see that "faithfulness, wisdom and economy" have gone into the acts of expenditure by public authorities.

Faithfulness: Faith in this context as defined by the dictionary is "duty or commitment to fulfil a trust, promise..." A main reason for the existence of public finance is that human beings living in society require certain things like roads, law and order, etc. that cannot be enjoyed exclusively. As the costs and benefits of such items cannot be internalised, they will not be supplied through the free market mechanism. Governments exist to provide these common requirements. Citizens in democratic forms of government are promised by their representatives to improve their welfare by judicious provision of such public goods and services, and they place their trust in the government by delegating authority to take taxation and expenditure decisions. How the individual acts of public spending results in the augmentation of social welfare may not always be obvious because of spillover effects and long gestation periods. When the citizens are not in a position to comprehend clearly the consequences of government action, it is so easy to mislead them by false claims. Hence it becomes all the more necessary for the government to be faithful to the original intentions. For example, if a certain sum is allotted to a centre for higher education to improve its facilities without specifying the item of expenditure, a more faithful way of spending would be on libraries, laboratories and other items of teaching and research rather than on frivolous things such as statues of past professors or air conditioned limousine for its vice chancellor.

Wisdom: The fidelity to the original intention must be tempered by 'wisdom'. For example, the original intention of the policy may be to spread appropriate information through expenditure on the activities of the DAVP or information departments. But such a policy when executed may be faithful to the intentions but may not be wise. In other words, expenditure should transcend the personal, the ephemeral and the showy, but must be done with circumspection and understanding of the deeper issues involved. While sagacity, prudence and common sense are the hallmarks of a just and wise ruler, he should also possess experience and knowledge that can be applied critically and practically in specific areas. In the context of a just utilisation of public funds, economic wisdom becomes a paramount necessity.

Economy: The importance of the third canon of public expenditure, i.e. economy takes a special meaning here. 'Economy' in public expenditure does not simply mean a low level of public spending, but it is the intelligent use of funds so that every paise fetches the most benefit. Those in charge of public funds must strive to evaluate alternative methods of achieving the objectives and see to it that leakages do not occur.

The remarkable thing about Ambedkar's canons is that they are ism-neutral. One can follow a policy of a large or a small public sector and yet the principles behind these canons are applicable. The canons are sufficiently flexible so that expenditure decisions can be related to the state of the economy. For example, what may be economic wisdom in undertaking a particular item of expenditure in one country may be economic stupidity at other times and other places. The canons emphasise that the expenditure decisions should closely relate to the specified objectives and the available resources besides ensuring economy, efficiency and effectiveness in the implementation of government decisions. While the determination of the aggregate level of expenditure is a matter of overall policy based on the democratic will of the people, allocation of that total among competing demands and the manner of utilisation fall within the domain of these canons. Following the canons scrupulously in individual items of expenditure cannot always eliminate problems arising out of the broader economic policy pursued by the government. But they can mitigate the harmful effects of ill-considered policies of our governments. In the present context of high fiscal deficits, a rigorous application of the Ambedkar canons can help reduce the quantum of public expenditure.

On Indian Agrarian Economy

In his paper *'Small Holdings in India and their Remedies'*[15] published in 1918, he analysed a problem that is still haunting Indian agrarian system. At that time, British administrators and academics in India who were used to their own country, where large agricultural land holdings were the norm, were appalled at the low productivity of Indian land. This they ascribed to the minuscule size of the farm land cultivated by Indian peasants. A number of suggestions emanated from sympathetic observers like H. S. Jevons of Allahabad University, Harold Mann and G. F. Keatinge of Bombay, and the committee appointed to make proposals on the consolidation of small and scattered holdings in the Baroda State (1917). They all proposed to consolidate and/or enlarge the holdings in the hands of individual farmers through interesting administrative measures. Ambedkar made a critical examination of the above, and in the process arrived at some very advanced conclusions.

On different occasions, Ambedkar delt with the problems of landless labourers, small holdings, Khoti system, Mahar Watan, collective farming, land revenue and abolition of landlordism.

(a) Land Reforms for Economic Holdings

Ambedkar dealt with the problem of fragmentation of holdings in his paper on *"Small Holdings in India and their Remedies"* in 1918.[16] He attributed the subdivision of land mainly to an enormous pressure of population on land, but not to the law of inheritance. He insisted that due to lack of alternative means of subsistence, large population is dependent on agriculture, which made sustenance of enlarged and consolidated holdings at a particular size impossible. He, further, insisted that **a land may become an economic holding on the basis of optimum combination of all factors including land, capital and labour in a proportion such that the *pro rata* contribution of each in conjunction with the rest is highest.**[17] Thus, he struck at the very root of the proposals by arguing that there can be no such thing as a correct size of agricultural holding. As he argued, land is only one of the many factors of production and the productivity of one factor of production is dependent upon the proportion in which the other factors of production are combined. In his words: "the chief object of an efficient production consists in making every factor in the concern contribute its highest; and it can do that only when it can co-operate with its fellow of the required capacity. Thus, there is an ideal of proportions that ought to subsist among the various factors combined, though the ideal will vary with the changes in proportions". From this he proceeds to say that if agriculture "is to be treated as an economic enterprise, then, by itself, there could be no such thing as a large or small holding". If this is so, what is the problem? Certainly it is not due to a want of efficiency in utilising whatever the peasant has. Ambedkar cites with approval of an English civil servant: "The ryots have a keen eye to the results of a good system of farming as exhibited on model farms". Ambedkar's answer rests on the inadequacy of other factors of production.

Ambedkar insisted that "subdivision and fragmentation involves waste of labour and cattle power, waste in hedges and boundary marks and waste of manure. It renders impracticable the watching of crops, sinking of wells and the use of labour saving implements. It makes difficult changes in cultivation, preparing roads, water channels etc., and increases cost of production."[18]

Ambedkar suggested two interrelated remedial 'curative' and 'preventive' measures:

(i) ***The curative measure*** is consolidation of holding, which means, the substitution of exchange of fields of the farmers in any area in such a way as to make the holdings held by each of them more compact. On consolidation, the number of fragments in the holding can be reduced. While rejecting Prof. H.S. Jevons' concept of voluntary exchange of land, Ambedkar suggested for the restricted sale of the right of occupancy.

(ii) Regarding ***the preventive measure*** Ambedkar preferred an amendment in the Civil Procedure Code "so as to make it obligatory on the courts to refuse partition whenever it would reduce a field beyond the economic unit fixed in advance."[19]

Ambedkar's analysis of agrarian reforms will not be complete without a reference of abolition of the Khoti System.

(b) Abolition of Khoti System

Ambedkar introduced a bill in Bombay Provincial Legislative Council seeking the abolition of Khoti sysytem on September 17, 1937. The Khoti system denotes the existence of minor land tenures in Ratnagiri, Ranged (then Colaba) and Thane districts of the then Bombay presidency. The Khoti system was different from Ryotwari system of land tenure. Under the widely prevalent Ryotwari system, the cultivators were directly paying the land revenue to the government; whereas under the Khoti system, there was an intermediary collecting land revenue on behalf of the government. A Khoti would imply in superior land holder and a tenant would represent an inferior land owner. The Khoti, superior land holder would collect land revenue on behalf of the government from tenants, the inferior land holders. Thus, there was some resemblance between zamindari system of land tenure existing under the Permanent Settlement Act and Khoti system.

While condemning Khoti system, Ambedkar made an early attempt towards land tenure reforms in India. Under the system, Khoti was obliged to collect revenues from the tenants and to pay a certain part of it to the government. Once such payment was made, the Khoti enjoyed unrestricted freedom to do whatever he liked to the tenant. This freedom, in fact, was misused and the tenants were subjected to all kinds of exactions.

By introducing the Bill to abolish the Khoti system, Ambedkar sought to put an end to the exploitation of the actual tillers of the land and to establish a direct relationship between them and the government. In the Bill, he also made the provision of paying reasonable compensation to the Khoti. Ambedkar's bill on the abolition of the Khoti system, thus, proved to be a forerunner to the land reforms legislation in the post-independent India.[20]

(c) Collective Farming

Ambedkar asserted that Indian agriculture should be a State Industry. He felt that neither consolidation of holdings nor tenancy legislation contributes to agricultural productivity nor do they help in solving the chronic problems of landless farmers and small farmers. He thought that a panacea is nationalisation of whole agricultural land with collective farming. Such a reorganization of agriculture, Ambedkar believed, helps to guarantee employment opportunities, weaken the economic strength of the landlords and reduce the extent of excessive exploitation of these labourers, belonging mostly to depressed class, and in turn, help their upliftment to a desired economic standard.[21] He insisted for agricultural labour to be treated as industrial workers with fixed P.F., fixed hour of work, health, insurance, workmen's compensation etc.[22]

The agriculture industry shall be organised on the following lines:

- The state should divide the land acquired into farms of standard size and let out the farms for cultivation to residents of the villages as tenants (made of group of families). These tenants may cultivate the land on the following conditions:

  (i) The farm should be cultivated as a collective farm;
  (ii) The farm should be cultivated in accordance with the rules and directions, issued by the government; and
  (iii) The tenants should share among themselves in the manner prescribed, the produce of the farm left after the payments of charges leviable on the farm.

- The land should be let out to villagers without any distinction of caste or creed and in such a manner that there should be no landlord, no tenant, and no landless labourer.

- It should be the obligation of the state to finance the cultivation of the collective farm by way of supplying water, draught animals, manure, seeds, etc., in order to increase the agricultural output.
- The state should be entitled—

(i) To levy the follwing charges on the produce of the farm: (1) a portion for land revenue, (2) a portion to pay the debenture holders, (3) a portion to pay for the use of capital good supplied, and

(ii) To prescribe penalties against tenants, who break the conditions of tenancy of wilfully neglect to make the best use of the means of cultivation, offered by the state or otherwise irk prejudiciously to the scheme of the collective farming.[23]

(d) Surplus Labour Utilization and Capital Formation

Ambedkar stated that a large agricultural population in relation to agricultural land in actual cultivation meant that a large part of the agricultural population was superfluous and idle. The economic consequence of the idle labour was twofold. First, given the lack of alternative job opportunities, the enormous population pressure led to subdivision of land into small and marginal holdings. Secondly, since idle labour continued to depend on agriculture, it reduced the income per worker to barely subsistence level and left no scope for saving and capital investment in agriculture. Productivity of agriculture could be increased, according to Ambedkar, by simultaneously expanding capital and capital goods, and reducing labour to raise land and labour productivity. If the stock of capital goods alone was increased, without reducing surplus labour, the problem of small and scattered land holdings would not be solved. Ambedkar, therefore, argued for a strategy of transferring labour from agriculture to other sectors of the economy.

Ambedkar was of considered view that problems of agriculture may not be resolved merely with consolidation or enlarging of holdings, but manual increase of the capital and capital goods. The insufficiency of capital which is needed for acquiring "agricultural stock and implements" arises from savings. But as Ambedkar remarks "that saving is possible where there is surplus in a common place of political economy".

The important policy implications of Ambedkar's assertion for surplus labour utilization and capital formation are as under:[24]

- The surplus agricultural labour shall be transferred to and productively employed in non-agricultural sectors with a view to reduce population pressure on agricultural land;
- Such a labour transfer would not only generate adequate earnings for its maintenance but it will also create surplus outside agriculture. This surplus is the source of additional capital formation;
- The increase in capital and capital goods supply shall favourably affect the agricultural sector by creating the necessary incentives for enlarging the size of economic holdings;
- Industrialization promoting the formation of economic holdings is treated as a far better remedy to legal measure of fixing the size of economic holdings. This implies that Ambedkar was convinced that market process of growth is a best remedy than legal measure.

(e) Industrialisation as a Remedy for Agricultural Problems

Even if the lands are consolidated and enlarged and cultivated through capitalistic enterprise, it will not solve the problem as it will only aggravate "the evils by adding to our stock of idle labour". The only way out of this impasse is to take people away from land. This will automatically "lessen and destroy the premium that at present weighs heavily on land in India" and large "economic holding will force itself upon us as a pure gain". He concludes that **"Industrialisation of India is the soundest remedy for the agricultural problems of India".**[25]

This can generate adequate surplus that will also eventually benefit the agricultural sector. Indeed a shift from primary industry to secondary industry is vital and it must be attempted seriously to prevent the present enlargement of the rural population that was being witnessed and remedies based on what he calls "faulty political economy" were being advocated.

According to Ambedkar, the cumulative effects of industrialisation, namely a lessening of pressure on land and increasing amount of capital and capital goods would forcibly create the economic necessity of enlarging the holding. Moreover, industrialisation by cancelling the premium on land would give rise to few occasions for subdividing and fragmenting it. It would be most effective barrier against subdivision and fragmentation. Ambedkar did not rule out direct capital investment in agriculture to improve land productivity, but believed that improvement in labour productivity would be a better source of surplus and capital investment in agriculture. In his theoretical formulations, one can see his affinity to Arthur Lewis model of economic development based on the existence of unlimited supply of labour, to others based on inter-sectoral linkages of labour and capital, and also to the underlying economic assumptions of the Indian strategy of planned economic development.[26]

Measures for the Industrial Labour: Trade Unions

Taking inspirations from labour movements led by Jyotiba Phule and Narayan Meghaji Lokhande, Ambedkar advocated for the cause of industrial labour. As all workers cannot come out for discussions, there must be a representative or a group of representatives to present the grievances of the workers. Ambedkar talked about two categories of unions. The first is a union which has 20 per cent of the workers as its members and second is a union whose membership is more than 50 per cent and can represent labour in the conciliation proceedings.

According to Ambedkar, a trade union may have three different objectives:

(i) Purpose connected with the promotion of their particular interest as workers, wages, hours of work, promotions in industry, etc.
(ii) Social purposes conferring certain benefits, giving old age pension, giving unemployment benefit to these members, providing pensions for their widows, etc.
(iii) Political purpose, viz. freedom to promote a particular line of politics, which the union thinks best suited for the protection of its economic and social position.[27]

Addressing the Conference of Regional Labour Commissioners in Bombay in December 1945, Ambedkar asserted that three things were necessary to mitigate or prevent industrial disorder: (i) a machinery for reconciliation; (ii) an amendment to the Trade Disputes Act, and (iii) minimum wage legislation. Ambedkar insisted that the employer must pay reasonable wages, which was another name for elimination of exploitation, and provide comfortable conditions of work, which was another name for labour welfare.[28]

Multi-purpose River Projects in India

Influenced by Tennessee Valley Project in America, Ambedkar put forth the idea of starting multi-purpose river projects in India. Ambedkar was of the considered view that such river projects combine the multi-purpose engineering to harness water resources providing navigation, controlling floods, and bring sufficient water to make production of power, a profitable undertaking. To a great extent Damodar Valley Project was the outcome of the efforts of Ambedkar. Moreover, while drafting the Constitution of India, he did not leave water management entirely to the states, but brought this subject under the provision of Central control to resolve the inter-State water problems.

Social Measures

(a) Economic Consequences of Hindu Social Order

The manner in which the formal economic rights concerning the private property, occupation, employment, wages, education and informal rights (i.e. norms, custom, values etc.) concerning dignity of labour were devised and evolved under the Hindu Social Order, it produced immense economic inequality and general atmosphere of backwardness.[29] The adverse impact on the motivation to work and invest was quite obvious. The rules governing employment reduced incentive to work. The restriction on occupational mobility and, hence, on labour, capital and entrepreneurship across economic activities for generality of people discouraged investment. Such restrictions on factor mobility reduces the competition and create imperfect and monopolistic situation in the markets. Further, the restriction on the choice of occupation as well as the social status of high and low attached to each one of them generate voluntary unemployment. The system, in fact, crippled the untouchable as it denied economic security and independence.

(b) Mahar Watan Abolition Bill

The Mahars were required to slave all day and night. For his hard arduous and ceaseless work, he got a piece of land called 'watan', some corn from villagers and a paltry pittance. Thus, 'Mahar Watan' was a worst kind of serfdom of agricultural tenant. In the absence of a Mahar servant, his father or any other male member of his family was pressed into service. In order to break the shackles of his serfdom, Ambedkar introduced a bill in Bombay Legislative Committee on 3rd August, 1928 to abolish Watan Act. In the Bill, he covered only inferior hereditary officers, particularly the Mahars in the Deccan, the Vethias or the Varthanias in Gujarat, the Rameshis or the Juglias and the Holi in Karnataka.

State Socialism

Ambedkar suggested the economic framework of Socialism in which he proposed state ownership in agriculture with collectivised method of cultivation; a modified form of State socialism in the field of industry; and nationalisation of insurance; leaving other activities to private sector. Here, the basic tenets of 'State Socialism' involve ownership of land and key industries by the state and collective maintenance and just distribution of common produce. Ambedkar also proposed the nationalisation of insurance to provide greater security to the individual. It was probably more due to functional reasons than any fundamental change in his enlightened economic ideology, as he felt that private sector had not achieved growth and his rational mind told him that we should "put an obligation on the state to plan the economic life of the people on lines which would lead to highest point of productivity without closing every avenue to private enterprise, and also provide for the equitable distribution of wealth".[30]

As the President of the All India Scheduled Caste Federation, he submitted a memorandum, *State and Minorities: What are their Rights and How to Secure them in the Constitution of Free India* in 1947 to the Constituent Assembly, demanding not only the inclusion of 'State Socialism' under the Fundamental Rights of the Constitution, but also a provision to enforce it within a period of 10 years from the date of promulgation of the Constitution. Though his proposal could not be accepted due to opposition from some prominent members of the Constituent Assembly like Sardar Patel, Acharya Kriplani, Dr. Rajendra Prasad and Pt. Jawaharlal Nehru etc.;[31] yet planned economic development with the state acquiring the commanding heights of the economy has been recognised as one of the important measures flowing directly from the Directive Principles of State Policy.

Ambedkar's views regarding the elements of state socialism and social welfare are contained in the *Independent Party Menifesto* (1936) and *State and Minorities*. Ambedkar's state socialism includes the following measures:[32]

- Industries which are key industries or which may be declared to be key industries shall be owned and run by the state;
- Industries which are not key industries, but which are basic industries shall be owned by the state and shall be run by the state or by corporations established by the state;
- Insurance shall be a monopoly of the state and that the state shall compel every adult citizen to take out a life insurance policy commensurate with his wages as may be prescribed by the legislature;
- Agriculture shall be state industry;
- State shall acquire the subsisting rights in such industries, insurance and agricultural land held by private individuals, whether as owners, tenants or mortgages and pay them compensation in the form of debentures equal to his or her right in the land. Provided that in reckoning the value of land, plant or security no account shall be taken of any rise therein due to emergency, of any potential or unearned value for compulsory acquisition.
- State shall determine how and when the debenture holder shall be entitled to claim cash payment.
- The debenture shall be transferable and inheritable property, but neither the debenture holder nor the transferee from the original holder nor his heir shall be entitled to claim the return of the land or interest in any industrial concern acquired by the state or be entitled to deal with it in any way.
- The debenture-holder shall be entitled to interest on his debenture at such rate as may be defined by law, to be paid by the state in cash or in kind as the state may deem fit.

Constitutional State Socialism with Parliamentary Democracy

To attain triple objective to establish socialism, retain parliamentary democracy and avoid distatorship, Ambedkar suggested for state socialism by the Law of Constitution to make it out of reach of a parliamentary majority to "suspend, amend or abrogate" it.[33] Ambedkar proposed a political and economic structure for India in the form of "constitutional state socialism with parliamentary democracy".[34] Ambedkar's negation of capitalism and preference for socialistic economy has grown out of his interpretation of democracy and urge for liberty. Ambedkar visualised the social transformation and democratisation of Indian society through constitutional means. As the Chairman of the Drafting Committee of the Constituent Assembly, Ambedkar tried to give expression to his philosophy of economic reorganisation of society in free India. In the context of India with its graded inequalities, the ascent of the ascended castes and economic degradation of the down trodden with some possessing immense wealth and others experiencing abject poverty, according to Ambedkar, political democracy cannot succeed in the absence of social and economic democracy at the base. As social and economic democracy are the tissues and the fibre of political democracy.

Ambedkar systematically developed a linkage between individual liberty and the shape and form of economic structure of society. In respect of social inequality, Ambedkar observed that any sort of privilges to some, tilt the balance of social action in favour of possessors. Hence, more equal the social rights of citizens, the more able they will be to utilize their freedom. Therefore, if liberty is to take its appointed end, it is important that there should be social equality in the first place. Realising significance of economic security, Ambedkar asserted that a man may be free to enter any vocation he may choose, but if he is deprived of security in employment, he becomes a pray of mental and physical servitude, incompatible with the very essence of liberty.

Ambedkar believed in material progress, constitutional approach to solving problems, rule of law, right to property, civil liberties, democracy based on the liberty, equality and fraternity—principles enunciated by the French Revolution. His extensive critique of the caste system is also based on enlightenment principles of economic efficiency through private initiative, individual liberty and human equality.

Ambedkar placed much value on democracy and individual liberty, which he thought could be preserved by judicious state action. Ambedkar defined democracy as "a form and method of Government, whereby, revolutionary changes in the economic and social life of the people are brought about without bloodshed."[35] Ambedkar envisioned democracy not as an end in itself, but as an effective means of bringing about the desired socio-economic transformation. In a sense this conforms to the classic Smithian position. The causal chain that Adam Smith envisaged was that economic and social freedom/ equality will propel the society towards political equality/ freedom. And this is long lasting than the other way round where first you get political freedom and strive to achieve economic and social equality/freedom. In almost all his writings, Ambedkar, while fighting for political emancipation, did not forget the need for social and economic reforms.

Again, it was Ambedkar's strong belief in the primacy of rationally directed social and economic development that he advocated centralisation of economic activities. Whether it is his single achievement in formulating a coherent national water policy (done during his membership of Viceroy's Council 1942-1946)[36], or his helping to give a unitary bias to the Indian Constitution, Ambedkar's anxiety was to promote economic and social development of the Indian nation as quickly as possible. Indian Constitution is more unitary than federal which in a sense is a reflection of Ambedkar's long standing bias as he said in 1939 at the Gokhale School of Politics while delivering Kale Memorial Lecture: "I am not opposed to a Federal Form of Government. I confess I have a partiality for a Unitary form of Government. I think India needs it".[37]

Ambedkar, in fact, placed an obligation on the State to plan the economic life of the people on lines, which would lead to highest point of productivity without closing every venue to private entreprise and also provide for equitable distribution of wealth. He advocated an economic policy framework specially aimed at providing protection to the vulnerable sections of society against economic exploitation.

While drafting the Constitution, Ambedkar strongly recommended democracy as the governing principle of human relationship, but emphasised that the principles of equality, liberty and fraternity, which are the cornerstones of democracy should not be interpreted narrowly in terms of the political rights alone. He emphasised the socio-economic dimensions of democracy by incorporating the Directive Principles of State Policy in the Constitution.

Relevance of Ambedkar's Ideas

A careful analysis of Ambedkar's views brings out a well-articulated theoretical framework for economic development.[38] Ambedkar's perspective on economic planning and development left imprint on the objectives and strategy of post-war economic plan. These ideas of Ambedkar include: emphasis on capital investment in agriculture; priority to industrialisation; more active and positive role for the State in planned development; emphasis on planning and public sector with a definite place for the poor and the socially oppressed sections in the planned economic development of the country and the need of social policy for down trodden.

The acceptance of the planning as an instrument for economic and social development of the country was a major step undertaken after independence. Realising that the problems of reconstruction differ from country to country, Ambedkar argued that in other countries, the problem of reconstruction is a problem of rehabilitation of industry during post-war period, whereas the problem of reconstruction is a problem mainly of the industrialisation of India. Ultimately, the reconstruction plan for India did cover measures both for rehabilitation and economic development.

Ambedkar appears to have significantly influenced the decision on the strategy of economic development as well. He emphasised the need for industrialisation for overall economic development as well as for development of the agricultural sector. He laid emphasis on direct capital investment in the agricultural sector. What Ambedkar insisted in 1944 (as statement of Objectives in the Plan paper) is equally relevant even today:

> "The ultimate object of all planning must be to raise the standard of living of the people as whole and to ensure employment to all. To that end, the purchasing power of the people must be increased by improvement in the efficiency and consequently the productivity of labour on the one hand, and simultaneous development and a reorganisation of agriculture, industries and services on the other. And further, agriculture is and will remain India's primary industry, but the present imbalanced economy has to be rectified by intensive development of the country's industries so that both agriculture and industry may develop side by side. That will enable the pressure of population on the land to be relieved and will also provide the means required for the provision of better amenities for the people in the way of education, sanitation, public health, housing etc."

Ambedkar's economic ideas have influenced the process of Indian Planning both explicitly and implicitly:

- The social theory of labour exploitation formulated by Ambedkar resulted in incorporation of a comprehensive scheme of total reservation in education, employment and civic amenities. This was accepted by the founding fathers of the Constitution of India without any protest or any kind of dissent note.
- On account of above item, under various components of development schemes and welfare programmes, the Scheduled Castes and Scheduled Tribes population is given priority. Purticularly TRYSEM, Self-employment Financing Scheme, DIR Scheme, Housing, rural employment programmes etc.
- Ambedkar's production oriented definition of economic holdings in agriculture has been accepted under our land reforms. Further, priority is given to landless agricultural labourers belonging to SC/ST groups while allocating the surplus land obtained by

the government. Thus, efforts have been made to promote the farm entrepreneurship among SC/ST people living in rural areas.

- Ambedkar favoured multi-purpose river-valley projects to provide canal irrigation to agriculture and generate energy to promote industrial development and also to provide a permanent solution to problem of flood and its devastation. In fact, he was associated with the study team which has examined the feasibility of constructing Damodar Valley River Project as early as in 1945.
- Ambedkar had clearly recognised the 'right to strike' by the workers. He suggested a tripartite tribunal system—workers, employers and government representative—to resolve the industrial disputes and unrest. This is the mostly accepted and widely practiced method of solving industrial problems in free India.
- Ambedkar had voiced in a few farmers' movements in Maharashtra and Uttar Pradesh and has supported the demand for farmers for better and remunerative prices for products and abolition of different forms of tenancy and landlord systems. Though Ambedkar had not written elaborately and separately on these subjects, he was aware of the unfavourable terms of trade for agriculture as against industry; therefore, he supported the demand of farmers for better farm prices.
- By including 'Directive Principles of State Policy', Ambedkar provided 'welfare state' orientation to our governmental structure and defined its economic goals concerning education, nutrition, housing, health, wages, labour, welfare etc.

Analysing the problem of centre-state relations, Ambedkar asserted that even though every government wants higher revenue through taxation, but a poor and under-developed country like India has limits to the widening of taxation and this burden has to be shared equitably between Central Government, provinces and local governments. His detailed study of principles, on provincial finance or centre-state financial relationship, had actually helped successive finance commissions in India after 1947. There is every need to lay strong foundation through sound principles for smooth functioning of centre-state relations, lest the states should follow the path of non-cooperation with centre. Realising such possibility, Ambedkar suggested concrete steps for amicable settlement of centre-state disputes by a judicious sharing of revenues so as to easily bear the every expanding developmental and welfare burdens of the states.

His writings on monetary economics, his statements of evidence before the Royal Commission on Indian Currency and Finance (1924-25) paved the way for the Reserve Bank of India in April 1935.

Likewise, relevance of Ambedkar's arguments can be realised through his assertion for a regulatory mechanism to restrain the discretionary powers invested with the issuer of currency. In the present context of heavy fiscal deficit and automatic monetisation there is need for strong and strict regulation, so that a stability in prices and a stable currency standard be achieved.

Ambedkar's own perspective on economic development and political issues had a profound impact on the policy perspective on irrigation and electricity development. As early as 1918, he realised that the root cause of economic backwardness was the persistent evil of maladjustment in India's social economy, characterised by scarcity of capital in agriculture along with the existence of disproportionately high magnitude of labour force. This had depressed the land and labour productivity. Agriculture productivity could be raised by simultaneously expanding capital investment and reducing idle labour by transferring it to non-agricultural industrial activities.

To solve the problem of unemployment, contrary to Gandhi, who advocated labour intensive method of production, Ambedkar preferred capital intensive agriculture and industry. The same was adopted by Nehru during the three initial five year plans. He preferred industrialisation within the mixed economy model, with state having dominant position. However, this model could not absorb the surplus labour from agriculture as assumed by Ambedkar.

In short, as a strategy of economic development of India, Ambedkar emphasized the eradication of poverty, elimination of inequalities and ending exploitation of the masses, weaker sections and *dalits* in purticular. He preferred industrialisation for absorbing surplus agricultural labour and land reforms to increase agricultural production. He considered agriculture as industry, and gold standard for maintaining stability of the value of Indian currency, smooth centre-state relations for coordinated economic development and state intervention for an orderly growth of the Nation. Thus, Ambedkar's economics is a vivid combination of *dalit* emancipation, socialism and nationalism.

NOTES

1. *Babasaheb Ambedkar: Writings and Speeches,* Bombay: Education Department, Government of Maharashtra, 1979-1991, Vol. 1-15.
2. *Ibid.*, Vol. I, 483.
3. *Ibid.*, Vol. XII, 115.
4. Odeyar D. Heggade, *Economic Thought of Dr. B.R. Ambedkar,* New Delhi: Mohit Publications, 1998, 43.
5. *Supra n.* 1, Vol. VI, 563.
6. *Supra n.* 1, Vol. VI, 627.
7. Narendra Jadhav, *Dr. Ambedkar's Economic Thought and Philosophy,* Bombay: Popular Prakashan, 1993,19.
8. *Supra n.* 1, Vol. VI, 137.
9. *Ibid.*, Vol. VI, 170-71.
10. Dr. Bhim Rao Ambedkar, *The Evolution of Provincial Finance in British India—A Study in the Provincial Decentralisation of Imperial Finance,* London: P.S. King & Son Ltd., 1925.
11. *Supra n.* 1, Vol. I, 347.
12. *Ibid.*, Vol. VI, 302.
13. *Ibid.*, Vol. VI, 303.
14. *Ibid.*, Vol. VI, 307.
15. *Ibid.*, Vol. I, 453.
16. *Ibid.*, Vol. I.
17. *Ibid.*, Vol. I, 468.
18. *Ibid.*, Vol. I, 459.

19. *Ibid.*, Vol. I, 459-462.
20. *Supra n.* 4, 94-95.
21. K. Sateesh Reddy and P. Ramaiah, "Dr. B.R. Ambedkar's Ideology and Land Reforms and Agricultural Development", in P. Ramaiah and K. Sateesh Reddy (ed.), *Dr. B.R. Ambedkar's Economic Philosophy*, New Delhi: Delta Publishing House, 1994,1-12.
22. *Constituent Assembly Debates*, Vol. IX, 944-45.
23. *Ibid.*, Vol. I, 396-97 and 408-12.
24. *Supra n.* 4, 92-93
25. *Supra n.* 1, Vol. I, 477.
26. Sukhadeo Thorat, *Ambedkar's Role in Economic Planning and Water Policy*, Delhi: Shipra Publication, 1998, 26.
27. *Supra n.* I, Vol. II, 227.
28. M.L. Kasare, *Economic Philosophy of Dr. B. R. Ambedkar*, New Delhi: B.L. Publications Pvt. Ltd., 1996,183.
29. *Supra n.* 26, 34-35.
30. *Ibid.*, Vol. I, 408.
31. G.S. Lokhande, *Bhim Rao Ramji Ambedkar—A Study in Social Democracy*, New Delhi: Sterling Publishers Pvt. Ltd., 1977, 34.
32. J.S. Narayan Rao, Y. Pushpalatha and B.N. Vinod Rao, "A Note on Ambedkar, Economics: Liberation Economics", *Supra n.* 21, 83-92.
33. V.D. Nagar and K.P. Nagar, *Economic Thought and Policy of Dr. Ambedkar*, New Delhi: Segment Books, 1992, 147-48.
34. *Supra n.* 26, 29.
35. Bhagwan Das (ed.), *Thus Spoke Ambedkar*, 1977, 61.
36. *Supra n.* 26, 22.
37. *Ibid.*, Vol. I, 353.
38. *Supra n.* 26, 23.

9

Dr. B.R. Ambedkar and the Vision of Social Justice

SUSHMA YADAV

Indian society has been caste ridden. In the past, there existed no such area of social existence and governance where caste as political, social, economic, educational and cultural factor was not present. Even today, after more than five decades of introduction of Republican Constitution, the caste factor is dominant in every sphere of life of the people of this country[1]. Before the commencement of Ambedkar era, there were the untouchable Hindus in India, who due to Hindu social system, had, remained socially graded, economically impoverished, politically suppressed, religiously ostracized and indefinitely excluded from educational and cultural opportunities[2]. They were condemned to the lot of serfs and deprived of all human rights.

Dr. B.R. Ambedkar's birth in an untouchable community and in a system based on the graded inequality and injustice and deprivation of basic human rights to his brethren was responsible for giving a purpose and a mission of his life. "Ambedkar was all sound and fury against social injustice. His weaponry was legal-political, his anathema Hindu caste exclusivism and his ambition social democracy...His life was a planning forge, his commitment was to free the ancient un-free, his economics, law and politics were welded into a constitutional militancy and geared to social emancipation movement."[3] Recalling his struggle for Social Justice, both in pre-Independent India, and in Constituent Assembly and more importantly to ponder over its continued relevance today is always an enriching exercise.

One of the key themes of the writings of Dr. B.R. Ambedkar was the attainment of Social Justice and establishment of a just society[4], which, for him, was essentially also a casteless society. He not only provided a ruthless criticism of the existing social order but also came up with an alternative vision and alternative model of social order based on justice, liberty, equality, fraternity and annihilation of caste[5]. Ambedkar was convinced that a good social order or society has to go through two tests, namely 'the test of justice' and the 'test of utility'. His judgemental analysis of the caste based Hindu social order was based on these two tests.

The term "social justice" was first used in 1840 by a Sicilian priest, Luigi Taparelli d'Azeglio, and given prominence by Antonio Rosmini-Serbati in *La Costitutione Civile Secondo la Giustizia Sociale* in 1848[6]. Later, British authors such as John Stuart Mill, Leslie Stephen and Henry Sidgwick referred from time to time to social justice, although without marking it off sharply from distributive justice generally[7]. John Stuart Mill gave this anthropomorphic approach to social questions almost canonical status for modern thinkers thirteen years later in ***Utilitarianism*** when he observed that society should treat all equally well who have deserved equally well of it, that is, who have deserved equally well absolutely. This is the highest abstract standard of social and distributive justice; towards which all institutions, and the efforts of all virtuous citizens, should be made in the utmost degree to converge[8].

At the end of the nineteenth century, when the term "social justice" came to prominence, it was first used as an appeal to the ruling classes to attend to the needs of the new masses of uprooted peasants who had become urban workers. Theorizing about social justice became a major concern in the early years of the twentieth century, and the first book actually called Social Justice was published in New York in 1900[9]. Its author was Westel Willoughby, a professor of political science at John Hopkins University who was influenced by the late idealist philosophy of the school of T.H. Green. Willoughby brings by observing that in an era of popular sovereignty we cannot avoid subjecting our existing social and economic institutions to critical appraisal, and, in particular, asking whether they treat individuals justly. The quest for social justice is a natural consequence of the spread of enlightenment: "the peoples of all civilized countries are subjecting social and economic conditions to the same tests of reasonableness and justice as those by which they have questioned in the past the rightfulness of political institutions"[10].

In the writings of most contemporary political philosophers, social justice is regarded as an aspect of distributive justice and indeed the two concepts are often used interchangeably[11]. Social justice rightly understood is a specific habit of justice that is "social" in two senses. First, the skills it requires are those of inspiring, working with, and organizing others to accomplish together a work of justice[12]. These are the elementary skills of civil society, through which free citizens exercise self-government by doing for themselves (that is, without turning to government) what needs to be done.

The second characteristic of "social justice rightly understood" is that it aims at the good of the society, not at the good of one agent only[13]. Citizens may join together to start a school or build a bridge. One significant characteristic of this definition of the virtue of social justice is that it is ideologically neutral. It is as open to people on the left as on the right or in the centre. Its field of activity may be literary, scientific, religious, political, economic, cultural, athletic, and so on, across the whole spectrum of human social activities.

This conception of "social justice" rules out any use of the term that does not attach to the habits (that is, virtues) of individuals. According to this conceptualization, social justice is a virtue and an attribute of individuals. And if Tocqueville is right that "the principle of association is the first law of democracy", then social justice is the "first virtue of democracy", for it is the habit of putting the principle of association into daily practice.

Functionally, "justice" is a set of universal principles which guide people in judging what is right and what is wrong, no matter what culture and society they live in. Justice is one of the four "cardinal virtues" of classical moral philosophy, along with courage, temperance (self-control) and prudence (efficiency). (Faith, hope and charity are considered to be the three "religious" virtues.) Virtues or "good habits" help individuals to develop fully their human potentials, thus enabling them to serve their own self-interests as well as work in harmony with others for their common good.

The ultimate purpose of all the virtues is to elevate the dignity and sovereignty of the human person. The highest aim of justice is to elevate each person. The roots of social justice lie in the thought process of Enlightenment. The development of a scientific and rational viewpoint led to corresponding changes in the social thought process which, in turn, initiated radical changes in the political and social structures of Europe, especially during the Renaissance[14]. The underlying thesis of the thinking process of the Renaissance was that man was born free with equal rights and dignity. Hence, all sorts of bondages imposed on him by society on the basis of birth, colour, creed or sex must not exist.

The basic premise of social justice is the emancipation of the underprivileged, exploited, and oppressed sections of society. Its main aim is to liberate mankind from traditional bondages of social and economic exploitation and discrimination. It postulates a social order which can guarantee freedom and equal rights to all sections of society[15]. The concept of social justice is closely linked with human rights as envisaged by the United Nations in its 1948 declaration and fundamental rights as provided in the Constitution of India but they are not synonymous. Fundamental rights, i.e. the right to freedom and equality, the right against exploitation, and right to constitutional remedies, etc. are essential for the free and natural development of the human personality and hence are the backbone of a just social order but they are subject to control or limits if they adversely affect the pattern of social justice in society.[16]

Social Justice encompasses economic justice. It is the virtue which guides us in creating those organized human interactions which we call institutions. Social justice is also equated with equality, liberty and dignity; which mean that all three are essential for social justice and that denial of anyone of them is a denial of justice[17]. Dignity is generally coterminous with freedom and equality. An illiterate, poor and ill fed person is hardly said to have any dignity.

Ambedkar cited that untouchability was unique in Indian society. Even the British Government had not done any good for improving the plight of untouchables. They had also denied them the political rights. He said that untouchables were:

1. Socialized in such a way as to never to complain of their low status.
2. Never allowed to dream of improving their lot by forcing the other castes to treat them with common respect.
3. Made to think that they had been born so low that their fate was anything but irrevocable.
4. Given to believe that nothing could ever persuade them that they have the right to insist on better treatment than that meted out to them.

Ambedkar had taken a vow to expose and finally, do away with the abominable conditions and inhuman injustice under which the class, into which, he was born had been groaning. He never failed in highlighting that the untouchable was prohibited from using the public road. If some high caste man happened to cross him, he had to be out of the way and stand at such a distance that his shadow will not fall on the high caste man. Helplessness made the untouchables live like slaves in Hindu society. The charter of fundamental rights and the Directive Principles of State Policy sought to incorporate the ideas of Human Rights in the Constitution of India.

Ambedkar believed in the maxim, "Tell the slave that he is a slave and he will revolt against his slavery" and often quoted this to arouse the consciousness amongst the untouchables for securing human rights. He established the ***Bahishkrit Hitakarini Sabha*** to promote the spread of education among the depressed classes by opening hostels; and by opening social centres, study circles and libraries. The Sabha also sought to improve economic conditions of the depressed classes by opening agriculture and industrial schools; as well as to provide a platform represent their grievances.

Ambedkar told his fellow untouchables in no unclear terms—Whoever has knowledge, wisdom and strength is capable of tyrannizing those who do not have either of them. Therefore, the particular code of conduct was assigned to us by those who had knowledge, wisdom and strength. He always felt bad about the fact that because of the ignorance, gullibility and utter submissiveness, the untouchables were suffering the injustices. As they were not conscious of the heritage acquired by the humanity they made their position deplorable, helpless, and therefore, they kept facing the difficulties of food, cloth and shelter even though India remained a country, which was called a golden sparrow. In the midst of plenty, the untouchables remained poverty-stricken.

In the Indian context, justice as seen was an important social value in terms of the strict observance of *dharma* or the enforcement of a social order based on the *varna-ashram vyavastha* reflected in an elaborate caste system. This established order, according to Ambedkar, was based on graded inequality and was legitimized by Hindu Law, which completely neglected equality, fraternity, liberty, democracy and human rights. He was also of the view that the system of graded inequality was not notional but legal and penal as it entailed strict enforcement of Hindu Law which meant different things to different castes and people and contained no notion of equal treatment to all. This fact has been highlighted by Ambedkar thus: "Hindu Law is the Law of the established order and was made by the touchable. The Untouchables had nothing to do except to obey it and respect it. The untouchables have no right against the Touchables. For them there is no equal right, no justice, which is due to them, and nothing is allowed to them. Nothing is due to them except what the touchables are prepared to grant. The Untouchables must not insist on rights.

They should pray for mercy and favour and rest content with what is offered".[18]

Obviously, such conceptualization of justice was characterized by a pattern, which gave preference to hierarchy, rather than equality, which underlined the importance of respecting traditional rights and performing traditional duties and did not contain any notion of equal treatment to all men. It was almost like what Anatole France had warned: "Justice is the means by which established injustices are sanctioned".[19]

Such kind of injustice prevailed in India for centuries because according to Ambedkar the untouchables lacked social conscience and it was futile to expect any compassion from them who were pledged to Brahmanism and their sense of obligation was restricted to a limited class of people, mainly the members of their caste. Consequently, their conduct, also is marked by a moralistic unconcernedness which makes them oblivious of the inequalities and injustices from which the Untouchables have been suffering. They also fail to see anything wrong in these inequities and injustice. Rather, Ambedkar felt that Brahminical values were used by upper castes to deny untouchables the social justice. It is this caste consciousness among Touchables that made Ambedkar suspicious about the validity of the legal concept of justice which involves punishment of wrong doing and the compensation of injury through the creation and enforcement of a set of rules.

However, Ambedkar maintained the view that legal justice at the formal or at theoretical level would be ineffective at the practical level. He observed:

> "It might have been thought that this principle of equal justice would strike a death blow to the established order. As a matter of fact, far from suffering any damage, the established order has continued to operate. It might be asked why the principle of equal justice has failed to have its effect. The answer to this is simple. To enunciate the principle of justice is one thing. To make it effective is another thing. Whether the principle of equal justice is effective or not must necessarily

depend on the nature and character of the civil services who administer the principle. If the civil services are by reason of class bias the friend of the established order and the enemy of the new order, the new order can never come into being. That a civil service in tune with the new order was essential for the success of the new order was recognized by Karl Marx in 1871 in the formation of the Paris Commune and was adopted by Lenin in the constitution of Soviet Communism. Unfortunately, the British government never cared about the personnel in the civil service. Indeed, it opened the gates of the administration to those classes who believed in the old established order of the Hindus in which the principles of equality had no place. As a result of this fact, India has been ruled by the Britishers but administered by the Hindus."[20]

Illustrating his point a little further, Ambedkar expressed with anguish:

"From the capital of India down to the village the whole administration is rigged by the Hindus. The Hindus are the omnipotent almighty pervading all over the administration in all its branches having its authority in all its nooks and corners. There is no loophole for anyone opposed to the old order to escape. If the established order has continued to exist, it is because of the unfailing support it received from the Hindu officials of the state. The Hindu officials are not merely administrators administering the affairs on the merit, they are administrators with an eye to their affairs on the merit, they are administrators with an eye to their parties. Their principle is not equal justice to all. Their motto is justice consistent with established order. This is inevitable. For they carry over into administration, the attitude towards different classes in society under the established order. This is well illustrated by the attitude of the state officials towards the untouchables in the field of administration. As every untouchable

> will be able to testify, if an untouchable goes to a police officer with complaint against the caste Hindu, instead of receiving any protection he will receive plenty of abuses. Either he will be driven away without his complaint being recorded or if it is recorded it would be recorded quite falsely to provide a way of escape to the Touchable aggressors. If he prosecutes his offenders before a Magistrate the fate of his proceeding could be foretold. The Untouchables will never be able to get Hindus as witness because of the conspiracy of the villagers not to support the case of the Untouchables however just it may be. If he brings witness from the Untouchables, the Magistrate will not accept their testimony because he can easily say that they are interested and not independent witness, or, if they are independent witness the Magistrate has an easy way of acquitting the accused by simply saying that the Untouchable's complaint did not strike him as a truthful witness. He can do this fearlessly knowing fully that the higher tribunal will not reverse his findings because of the well established rule which says that an appellate court should not disturb the findings of the trial Magistrate based on the testimony of witness whose demeanour he had no opportunity to observe."[21]

Thus, according to Ambedkar upper-caste administrators have a Hindu bias and an antipathy towards untouchables, which results in the denial of protection and justice to the latter. Ambedkar also made several attempts to gain religious and social rights for the untouchables, by using the Gandhian technique of *satyagraha*; drinking water from a public tank in Mahad (1927), temple entry to the Parvati temple at Poona (1929), and then the Kala Ram temple at Nasik (1930-35).[22] The failure of these movements demonstrated, according to Ambedkar, that the untouchables were not really a part of Hindu society and would never be accepted as equals by Hindus within that framework. It was quite obvious that this low threshold concept of a legal conception of equality does not allow for a corresponding conception of political citizenship. Thus, from a position of questioning the brahmanical social order, Ambedkar moved towards its rejection: raising the issue of conversion by the untouchables in 1935. At the Yeola Conference in the Nasik District of Maharashtra held on October 13, 1935, Ambedkar declared that he would not die a Hindu[23].

But there was another reason. The second occasion was the Round Table Conference held in 1930 in London, where Ambedkar confronted Gandhi and Congress on the issue of the political rights of depressed classes[24].

Earlier, in the 'Evidence before the Southborough Committee on Franchise' (1919), Ambedkar (invited as a delegate of the depressed classes) had argued eloquently for uniform franchise, for securing access for the depressed classes to the public sphere—to public wells, roads, schools, temples, and cremation grounds—and for special provisions for their adequate representation of their interests and opinions[25].

The road to social justice in the opinion of Ambedkar was to be led by education. He firmly believed in the efficacy of education as a panacea for the social evils and injustice because the problem of social injustice in India is not only economic but also cultural[26]. Here, it is not enough to house the untouchables/deprived sections of society, feed them and then leave them to serve the higher classes as was the ancient ideal of this country. It was even more necessary to remove from their minds/psyche that feeling of inferiority which has shunted their growth and made them slaves of others and to create in them a consciousness of significance of life for themselves and for their country of which they have been cruelly robbed by the Indian social order. Ambedkar was convinced that nothing could achieve this better than the spread of higher education and the fact remains as true in present times as it was when Ambedkar wrote.

Social justice—a categorical imperative for establishing social harmony can be achieved only by a general development and empowerment of the masses of the underprivileged and deprived sections of our society, the poorest of the poors as they are. For this, jobs and education are extremely important as Ambedkar emphasized. But, for Justice Krishna Iyer, equality and homogeneity—the two pillars of social justice would remain a far cry if the landless *dalit* is not given land, the penniless Pariah is not given opportunity to start small scale factories, the bonded woman is not liberated from servitude so as to enable her to pursue a vocation and the *dalit* youths, often illiterate and disorganized and drawn into delinquent and destitute situations, are given effective opportunities to enter the professional echelons and public services in large numbers[27].

Regarding Indian society, Ambedkar felt that, if the lower strata of the Indian society which is interested in blowing up the caste system is educated, the caste system will be blown up. Giving education to those who want to blow up caste system will improve prospect of Democracy in India and put Democracy in safer hands. To him, "it is very important to educate the poor masses and develop in them a genuine sense of political consciousness and constitutional temper. Their education means the maintenance of democracy and political order in peace and justice". He thought so highly of education that in his tri-worded slogan—Educate, organize, and agitate, he gave top priority to it[28].

Ambedkar fought against caste and injustice. He struggled hard to create human rights. He wanted to vitalize the conscience of the people and to mobilize the masses in India, for equal human rights. His ultimate aim of life was to establish a real social democracy. To him, "A Democratic form of Government presupposes a Democratic form of Society. The formal framework of Democracy is of no value and would indeed be a misfit if there was no social democracy". The political leaders never realized that Democracy was not only a form of government; it was essentially a form of Society.

To Ambedkar, the aim of democracy is essentially the practical interests of society as a whole, and not of any class group or community. He regards democracy as the social organization of the people in the sense that the people include all members of society. To him, real democracy is opposed to the suppression of minorities[29].

Democracy was an essential ingredient of Ambedkar's vision of Social Justice. For this, there is no denying that self-government must be good government, otherwise it is not worth having. The primary concern of his life had always been to study and understand the nature of good government. He stood for a self-government which should be both efficient and good government. To him, the ability and efficiency of the governing class are not enough for good government. "What is necessary is to have in the governing class the will to do good or, to use Dicey's language, freedom from internal limitations arising out of selfish class interests. Efficiency combined with selfish class interests instead of producing good government is far more likely to become a mere engine of suppression of the service classes."[30] He argued, therefore, not only for self-government but also for a good government. He had a deep faith in self-government and good government, which, in his view, could go a long way in ensuring social justice.

Ambedkar's vision of social justice also includes a strong faith in the separation of the government's power and of the allocation of functions to various departments. He regards rights as natural and inherent in the individual. He builds his theory of Social and Political Organization around his central concept of the individual and his rights. To him, the State exists only to prevent injustice, tyranny and oppression. He wants that no state should violate the fundamental rights of man. He is opposed to all kinds of discrimination in administration. He holds that society can do nothing without some organized power. He stresses the need of constitutional morality and some conventions for the practical success of a constitution. He wishes a good, moral government, to protect the rights of the people in all their legitimate functions. He fought for these rights in his life[31].

According to Ambedkar, law is an important factor in maintaining social peace and justice among different groups of people. It is a guardian of equality and liberty. For him, law was not only a legal function. It also regulated the life of the whole society and nation as well. He categorically declared,

"All citizens are equal before the law and possess equal civic rights. Any existing enactment, regulation, order, custom or interpretation of law by which any penalty, disadvantage or disability is imposed upon or any discrimination is made against any citizen shall ... cease to have any effect."[32] His faith in individual liberty and dignity leads him to the rule of law.

Ambedkar had to fight against tyranny, injustice and false traditions in order to release the suffering people from bondage. Poverty was the greatest enemy of his political ideals. He vigorously struggled against injustice, social slavery, inequality and poverty and for their removal from among the down-trodden. He represents a combination of both love and hate—love for knowledge and hate for ignorance and poverty. He condemns everything that extols poverty. His idea of socialism is also an attack on poverty[33]. He does not agree with those men who develop a sort of stoic endurance and resignation towards poverty.

Ambedkar stood against all kinds of social discrimination. He advocated an urgent need of bringing about equality of opportunity to the needy and the weak. He condemned discrimination against citizens by government officers or by private employers in factories and commercial concerns on the ground of race, creed and social status. To him, any kind of discrimination is a menace to social progress. He also revolted against the social boycott. Social discrimination and social boycott are the enemies of his concept of socialism, because his socialism lays a stress on the need of equal behaviour and individual liberty and respect[34]. To him, a true socialist would not tolerate ill-treatment and oppression, because these are opposed to socialism. He also believed that the present social order is not suited to create a socialist spirit among the people.

It is significant to note that Ambedkar's Vision of Social Justice encompasses Nationalism as well. Ambedkar says, "Nationalism is a fact which can neither be eluded nor denied. Whether one calls it an irrational instinct or positive hallucination, the fact remains that it is a potent force which has a dynamic power to disrupt empires."[35] Whether nationalism is the cause or the threat to nationalism is the cause, is a difference of emphasis only. He regards nationalism as a real force in human life. The starting point of his nationalism was startling, which was entirely misunderstood and was looked upon as anti-national, although his attitude was always purely national.

His attitude towards social justice was humanistic as well as nationalistic. His approach was twofold. He wanted not only freedom from foreign domination, but also internal freedom for the people to whom it was denied. He says, "We must have a Government in which men in power knowing where obedience will end and resistance will begin, will not be afraid to amend the social and economic code of life which the dictates of justice and expediency so urgently call for. This role the British Government will never be able to play. It is only a Government which is of the people, for the people and by the people that will make this possible."[36]

During the British period Ambedkar was undoubtedly the most articulate spokesman of the exploited and downtrodden in Indian society, particularly of the Depressed Classes. He held pragmatic and uncompromising views on the amelioration of the sufferings of these classes and the role of the government in this regard. He came out vociferously and eloquently in support of adequate representation and constitutional safeguards for the Depressed Classes in his innumerable statements, representations and evidences.

For instance, on May 29, 1928, he submitted a statement before the Indian Statutory Commission (Popularly known as Simon Commission) on its arrival in India. Ambedkar demanded protection through adequate representation to the Depressed Classes in his "Statement Concerning the Safeguards for the protection of their interests in the Bombay Presidency, and the changes in the composition of and the guarantees from the Bombay Legislative Council necessary to ensure the same under Provincial Autonomy".[37] He was in favour of taking into consideration population and social status to indicate the quantum of representation. Moreover, it was the responsibility of the government to ensure the spread of education, to make no discrimination in recruitment and to provide for adequate safeguards.

The essence of his demands for constitutional rights and social justice for the untouchables during British rule may be stated as follows: "All educational facilities should be provided to the Depressed Classes; Depressed Classes should be given representation in state and central legislative councils on the basis of their population, needs and importance; Jobs in the state and central government services should be reserved; Depressed Classes should be given representation in all democratic bodies of the country; Provision of separate electorate should be made for the Depressed Classes; Separate settlements should be established for the Depressed Classes."[38]

Ambedkar envisioned that democratic society of India would flourish only when the untouchables would enjoy basic human rights. It was an irony that in Hindu society untouchables not treated as citizens and were denied social rights. The Hindu society insisted on segregation of the quarters of untouchables. The Hindus did not live in the quarters of the untouchables and did not allow the untouchables to live inside Hindu quarters. This was a fundamental feature of untouchability as practiced by Hindus. It is not a case of social separation, mere stoppage of intercourse for a temporary period. It was a case of territorial segregation as well. Every Hindu village had a *ghetto.* The Hindu lived in the village and the untouchables in the *ghetto*[39].

Ambedkar resorted to the theory of basic human needs according to which the basic human needs of the *dalits* were not only material (wealth, property occupational mobility) but also non-material. He also eloquently pleaded the case of necessary priority of community claims over individual rights on the grounds that these departures from formal equality could be justified on the basis of the following principles:

The anti-discriminatory view: The anti-discriminatory principle's main purpose is to prevent private practices and legal procedures from stigmatizing the individuals involved. This was viewed as necessary given that structural forms of oppression against the *dalits* were well entrenched. To remedy this social malaise Ambedkar raises the possibilities for political participation of *dalits* through reservations. It was his view that a legislature "mainly composed of high caste men, will not pass a law removing untouchability, sanctioning inter-caste marriages, removing the ban of the use of public streets, public temples, public schools..."[40]

The reparation ideal: The other objective was related to the historic injustice suffered by the *dalits*. This theme was proposed to offset the systematic and cumulative deprivations suffered by lower castes in the past. Ambedkar argues that some oppressive cultural practices and social institutions result in injustice and accumulated disabilities for untouchables.[41]

His vision of social justice also included redistribution of surplus and waste land to untouchables' schools and colleges to provide education to untouchables and formation of the Republican Party of India. As an Elephant is easily recognized, he chose Elephant as his party symbol and also because the Elephant is taken to be a symbol of wisdom, strength and courage.

The social and constitutional vision of Ambedkar, the greatest well-wisher of the socially backward and the exploited, offered them, not the way of despair and dejection, but of the wonderful opportunity to assert themselves in the national affairs. The deprived people had to practice it, not in any fear, but in all happiness of spirit and courage. By practicing the democratic ideals, the depressed classes shall lose nothing except the stigma of caste and untouchability. They must go forward firm in their faith, steadfast in their purpose; however, they have to be cautious of the reactions and dangers from the orthodox sections of our society. What kind of society they shall be making, whether they will shape the future in the way they have adopted, is, and ought to be, the task and determination of all those who stand for progressive change and revolutionary transformation. In other words, Ambedkar wanted the people of depressed classes to be vanguard of revolution—social, economic, political and religious in modern India.

The central theme of Ambedkar's social and legal vision is the empirical man and the establishment of right relations between man and man in this life. From the relations based on justice, liberty, equality and fraternity, would emerge a democratic and humanistic society of moral understanding and mutual respect. Ambedkar was fully convinced that the education is one of the best resources to connect the destitute with the main stream of national development. Hence he laid utmost stress on the expansion and promotion of education. The introduction of free and compulsory system of primary education in the Constitution of India is the happy result of this objective.

He thought that Hindu society should be reorganized on the basis of two cardinal principles of equality and castelessness. He demanded that the prevailing system of priesthood and *purohitism* should be democratized so that everyone may enjoy the freedom in the choice of his profession according to his liking. He was convinced that this process would not only do away with the evils of casteism, untouchability and discrimination between the high and the low but also foster the feelings of unity and equality in society.

It becomes very clear that Ambedkar was not just a critic or an intellectual having some new ideas, but he also at the same time had concrete suggestions for the implementation of the same. For example, in his analysis of the existing social order based on the caste, he was very clear what evils it carried, he was also very clear, about 'justice' as the basis of his envisioned society. *Varna* system was the basis of the existing Indian social order and it was this system, which was responsible for all the evils of the existing order. Because of this analysis, he talked about the annihilation of caste. But he was also very clear that it "is not possible to break caste without annihilating the religious notions on what it, the caste system, is founded".

Ambedkar pleaded for constitutional safeguards to scheduled castes and scheduled tribes not as altruistic concessions or humanitarian doles. He wanted historical oppression and miseries caused to the depressed classes to be corrected through the reservation policy and its application. He wanted the scheduled castes and scheduled tribes to lift themselves with their bootstrap and stand up to the competition of the world at large. That is why he accepted the stipulation of 10 years time for the minorities to cope up. He believed that it is wrong for the majority to deny the existence of minorities and it is équally wrong for the minorities to perpetuate themselves. The movement the majority loses the habit of discriminating the minority; the minorities will have no ground to exist. It is obvious from this that Ambedkar did not want the minorities nor the scheduled castes and scheduled tribes to develop a "permanent interest" in the "backwardness".

Thus, Ambedkar's conception of political power was aimed at securing social justice for the deprived on more equitable and honourable terms. But for him, political justice was not enough for the welfare and well-being of the Untouchables. He considered socio-economic justice as the precondition for redeeming political justice. Moreover, his vision of social justice involves a normative element also inasmuch as it aims at the desirability of goodness in social life, dignity of the individual, equal rights of man and woman, promotion of social progress and better standards of life with peace and security in all spheres of human life.

NOTES

1. See for a comprehensive analysis, G.S. Ghurye, *Caste and Class in India*, Bombay, Popular Book Depot, 1957; Ghanshyam Shah, (Ed.) *Caste and Democratic Politics in India*, New Delhi, Orient Longman, 2002; B. Nicholas Dirks, *Castes of Mind: Colonialism and the Making of Modern India*, New Delhi, Orient Longman, 2003 and Rosa M. Perez, *Kings and Untouchables: A Study of the Caste System in Western India*, New Delhi, Chronicle Books, 2004.
2. See, B.R. Ambedkar, *Who Were the Sudras? How They Came to be the Fourth Varna in the Indo-Aryan Society*? Bombay: Thacker & Co., 1946; and B.R. Ambedkar, *The Untouchables—Who Are They and Why They Become Untouchables*? New Delhi: Amrit Book Co., 1949.
3. Bansanta Kumar Mallick, "Ambedkar and his Movement for Social Equality", *Mainstream*, Vol. 29, No. 25, April 1991, p. 4. Also see, Alva, Joachim, *Man and Superman of Hindustan*, Thacker & Co. Ltd., 1943, Keer, Dhananjay, *Dr. Ambedkar: Life and Mission*, Bombay Popular Parkashan, 1971 and Rao D. Venkateswara, *Dr. B.R.*

Ambedkar: Champion of Human Right in India, New Delhi, Manak Publications, 2006.

4. See for details, James Massey, *Dr. B.R. Ambedkar: A Study in Just Society*, New Delhi, Manohar Publications, 2003 and P.V. Rathnam, *Socio-Political Philosophy of Dr. B.R. Ambedkar*, Hyderabad, Ambedkar-Lohia Socialist Centre, 2003.
5. Ambedkar, Dr. B.R., Castes in India: Their Mechanism. Genesis and Development, (A paper read before the Anthropology Seminar of Dr. A.A. Goldenweizer at the Columbia University, U.S.A. on 9 May 1916) *Indian Antiquary*, May 1917, Vol.XLI, Quoted in *Dr. Babasaheb Ambedkar: Writings and Speeches.* (WS) Vol.-I, Education Department, Government of Maharashtra, Bombay, 1979, and B.R. Ambedkar, *Annihilation of Caste: With a Reply to Mahatma Gandhi*, Address before the Annual Conference of Jat-Pat-Todak Mandal, Lahore, 1935.
6. Novak, Michael, "Defining Social Justice," *First Things*, 108. December 2000, p. 11.
7. See, for example, J.S. Mill, Utilitarianism, chap.5 in J.S. Mill, *Utilitarianism; On Liberty; Representative Government*, ed. H.B. Acton, London: Dent, 1972; L. Stephen, "Social Equality", in *Social Rights and Duties*, Vol. 1, London: Swan Sonnenschein, 1896; and H. Sidgwick, *Principles of Political Economy*, London: Macmillan, 1883, book 3, chapters, 6-7.
8. J.S. Mill, *Utilitarianism*, Chapter 5.
9. W.W. Willoughby, *Social Justice*, New York: Macmillan, 1900. Other American texts from this period include T. N. Carver, *Essays in Social Justice*, Cambridge, Mass.: Harvard University Press, 1915; and J.A. Ryan, *Distributive Justice*, New York: Macmillan, 1916.
10. Willoughby, *Social Justice*, p. 7.
11. See, for instance, J. Rawls, *A Theory of Justice*, Cambridge, Mass: Harvard University Press, 1971, in which he talks indiscriminately about justice, distributive justice and social justice.
12. Michael Novak, *op. cit.*, p. 11.
13. *Ibid.*, p. 12.
14. See, for instance, J.Y. Calvez and J. Perrin, *The Church and Social Justice*, London: Burns and Oates, 1961, Chap. 6; and L.W. Shields, *The History and Meaning of the Term Social Justice*, Ph.D. Diss., University of Nottre Dame, Indiana, 1941, Chap. 3.
15. See for details, Miller David, *Principles of Social Justice*, Cambridge, Harvard University Press, 1999, pp.1-20.
16. Chandy, K.T., "Social Justice and Requirements for Development", *Legal News and Views*, No. 6123, 1992, pp. 42-44.
17. Rajasekhriah, A.M., *B.R. Ambedkar: The Quest for Social Justice*, New Delhi, Uppal, 1989.
18. *WS*, *op. cit.*, Vol. 5. p. 99.

19. Quoted by Justice Iyer, V.R. Krishna, *Ambedkar Centenary: Social Justice and Undone Vast*, Delhi BRPC, 1991, p. 28.
20. *WS*, *op. cit.*, Vol.5, p.252.
21. Quoted by Khairmode, G. B. in *Bhimraro Ramji Ambedkar* (Marathi), Pune: Sugawa Publications, 1989, Vol. 4, p. 265.
22. See for details, Rao, D. Venkateshwara, *op. cit.*, pp 27-40.
23. *The Times of India*, 14.10.1935.
24. *Proceedings of the Round Table Conference*, Second Session, Government of India, Central Publication Branch, Calcutta, 1931, and also see, Ambedkar: *What The Congress and Gandhi have Done to the Untouchables*, Bombay, Thacker & Co., 1965.
25. *Report of the Franchise Committee, (1918-1919)*, (Chairman: Lord South Borough), Government of India, Central Publication Branch, Calcutta.
26. Dr. Ambedkar On Bombay University Amendment Bill: II, published in *WS*, Vol.2, Education Department, Government of Maharashtra, 1982.
27. Justice V.R. Krishna Iyer, *Ambedkar Centenary: Social Justice and the Undone Vast*, Delhi, BRPC, 1991, p.76.
28. *Dalit Education*, Dr. Babsaheb Ambedkar Research and Document Centre, Samata Prakashan, Nagpur, 1994, pp.118-122.
29. See for details, *States and Minorities*, Bombay, Thacker & Co., 1947.
30. B.R. Ambedkar, *What Congress and Gandhi Have Done to the Untouchables*, Bombay, Thacker & Co., 1945, p. 240.
31. See, D.R. Jatava, *The Political Philosophy of Ambedkar*, Agra, Phoenix Publishing Agency, 1965; Rathnam, P.V., *op. cit.*, pp. 101-156; and Rao, D. Venkateswara, *op. cit.*, pp. 120-160.
32. See for instance, Constituent Assembly of India, *Draft Constitution of India*, Government of India, New Delhi, 1948, pp.4-9.
33. See P.V. Rathnam, *op. cit.*, pp.201-217. For a contemporary analysis, also see, Anand Kumar, *Political Sociology of Poverty in India: between Politics of Poverty and Poverty of Politics*, New Delhi, IIPA, 2004.
34. Dr. B.R. Ambedkar, *States and Minorities*, *op. cit.*, pp. 408-412.
35. Dr. B.R. Ambedkar, (*WS*), Vol. 2, *op. cit.*, pp. 257-258.
36. Das Bhagwan, *Thus Spoke Ambedkar*, Speeches, Vol. 1, 1963, p. 8.
37. See *Dr. B.R. Ambedkar with Simon Commission* and 'Evidence before the Indian Statutory Commission on 23rd October, 1928' in *WS*, Vol. 2, 1982; and Jeanette Robbin, *Dr. Ambedkar and His Movement*, Hyderabad, Dr. Ambedkar Publication Society, 1964, p. 131.
38. See, B.R. Ambedkar, *WS*, Vol. 1, pp. 252-253.
39. Ambedkar, 'Untouchables of the Children of India's *Ghetto*', in *WS*, Vol. 5, 1989, pp. 108-09.
40. Ambedkar, 'Evidence before the Southborough Committee', in *WS*, Vol. 1 (1979), p. 264.

41. See Ambedkar, 'Who were the Shudras? How They Came to be the Fourth Varna in the Indo-Aryan Society', *WS*, Vol. 7, (B:ED, 1990). For a critical examination of these themes in the Indian context see also Marc Galanter, 'The Compensatory Discrimination Theme in the Indian Commitment to Human Rights' in U. Baxi (ed), *The Right to be Human* (New Delhi:Lancer International, 1987), pp. 77-94.

10

Dr. Ambedkar on Annihilation of Caste

ASHOK KUMAR SINGH

"The outcaste is a by-product of the caste system. There will be outcaste as long as there are castes. Nothing can help emancipate the outcaste except the destruction of the caste system. Nothing can help to save Hindus and ensure their survival in the coming struggle except the purging of the Hindu faith of this odious and vicious dogma", so wrote Dr. Ambedkar in a letter dated February 7, 1933 to Gandhijee.[1]

Gandhijee asked Ambedkar for a message for the first issue of his journal: *Harijan*. It is an eternal message to every Indian who has common sense and conscience of his or her own, from one of the greatest social reformers of the country. It was for the emancipation of the outcaste from the social tyranny, that Dr. Ambedkar devoted his whole life. He personally experienced the indignity and humiliation of having been born among one of the lowest castes in the graded society. It was this single most ugly feature of Hindu social order that urged him to embark upon scathing indictments in his writings and speeches. Dr. Ambedkar never compromised either with Hindu social order or with the Hindu philosophers and social reformers who attempted to seek reasons and justifications for the iniquitous and inhuman social order: *Varnashrama*.[2] As he said it: "To me the *Chaturvarna* with its old lebels is utterly repellent and my whole being rebels against it".[3] It is this revulsion against the unjust system that placed him as the foremost among the pioneers and social reformers in India. No author, scholar or reformer has written so many volumes on the subject of caste and untouchability as did Ambedkar.[4]

The existence of the caste in Indian society is actually a very perplexing problem. However, on the question as to why caste persists in our society, there have been many attempts to find out the true reason. Some have tried to perpetuate caste system for obvious ulterior motives while others have tried to do away with it. But the reality is that the caste system exists and persists even today. The problem has more compounded than before and the nature of caste and its role have changed with the change of time. In order to see the different political and social ramifications that caste has for our country, this chapter is an attempt to look at the structure of caste system. The problem is of course not so simple. However, we are certainly not grappling with the caste problem in a very complete and uncontoured sense. Our interest in looking at caste is to see if Dr. Ambedkar's analysis of caste is adequate and his programme for its annihilation plausible. It is over five decades since India became independent and the original version of Dr. Ambedkar's casteless society in India remains very distant, perhaps farther than what it was at the time when India became independent. The nature and course of Indian history has made the understanding of caste even more difficult.

Castes obviously had their birth in ancient India. But one does not know the exact rationale behind the creation of the caste system. It is more often than not assumed that castes were deliberately created. There is one school of thought who subscribes the view that this system was created to establish patterns of domination. Another school of thought felt that originally the caste system was created as a division of labour and whatever perversities we find today crept into it much later. Yet another view is that the caste system is not something 'created' but is something which 'happened' as a result of the ancient Indian civilization. However, the entire discussion do not take one to the final solution. Causes or origin need not always be the cause of persistence as well. In the cast of caste system our perception is that the causes of persistence are not coterminus with the cause of origin. Our attempt is to establish this point in the course of future discussion.

This brings us now back to the question of Indian history. We refer to history and the twists and turns that it provides to Indian caste system for two reasons. The first is that history has shaped caste system in the form that it is today. The second is that Dr. Ambedkar himself is the product of this history and his own ideals and convictions were as much a result of his position in history as much as his own personality and intelligence. Due to the number of invasions that India suffered and also due to the incorporation of the invaders' culture into that of the indigenous Indian society did become very complicated. British colonialism and Western education gave Indian society a very peculiar twist. They gave some new ideas to the people of India and personally think that Ambedkar himself was a product of this age. There are many freedom fighters who wanted the establishment of an independent India but Ambedkar was slightly different from the rest. His task of emancipation of the Indian people did not end with the liberation from British colonialism but went to the extent of seeking to obliterate the structures of oppression within the Indian social system. This is where the notion of Ambedkar being a product of his time becomes pertinent. Western education, though incorporated in India to serve the administrative machinery set up by the British, also served the cause of enlightenment and unintended consequence (this is now a very familiar argument). The freedom movement actually threw up the French revolution ideals of Liberty, Equality and Fraternity in India. As already stated Ambedkar took this beyond the British-Indian relationship into the caste system and the relations that it posited in the Hindu society. In his reply to Mahatma Gandhi, Ambedkar stated that "the Hindu society must be reorganised on a religious basis, which would recognize the principles of Liberty, Equality and Fraternity."[5] For Ambedkar caste is the real reason why there is no equality in the Hindu society. Once again in his reply to Mahatma Gandhi he says "Caste has ruined the Hindus... the reorganization of the Hindu society on the basis of *Chaturvarna* is impossible because the *Varna Vyavastha* is like a leaky pot or like a man running with a nose. It is incapable of sustaining itself by its own virtue and has an inherent tendency to degenerate into a caste system unless there is a legal sanction behind it which can be enforced against everyone trespassing his *Varna*".[6]

According to Ambedkar, destruction of the caste system is the only solution of the problem. "In order to achieve this object (of Liberty, Equality and Fraternity) the sense of religious sanctity behind caste and *varna* must be destroyed."[7] Ambedkar suggests that unless there is destruction of scriptures, the destruction of caste and *varna* is not so simple. "The sanctity of caste and *varna* cannot be destroyed only by disregarding the divine authority of the *Shastras*". We cannot interpret this as anger of a man motivated by his own position in society. Ambedkar's assessment is not just passionate but quite logical too. He was trying to understand the true meaning of independence and freedom. In the annihilation of caste, he says, "Yours is more difficult than the other national cause, namely *Swaraj*. In the fight for *Swaraj* you fight with the whole nation on your side. In this, you have to fight against the whole nation and that too, your own. But it is more important than *Swaraj*. There is no use of having *Swaraj*, if you cannot defend it. More important than the question of defending the Swaraj is the question defending the Hindus under the *Swaraj*. In my opinion only when the Hindu society becomes a casteless society then it can hope to have strength enough to defend itself. Without such internal strength, Swaraj for Hindus may turn out to be only a step towards slavery."[8]

This view of Ambedkar is very important for those who try to understand Indian caste system. He is at his cogent best in his arguments against Gandhi's upholding of the caste system in its 'pristine form'.[9] Ambedkar did not see anything pristine in caste. We would think it significant to look at the rebuttals that Ambedkar provided to Gandhi's contentions. This would lead us to a better understanding of Ambedkar's analysis and mission.

Gandhi's rejoinder to Ambedkar on this issue is hardly convincing. "*Varna* and *ashrama* are institutions which have nothing to do with castes. The law of *varna* teaches us that we, each one of us, have to earn our bread by following the ancestral calling. It defines not our rights but our duties. It necessarily has reference to calling that are conducive to the welfare of humanity and to no other. It also follows that there is none called too low and none too high. All are good, lawful and absolutely equal in status. The calling of a Brahmin—spiritual teacher and "scavenger is equal and their livelihood and no more. Indeed one traces even now in the villages the faint times of this healthy operation of the law".[10] Let us spell out our reasons clearly for characterising this rejoinder as hardly convincing. By reading Gandhi one gets the impression that he had not fully grasped the crux of Ambedkar's reference to the scriptures, therefore, should not be seen as a summary rejection of God or the scriptures themselves. The fact that 'legitimacy' for the perpetuation of a society based on hierarchy came from the scriptures perhaps, due to this Ambedkar rejected the scriptures. It should nevertheless be remembered that the scriptures may never have explicitly talked about the hierarchy. What is pertinent is that the nature of society hinted at by scriptures made it possible to establish a segmented society where some could extend their authority over others. Perhaps, Gandhi missed this point and chose to attack Ambedkar. First, he tried to settle the issue by dwelling on the origin of the caste system. Even during Gandhi's time it was reasonably clear that there was very little correspondence between causes of origin and causes of persistence. In fact Gandhi himself provides us with a glimpse of this. In the above quotation he seems to say that what remains of the old *varna* system in some villages is only faint. The question there is, of what importance is the origin of the caste system which seems quite distant from the present situation. Second, he takes recourse to metaphysics. He indicates that performance of the duty carries equal merit before God. (This too can be seen in the passage quoted above). This does not mean that the *varna* system can be absolved of all guilt. Even if it were to be accepted that God recognised all service as equally meritorious, one still cannot afford to overlook the societal dimension, which is precisely what Gandhi is doing. Equality before God is in no way any justification for inequality in the society. Therefore, some of the arguments of Gandhi are fallacious. Ambedkar himself understood this very well and his answer to Gandhi is quite fitting. "What does it avail to anyone if the texts are interpolations and if they have been differently interpreted by the saints? The masses do not make any distinction between texts, which are genuine, and texts which are interpolations. The masses do not know what the texts are. They are too illiterate to know the contents of the *shastras*. They have believed that what they have been told is that the *shastras* do enjoin as a religious duty to observance of caste and untouchability."[11] Ambedkar is not prepared to accept that saints are true representatives of Hindu culture. He makes them ineffective, for two reasons. "First, none of the saints ever attacked the caste system. On the contrary, they were staunch believers in the system of castes. Most of them lived and died as members of the castes to which they respectively belonged; second reason why the teachings of the saints might break caste but the common must not. A saint, therefore, never become an example to follow." Thus Ambedkar...Raves the way for yet another questioning of Gandhi's belief about religion. Gandhi felt, "A religion has to be judged not by its worst specimens but by the best it might have produced."[12] The point then is that if there are too few who are the best and too many who are not the best, how can one judge religion and society on that basis. Ambedkar himself says, "the argument of Mahatma that Hinduism would be tolerable if only many were to follow the example of the saints is fallacious. By citing the names of such illustrious persons as Chaitanya, etc., what the Mahatma seems to suggest in its broadest and simplest form is that Hindu society can be made tolerable and happy without any fundamental change in its structure if all the high caste Hindus can be persuaded to follow a high standard of morality in their dealings with low caste Hindus. I am totally opposed to this ideology."[13] It must be said that Ambedkar, unlike the Mahatma, is not talking about the merits or demerits of Hindu religion itself, but is pointing to the demerits of social system which has sought its legitimacy from the Hindu religion. Therefore, the implication is that one aspect of Hinduism leads to the hegemony of one segment or caste in society over others. Ambedkar is more opposed to Hindu society than Hindu religion. "Hindu society seems to me to stand in need of a moral regeneration which is dangerous to postpone. And the question is who can determine and control this moral regeneration? Obviously only those who have undergone an intellectual regeneration and those who are honest enough to have the courage of their conviction born of intellectual emancipation."[14] About the possibility of this moral regeneration, Ambedkar is quite pessimistic about. This mainly seems to stem out of his conviction that it is not simply the masses who are ignorant but also that the leaders themselves are not enlightened. "Judged by this standard the Hindu leaders who count are in my opinion quite unfit to the task. It is impossible to say they have undergone the preliminary intellectual regeneration... The Hindu masses are of course incredibly leaders in the formation of their beliefs. But so are the Hindu leaders. And what is worse is that these Hindu leaders become filled with an illicit passion for their belief when anyone proposes to rob them of their companionship."[15] In perception of Ambedkar, social reforms in Hindu society would be very difficult. In the annihilation of caste Ambedkar wrote "The path of social reform, like the path to heaven at any rate in India, is strewn with many difficulties. Social reforms in India has few friends and many critics."[16] This perception of Ambedkar's seems to have slowly pushed him towards disgust with the Hindu society. Finding that reform may not easily be carried out in the Hindu society, Ambedkar preferred to leave the fold of Hinduism. This is quite obvious from his utterances in the last part of the Annihilation of Caste: "You must make your efforts to uproot caste, if not in my way, then in your way, I am sorry I will not be with you. I have decided to change. But even when I am gone out of your fold, I will watch your movement with active sympathy and you will have my assistance for what it may be worth. Yours is a national cause".[17] This is the most surprising step that Ambedkar took. He decided that the best way to avoid the caste system was to simply leave the fold of Hindu religion and society. This decision is baffling because it would have been very naive on Ambedkar's part to actually believe that the way out of castes system was the leaving of the fold of religion which propagated it. Here one cannot help but wonder as to how Ambedkar, who displayed such a sharp intellect and prowess of analysis in his debate with Gandhi, could persuade himself into such a simplistic belief. Another thing that is equally surprising is that Ambedkar's step is individualistic. It appears that perhaps Ambedkar preferred to move to other religion instead of reforming Hinduism. It is, however, quite correct that Ambedkar did exhort many of the oppressed Hindus to join the rank of Buddhism. However, even this does not solve the problem in front of us. The question now is: Can one escape the oppressive mechanisms of the caste system by discarding Hinduism?

Before answering this question one has to look at the nature of Indian society. It is true that it is mainly Hinduism which sees to the operation of the caste system and that other religions are relatively free of this. Caste system exists in Hinduism but its logic can also be found in other communities in India. The fact is that the relation between people are not necessarily on an horizontal plane, even though there are no obvious caste structures in other religions. This perhaps is due to the fact that while conversions took place from Hinduism to other religions, the people, who moved from one fold to other, carried with them their old or previous identities without totally inferring them. This did lead to emergence of hierarchy in other religions too, even though its existence is not so striking or glaring as it is in the case of Hinduism. Thus the emerging point is that though the other religions are free of actual caste structures, they are not, totally free from the 'logic of caste relations'. However, there is yet another point that has to be seen in conjunction with what we have just mentioned. Can one really assume that the taking up of a new identity would automatically result in the destruction of the old? Logically it appears that such an assumption would be quite contrary to reality. This means that due to the birth in a certain caste, if one were to leave Hinduism and take up a new religion, one cannot escape the social ostracisation. The angle that did not come for full exploration from Ambedkar in this. There is not much attention paid to the stigma of birth and the difficulty one faces in ridding oneself of it by taking up a new identity. To put it differently, even people relinquish caste, caste may not relinquish them. Ambedkar perhaps does not seem to have fully realised it. But what proves to be very interesting is that Ambedkar himself was not totally unaware of what we have just seen. He says "caste is no doubt primarily the breath of the Hindus. But the Hindus have fouled the air all over and everybody infected, Sikh, Muslim, and Christian".[18] The question arises in this context is why did not Ambedkar choose a more fundamental attack on Indian society? Why did he continue to believe that if emancipation was not possible from within one religion it was possible from another? The questions brook no easy answer. In this connection what can be said to be conjectural arid not indubitable or certain. Any exercise of that sort can only be one of interpretation. One possible explanation is that Ambedkar did not believe in the radical philosophy of that time which totally rejected religion and that is socialism. Ambedkar tended to view the premises of the socialists as being inverted. He asks "can you have economic reform without first bringing about a reform of social order? The scientists of India do not seem to have considered this question... Men will not join in a revolution for the equalisation of property unless they know what after the revolution is achieved they will be treated equally, and that there will be no discrimination of caste and creed."[19] Let us closely examine what we have just seen. Ambedkar is clearly saying that there will be very little possibility of revolution because revolution demands unity and that this unity is non-existent in India because of social schism. "Can it be said that the proletrariat of India poor as it is, recognise no distinction of caste or creed, high or low?"[20] The reason for Ambedkar's rejection of socialism are quite clear. But it is distressing to note that Ambedkar never went on to develop this line of thinking fully. He never got to the problem of why caste stands in the way of the realisation of a class-consciousness.

As a result, he chose a reformist path but there were many obstacles in the way. The situation then was that Ambedkar was a man who had a problem on his hand and he had good analysis of the nature of his problem, but he had no answer to this. Therefore, he sought an individualistic solution to this problem. At this stage an assumption could be made about Ambedkar's view on socialism. While Ambedkar may be justified in thinking that unity was not possible without the submerging of social schisms, he seems to have underestimated the role of the 'economic sphere' in this regard. The difference brought about by social structure might have led to compounding the difference created in society by economic status. In India what has been happening is that caste seems to be occasionally playing a class role. Many now argue that caste in India is playing a class role or that in India caste is class. We may take it up for consideration. While sociologically it does appear as if caste is playing a class role, culturally this argument becomes untenable.

In most parts of India the lower castes, who are by and large the economically depressed sections, have slowly been reduced to the position of peasantry. The small land holders slowly became extinct because of the growth of large farmers and became landless labours. Ideally the situation is ripe for the creation of a class of wage labourers who should have identical interests. To use a phrase from Karl Marx, there is ground to believe that there is now a class which has come into being 'objectively'. The fact is that this objective class which is in itself or class that has been enlightened about its own interests. Why has this not happened? Here caste becomes significant. We think that caste is a very strong reason, which has prevented the emergence of class-consciousness. In order to understand this point let us take a brief look at the structure of the caste system. It is needless to say that caste is hierarchical and has many elements of oppression. What is now very important is that in the caste structure there are the dominant and dominated. But this is not the end of the caste structure. Again within the dominated there are the dominant and dominated, which means just as the original dominator perceives himself to be superior to the dominated, the dominator from within the dominated considers himself to be superior to the dominated in the dominated. This is a confounding situation. There is no unity among the lower castes too. Thus, it is not just the upper castes who follow the caste system but the lower castes also. The oppressor-oppressed relations in the main caste system are sought to be duplicated and are duplicated in the auxiliary caste system of the lower castes. There is an urge to oppress in all castes. This is what we may call 'abstract consciousness'. The prevalence of this consciousness answers the survival of the caste system, because the lower castes are constantly trying to emulate the upper castes. This means that people are constantly trying to avoid being dominated without trying to remove domination itself. It follows that they do not mind being the oppressors or the dominators. No doubt sociologically situation is created for unity among lower castes, but culturally due to the intervention of this abstract consciousness such unity is thwarted. Therefore, the realisation of a subjective consciousness of a class of people is not very easy as long as caste exists. This analysis is as significant for Ambedkar as it is for the socialists. This demonstrates the reason why Ambedkar chose the path of reforms rather than revolution. It also shows why Ambedkar was frustrated in his attempts at reforms also.

The whole question of caste today is even more complex and perplexing than before. This is mainly due to the fact that caste has ceased to play only its 'traditional' role and has acquired a new one, that of mobilisation. There is now mobilisation of people or electorates on caste lines in order to seize power. Those interested in creating a vote bank try that the poison of caste system continues till it serves their political interest. As a result, as long as caste persists, social tensions and inequalities will persist. Therefore, it is only logical that the task begun by Ambedkar be completed.

NOTES

1. *Harijan*, dated December 11, 1933.
2. Ambedkar B.R., *Annihilation of Caste*, p. 59. Writings and Speeches of Ambedkar, Vol. 1, Education Department, Government of Maharashtra, 1988, Bombay.
3. *Op. cit*, 1988, p. 14.
4. *Ibid.*, p. 144.
5. *Ibid.*, p. 144.
6. *Ibid.*, p. 144.
7. Ambedkar, B.R., *Annihilation of Caste*, Jalandhar, *Bheempatrika*, 1982, p. 133.
8. Gandhi, M.K., *A Vindication of Caste* (Appendix II. Annihilation of Caste), Jalandhar, *Bheempatrika*, 1982, p. 138.
9. Ambedkar, B.R., *A Reply to Mahatma*, Ibid., p. 145.
10. *Ibid.*, pp. 145-146.
11. Gandhi, M.K., *op. cit.*, p. 148.
12. Ambedkar, B.R., *Ibid.*, p. 148.
13. *Ibid.*, p. 159.
14. *Ibid.*, p. 159.
15. *Ibid.*, p. 58.
16. *Ibid.*, p. 133.
17. *Ibid.*, p. 133.
18. *Ibid.*,p. 133.
19. *Ibid.*, p. 72.
20. Ambedkar and *Social Justice*, Vol. I, Director Publication Division, Ministry of Information and Broadcasting, Government of India, p. 92.

11

Making of Panchayati Raj Institutions and Dr. Ambedkar

SURESH MISRA

Introduction

In India, the parliamentary democratic form, was chosen by the founding fathers after deep thought and debate. In the Constituent Assembly Dr. Ambedkar, the Chairman of the Drafting Committee, explained that in choosing the Parliamentary system for India, they preferred more responsibility to stability which could slip into authoritarian exercise of power. He said accountability was still difficult to obtain thus the Parliamentary system was a deliberate and well thought out choice by the Constituent Assembly. It was not chosen in imitation of the British system or because of the familiarity with it that India had acquired during the colonial period.

Another factor to be borne in mind was the immensity of India, the perplexing variety and diversity of the country, the very size of its population and the complexity of the social and developmental problems. The parliamentary system would provide more than a system which prefers stability to responsibility and accountability. Dr. Ambedkar also explained that there were elements in our heritage which made it possible and easy for India to adopt the parliamentary system of democracy. What was clear is that the founding fathers were of the view that democracy based on justice and equality was most suited to India. To realize this they provided for democratic institutional mechanism at various levels with appropriate checks and balances. However, they did not envisage such a system of democratic governance at the district level and below, particularly the old age institutions at the village level.

Place of Village Panchayat

Before we analyze the relevance of panchayati raj system and the role of villages in India it would be appropriate to analyse the historical role played by the villages in India. According to the Report of the Congress Village Panchayat Committee in Ancient India, it is apparent, a relationship of a unique type had developed between the state and the village community and that intimate relationship then existed between the government and the panchayats. It was also pointed out that from ancient most times, villages in India have been the axle of administration. The position of towns in ancient Indian life was negligible. Villages in ancient India could attain such a decisive importance in the administrative machinery mainly because of the close unity in which they were knit through the panchayat institutions. A keen sense existed among the populace about their rights and duties. The panchayats functioned at a high level of justice, fairplay and efficiency. They also had confidence, commanded respect and inspired the village populace. This in turn could be possible because the state gave the village body the fullest and complete authority and rights over all affairs relating to the village, insisting, of course, on regular payment of taxes. The village panchayat was simply the continuation of a system coming down from Vedic times, though every successive century did witness adjustments and modifications, almost always for the better, till about 1800 A.D. when the British came and mercilessly destroyed them. The destruction of village communities in India was accompanied by the creation of superior interests in our villages where such superior rights had never existed. Apart from this there was a large scale destruction of industries and handicrafts, and the millions thus deprived of their traditional occupation, fell back upon land for their livelihood and thus the pressure on land increased.

Even the Royal Commission on Decentralization (1907) recognized that throughout the greater part of India the village constitutes the primary territorial unit of government organization, and from the villages are built up large administrative entities. The Report said the villages formerly possessed a large degree of autonomy, but this autonomy has now disappeared owing to the establishment of local civil and criminal courts, the present revenue and police administration, the increase of communication and the growth of individualism. However, the Commission recommended that it would be desirable to constitute village panchayat for the administration of local village affairs. No doubt the Commission also visualized certain difficulties in the success of such an effort, like caste and religious disputes and factions so common in village life. It also agreed that these difficulties are far from insurmountable but advised a gradual and cautious approach beginning from those villages in which circumstances are most favourable by reason of homogeneity. Therefore, we will be negating the contribution and the role of village panchayats if we only view them as dens of exploitation. Even the Royal Commission on Decentralisation wanted the continuance of these village institutions.

Panchayats and the Draft Constitution

India achieved its independence in 1947. The Draft Constitution for free India as settled by the Drafting Committee set up by the Constituent Assembly was released in February 1948, that is, after Mahatma Gandhi's death. In spite of village panchayats being in existence since ancient times, they did not find mention in the Draft Constitution. The Draft was formally placed before the Constituent Assembly on November 4, 1948 by Dr. B.R. Ambedkar, the Chairman of the Drafting Committee. Referring to the criticism against the Draft, that no part of it represented the ancient polity of India and that it should have been drafted on the ancient Hindu model built upon village panchayats and district panchayats, Dr. Ambedkar referred to the part of the villages in the destiny of the country as described by Metcalfe, who had said "Dynasty after dynasty tumbles down, revolution succeeds revolution. Hindu, Pathan, Moghul, Maratha, Sikh, English all are masters in turn, but the village communities remain the same. In times of trouble they arm and fortify themselves. A hostile army passes through the country. The village communities collect their cattle within their walls and let the enemy pass unprovoked". However, Metcalfe could hardly be expected to know that it was the inexorable law of capitalism and imperialism at work in India of which they were the agents. The English exerted in India their direct political and economic power as rulers and landlords for disrupting our age-old village panchayats and the destruction of handicrafts, which was an integral part of the small well-knit economic organization of the village, was accomplished simultaneously.

Ambedkar's Opposition of Village Panchayats

Dr. Ambedkar pointed out that this was the part that the village communities had played in the history of the country. Knowing this he asked "what pride can one feel for them". That they have survived, survived through vicissitudes may be a fact. But mere survival has no value. The question is on what plane they have survived. Surely on a low selfish level. I hold that these village republics have been the ruination of India. I am, therefore, surprised that those who condemn provincialism and communalism should come forward as champions of the village. What is the village but a stink of localism and a den of ignorance, narrow-mindedness and communalism? "I am glad that the Draft Constitution has discarded the village and adopted the individual as the unit".

We have to understand as to why Dr. Ambedkar was opposed to any role for the village panchayats in the new set-up. He basically saw them as institutions of oppression and inequality. Prof. Andre Beteille, the noted sociologist in an article on Village Republics published in *The Hindu*, has brought out this debate in a very scholarly manner. According to him the two most outstanding Indians of the period before Independence, Rabindranath Tagore and Mahatma Gandhi were both actively interested in the village and in its reconstruction. Yet, as the historian, Niharranjan Ray, pointed out, Tagore was born and brought up in the city of Calcutta. Gandhi's family too was town based rather than village based. Neither of them had experienced at first hand the harsh realities of village life in either childhood or adolescence. They turned to the village in adult life after they had formed a view of the world in which the village stood for the core values of Indian civilization. As against the benign views of the Indian village taken by Tagore and Gandhi. Dr. Ambedkar spoke about it bluntly and unsentimentally. He articulated a kind of experience that neither Tagore nor Gandhi could have possibly had in their formative years. Based on his experience as a member of the depressed caste and the exploited meted out to them in the village system he could hardly have any other view about the village panchayats. And when he told the Constituent Assembly, that "I hold that these village republics have been the ruination of India," and went on to ask, "What is the village but a sink of localism, a den of ignorance, narrow-mindedness and communalism?" has to be seen in that context. He was not portraying a romantic view of village republics but a realistic picture of what existed in them. Ambedkar showed in them the real image of Indian villages to the Constituent Assembly stating that Indian villages were devoid of equality, liberty and fraternity, and hence of democracy. "It is the very negation of republic. If it is a republic, it is a republic of Touchables, by the Touchables and for the Touchables. The republic is an empire of the Hindus over the untouchables," said Ambedkar. That is why he pleaded that the individual should be considered the unit of the Constitution.

Demand for Statutory Provisions for Panchayats

Dr. Ambedkar's opening speech on the Draft Constitution was hailed all-round as a masterly performance, but his reference to the villages was very much regretted. When on subsequent days the Constituent Assembly debated the Draft Constitution, speaker after speaker expressed disapproval of Dr. Ambedkar's remarks. His views were regretted at one stroke. Dr. Ambedkar had condemned the village panchayats. It was strongly urged that the constitution must be so amended as to make it useful for the millions of villages for whose sake freedom had been won. It was also pointed out that but for the villages India would have been in chaos. A demand for some statutory provisions for the recognition of village panchayats was made. It was also argued that a Constitution which gave no place to the village panchayats could not be suited for India.

The Constitution did not give sufficient importance to village communities which were an essential feature of India's social and political life. It was felt that villages or groups of villages must be recognized in the Constitution so that the villages would be trained to discharge their responsibilities under democracy. The Constituent Assembly did not approve of Dr. Ambedkar's summary dismissal of the village institutions in Indian history and polity, and left no doubt about its strong opinion that village panchayats must find a place in the Constitution. However, Dr. Ambedkar pointed out that there is no doubt that the Constitution does not contain any clause about village Panchayats. A good deal of criticism has been hurled at it for that reason, but may point out that the Constitution in no way rules out the development of the village panchayats? The Constitution doesn't put any obstruction whatsoever in the path of the development of those units of local self-government which will enjoy power for managing their own affairs and, therefore, that criticism also seems to me to be without any foundation. More than 80 per cent of the members in the Constituent Assembly were strongly of the view that the soul of India was not represented by this Constitution because the autonomy of the villages was not fully delineated there and that the Draft Constitution did not give a true picture of what many people would like India to be. Most of them felt that Dr. Ambedkar had drawn his inspiration from foreign Constitutions alone and he had deliberately failed to take even a casual glance at the historic spirit and culture of

India or take into consideration the Indian approach to life. Finally, most of them were of the view that Dr. Ambedkar's Constitution will only safeguard the bread of those whose hands were full of bread and not the hands of those whose hands were empty.

Gandhian Influence

The advocates of village panchayats were greatly influenced by the freedom struggle and the concept of Gram Swaraj as propounded by Gandhi. Gandhi said that the Indian Independence must begin at the bottom. Thus every village will be a republic or panchayat having full powers. It follows, therefore, that every village has to be self-sustained and capable of managing its affairs, even to the extent of defending itself against the whole world. It will be trained and prepared to perish in the attempt to defend itself against any onslaught from without. In this structure composed of innumerable village, there will be ever-widening, never ascending circles. Life will not be a pyramid with the apex sustained by the bottom. But, it will be an oceanic circle, whose centre will be the individual always ready to perish for the village.

Gandhi also said I regard village panchayats as an institution by itself. But thanks to the degradation of the caste system and the evil influence of the present system of government and the growing illiteracy of the masses, this ancient and noble institution has fallen into desuetude, and where it has not, it has lost its former purity and hold. It must, however, be revived at any cost, if the villages are not to be ruined. For Gandhi the village was of prime importance. His influence on governance was to be seen with the revival of village community. They also received great strength from the views expressed by the great constitutional lawyer Krishnaswamy Aiyer. While he paid tributes to Dr. Ambedkar for his lucid explanation of the Draft Constitution, he made it clear that he did not share his views and his general condemnation of village communities in India.

Public opinion in the country also expressed itself in no unmistakable terms. Sardar Patel in a speech delivered at

Sevagram said "when Bapu came to India, work was being done in a different way. Bapu said that real India was in the villages. Crores live in India and their interest must command out attention." The noted paper *Anand Bazar Patrika* added "if the village is and is allowed to remain stink of localism and a den of ignorance, narrow-mindedness and communalism, what chance is there of India ever achieving greatness and prosperity." For without a doubt the real India lives in villages. The *swaraj* that we have won will be worth little if it leaves the villages where they are immersed in poverty, ignorance and indebtedness.

Panchayats in Part IV of the Constitution

The countrywide repercussions to Dr. Ambedkar's remarks on village panchayats, as also the reactions inside the Constituent Assembly, at last succeeded in their objective. The Constituent Assembly started the discussion on the Directive Principles of State Policy and addition of a new Article declaring that the "state shall organize village Panchayats and endow them with such powers as might be necessary to enable them to function as units of self-government". The Directive Principles of State Policy are guidelines to the central and state governments to be kept in mind while framing laws and policies. They are not enforceable by any court, but the principles laid down therein are considered fundamental in the governance of the country, making it the duty of the state to apply these principles in making laws to establish a just society in the country. The concept of Directive Principles of State Policy was borrowed from the Irish Constitution, which influenced the makers of our Constitution. The amendment was based on the view which was shared by everyone in the House. It was also said that if village republics were properly organized and if they functioned properly as self-sufficient, self-governing units, they would help bring down inflationary trends and put the biggest check on black markets and profiteering. It was also highlighted that the villages fell into obscurity only during the British regime. Dr. Ambedkar accepted the Amendment.

Under the alien rulers, Instruments of Instructions were issued to the Governor-General, and they were meant to secure the foreign stronghold over our land. These Directive Principles in the Indian Constitution, issued to the legislatures and the executives, secure the sovereignty of the people and ensure good governance in the interest of the people. In commending these principles Dr. Ambedkar said "whoever capture power.... cannot ignore them. He may not have to answer for their breach in a court of law. But he will certainly have to answer for them before the electorate at election time. Directive Principles provisions will be realized well when forces of right contrive to capture power."

The incorporation of the panchayat idea in the Indian Constitution was an event of profound importance with great and far-reaching consequences on the very structure of the state. The decision was hailed all over the country. As an objective it involved recognition of a principle to which till then only lip service had been paid and on which the pure constitutional pedant still had many doubts. It is noteworthy that even Dr. Ambedkar while condemning the village communities for their conservatism and ignorance, could not deny them the virtue of stability, and stability combined with real social and economic progress will mean that the vagaries of parliamentary democracy will be under a brake. Way was opened for the village panchayats to become a useful focus for economic organization which ultimately would be the solvent for social malaise.

Working of the Panchayats

From not being even mentioned in the Draft Constitution to attaining constitutional status through the 73rd Constitutional Amendment, the nation and the panchayati raj institutions have travelled a long distance. It is more than 60 years that Dr. Ambedkar called the villages a stink of localism and a den of ignorance. Now it is time we evaluate the role of the panchayti raj institutions. The panchayats as part of the Directive Principles of State Policy could not attain the desired status and dignity that local institutions need to achieve. The panchayats remained dominated by the rural powerful elites who siphoned away the benefits that were meant for the poor and the deprived sections of the society. As far as power relations are concerned the *status quo* remained and the deprived sections of the society continued to be isolated and lost in their own village. The Scheduled Castes to be more precise did not have any representation in the panchayats and it was difficult for them to even get elected.

It would be appropriate to say that the State governments and the local MLAs and MPs also ensured that the panchayats remained deprived of powers, functions as well as finances. The local level bureaucracy ensured that the panchayats remained within the grip of the local administration. Elections were not held and most of the State governments superseded the panchayats on one pretext or the other. The village community became fragmented due to electoral politics. In large number of States the panchayats nearly ceased to exist. There were only island of success. A number of committees and commissions were set up to revitalize the panchayats but the fragmented nature of village polity ensured that the panchayats remained dormant.

The advocates of Panchayati Raj and village republic could not empower the panchayats and as time passed by the dream of Mahatma Gandhi was forgotten. The concept of Gram Swaraj faded away and modern India neglected its villages as never before. The panchayats in modern India became a den of corruption and exploitation of the poor by the rich and powerful rural elites. Perhaps Dr. Ambedkar was right in some respects as far as village community in India was concerned. None had visualized this role for the panchayats in Independent India. The Gandhian concept where each village would be a self-reliant republic remains a distant dream. The process of reforms continued and still continues even after the 73rd Amendment Act. No doubt a large number of members from the deprived sections of the society have come to occupy position of power by virtue of reservation of seats in the panchayats, but still the real empowerment of the depressed classes is still a long journey.

The panchayats need to reorient in their approach to solving rural problems and ensuring that the poor and the deprived sections of the society have a major role to play. If the village community cannot become an engine of social reengineering, in which the evils of social, economic and political order do not find place then there is little hope that India will change its destiny. The village would continue to remain in Dr. Ambedkar's words a stink of localism and a den of ignorance, narrow-mindedness and communalism unless it proves otherwise. Let us not idealize the village community and romantise the village life but have a realistic view and address the problems that face our village community.

We have to evaluate Dr. Ambedkar's contribution to Indian polity and society in terms of his desire to give a place of dignity and self-respect to the downtrodden in this country. He was a product of unjust and inequal social system which was hierarchical and discriminatory. His opposition to the villages and the village panchayats has to be seen in this backdrop.

REFERENCES

Ambedkar, B.R. *Untouchables and Untouchability (Social, Political, Religious): Writings and Speeches;* (Vol. 5) Ed. Department, Maharashtra Government, 1989.

Andre Beteille. Village Republics, *The Hindu,* Tuesday, September 03, 2002.

Desai, A.R. *Social Background of Indian Nationalism,* Popular Prakashan, 1991.

Gaikwad, S.M. Ambedkar and Indian Nationalism, *Economic and Political Weekly,* March 7, 1998.

Kashyap, Subhash C. *History of the Parliament of India,* Vol. II, Shipra Publications, Delhi, 1995, p. 49.

Kumar, Vivek. Ambedkar, The Nation-Builder, 28 April, 2004, *The Pioneer.*

Mookerji, Radha Kamal. *Local Government in Ancient India,* Oxford, Clarendon Press, 1919.

Narayanan, K.R. President's address to the Nation on the occasion of the 50th anniversary of the Republic of India.

Report of the Congress Village Panchayat Committee, New Delhi, AICC, 1954.

12

Ambedkar
A Champion of Human Rights

A.N. PANDA

The annals of mankind will record the contributions of Bhimrao Ramji Ambedkar with conspicuous fashion and the avid readers of *dalit* movement will study his life and works with passion. He has left an indelible mark in the struggle for the protection of rights of the downtrodden people in India; he has championed their cause in different forums and stood against the mighty people of his time to defend the exploited masses and their rights. Many may not agree with him with regard to what constitute the real interests of the oppressed classes and may not accept his method of safeguarding their rights as the apposite technique to achieve the goal; but nobody can nurture a doubt about his commitment for the emancipation of the subjugated people of India, who had been at the mercy of the powerful upper castes of the Indian society since time immemorial.

Born in the Mahar caste of Maharashtra, which was traditionally treated as an untouchable caste, Ambedkar realized what the stigma of untouchability meant. "He had experienced the agonies, anguishes, frustrations and humiliations of being born in the Mahar caste"[1]; he himself had suffered degradation many a time at the hands of the high caste people because of their superstitious beliefs and was treated shabbily even after he had proved his capability in different respects. He understood that if an adept person like him was not beyond disparagement of the higher castes people than others, who were more unfortunate, were likely to invite their wrath and suffer increasingly. He was conscious that the Indian social system was based on the defective principle of inequality and was against the interests of the people of lower birth; he was genuinely concerned about their welfare and wanted to remove inequality from the Indian society so that all could live with self-esteem. Therefore, Ambedkar carried on a relentless struggle against untouchability throughout his adult life and made strong endeavours to protect the interests of his own fellowmen.

Ambedkar felt that all human beings were equal and all had the right to be treated equally. Unlike many others who respected the prevailing notion of his time that inequality imposed by birth must be accepted as justified as it had religious sanction, Ambedkar held the view that all men were equal and all must be treated as human beings. In his opinion, all men had some basic rights as human beings. He aspired to provide the most essential rights to his fellow human beings and championed for their cause. He opposed others in his pursuits for the protection of the rights of *dalits,* who were his comrades. His other ideas were only the reflections of his concern for human rights and the activities he undertook throughout his life were only for attaining the goal of maintaining human rights of all. Thus, the different ideas of Ambedkar can be studied in the light of his interest in protecting human rights. He may be better understood as a champion of human rights.

Two of Ambedkar's most fundamental ideas are those of state and religion on which most of his political thoughts and actions are based. These two concepts can be analysed from the point of view of his concern for human rights. Ambedkar's opinions about these two ideas manifest his visions of an institution which protects the rights of citizens and of a system which guarantees the freedom of people to select and practice a religion of their choice that gives them their appropriate status. Thus, his commitment to the cause of human rights can be inferred from these two notions and both these concepts can be examined in this light.

Ambedkar's Concept of State

Ambedkar does not consider state as a creation of God and holds the view that state is a human institution. It is an organization meant to serve the interests of individuals. In his opinion, "the aim of the state is (i) to maintain the right of every subject to life, liberty and pursuit of happiness and to free speech and free exercise of religion; (ii) to remove social, political and economic inequality by providing better opportunities to the submerged classes; and (iii) to make it possible for every subject to enjoy freedom from want and freedom from fear"[2]. Ambedkar propagates for the freedom of men and differentiates between a good state and a bad state on the basis of the state's capacity and willingness to protect freedoms of citizens. He maintains that "a good state guarantees protection against persecution of one community by another and also internal disturbances, violence and disorder in any part of territory"[3]. He opposes discriminatory behaviour towards any group and exploitation of one by another.

Ambedkar does not find a supernatural source of law. For him, law is made by human beings to deal with human affairs. The ultimate aim of law is to serve the interests of human beings. He considers law as an instrument for providing happiness to man. To him, "Laws are made by man for man. Law has not created man; but man has created laws for his own happiness"[4]. Thus, Ambedkar believes that law is not above man and its objective is not to harass him. It has a human purpose and it must be applicable to all equally. "Law must be social and human i.e. universal in its effect"[5]. To maintain an ideal social condition there must be rule of law. If a society is governed by law and not by the whims of man then individual is able to enjoy his freedom. His unflinching "faith in individual liberty and dignity led him to emphasize rule of law"[6].

However, though Ambedkar underlines rule of law and points out the importance of law in providing a better condition to the people to avail their rightful position against the caprices of the vested interests, he does not accept the view that law alone can safeguard the rights of individuals, especially if the individuals are at the lower strata of the social ladder. Therefore, he invokes the conscience of society. If the social values are in favour of providing rights to all, including the lowest of the low, then only all can derive benefits from the social condition. "Rights are protected not by law but by the social and moral conscience of society. If social conscience is such that it is prepared to recognise the rights which law chooses to enact, rights will be safe and secure. But if the fundamental rights are opposed by the community, no law, no parliament, no judiciary can guarantee them in the real sense of the word."[7]

Ambedkar had experienced many humiliating situations in his life as a result of the misbehaviours of the upper class people and the state was unable to protect him from such conditions as it was being controlled by the very persons who were the perpetrators of those humiliations. He was convinced that if the state's power remained in the hands of a class then there could be no justice for all, especially for the people who were outside the decision making process. The controllers of decision making authority would likely to victimize those who had no such power.

Ambedkar's idea of state indicates some amount of autonomy from the hegemony of any class. He prefers a set of principles to be followed in the governance of the state. To him, the state is expected to act according to the principles of the Constitution and, therefore, he made attempts to incorporate certain principles into the Constitution which he considered favourable to his fellow men. Many of the provisions found in the Constitution are all for the downtrodden people of India and aim at implementing affirmative actions for them.

Ambedkar also understood that the state might be an instrument in the hands of the ruling classes to serve their interests and until the subjugated people themselves became the rulers, the state might not work for them. Therefore, Ambedkar wanted to make the lower caste people politically powerful. He argued for reservation of seats for the Scheduled Caste people of India long before India attained independence and in the process, he encountered opposition from many other

Indian leaders. The First Round Table Conference held in 1930 marked "the beginning of the claims of the untouchables in the arena of the devolution of political power from the British rulers to the Indian natives."[8] Gandhi refused to consider separate electorate for the depressed classes and opposed any form of representation involving reserved seats. He said in the Second Round Table Conference held in 1931, "I do not mind the untouchables being converted to Islam or Christianity. I should tolerate that, but I cannot possibly tolerate what is in store for Hinduism if there are these two divisions set up in every village. Those who speak of political rights of untouchables do not know India and do not know how Indian society is today constructed. Therefore, I want to say with all the emphasis that if I was the only person to resist this thing I will resist with my life."[9]

However, there were also contrary opinions with regard to reservation of seats for the Scheduled Castes. While the Constituent Assembly held its first and second meetings on 9th and 13th December, 1946 for making resolution to provide constitutional reservations, Ambedkar expressed the hope that given the "time and circumstances, nothing in the world will prevent the country from being one."[10] G.B. Pant supported this idea and said, "We find that in our country we have to take particular care of the depressed classes, the Scheduled Castes and the Backward Classes. We must do all that we can do to bring them up to the general level and it is real necessity as much in our interest as in theirs that the gap should be bridged. The strength of the chain is measured by the weakest link of it and so until every link is fully revitalized, we will not have a healthy body politic."[11] Reservation of seats for Scheduled Castes and Scheduled Tribes was termed by Nehru as a "historic turn in our destiny."[12] K.T. Shah told in the Constituent Assembly, "This discrimination is in favour of particular classes of our society, which owing to our unfortunate legacy of the past, suffer from disabilities or handicaps. Those, I think, may require special treatment and if they require it they should be permitted special facilities for some time so that real equality of citizens be established."[13]

Ambedkar was conscious of the need for political empowerment as he felt that without political power there could be no social and economic power. He considered that the lower caste people were controlled and exploited by the higher caste people as the latter has the power to govern and regulate the social system. Without decision making power it was not possible to thwart the domination of the higher castes. He thought, real equality might be attained only if there could be political power or decision making power at the hands of the intimidated mass. Therefore, he encouraged and motivated his followers to capture political power so that the hold of the upper caste people over different social structures would end and there would be equality for all in different fields. However, unlike many others, Ambedkar considered political power only as a means and not an end. He desired political power to attain some better conditions for his own people.

Ambedkar had firm faith in democracy. He visualised the establishment of a society free from any kind of exploitation through democracy. His conception of democracy appears to be purely people oriented which allowed involvement of all in the decision making process. It envisaged complete abolition of inequality. He set in motion a social revolution to lay the foundation of an egalitarian social system; he believed that through this revolution the traditional Indian society would be transformed into a classless society in which there would be perfect social justice and no place for untouchability. For this purpose he wanted to empower the downtrodden people of India. He held the view that "devoid of power and knowledge, the non-brahmins and the depressed classes could not make any progress."

Ambedkar's Concept of Religion

Ambedkar was against the Brahminic tradition which perpetuated the domination of the upper castes over the backward people. He felt that the upper caste people had spread their brand of religion so that they could continue their hold over the various structures of the social system and monopolize all the benefits. According to him, there was an upper class bias in Hindu religion. As a result, Hindu religion defended only the interests of the upper castes and completely disregarded those of the backward classes. The low born people of Hindu society were subjected to different kinds of cruelty and humiliation and these degrading acts had the support of various religious sanctions.

He also rejected the doctrine of the infallibility of the *Vedas*, the holy scriptures of Hinduism and the *varna-vyavastha*, which divided the society into four *varnas* or orders such as *Brahmins, Kshatriyas, Vaisyas* and *Shudras* and which occupied positions in society in the descending order. Ambedkar held the *varna* system responsible for social inequality in India. Ambedkar felt that so long as Hindu religion reigned Indian society or the low caste people were part of Hindu society there was no remedy for the exploitation of the lower caste people. He had a firm belief that Hinduism would never end the domination of Brahmins as the religion itself was controlled by the Brahmins and the inequality persisting in Indian society would continue indefinitely. Therefore, he encouraged his followers to prefer for another religion which would provide them an equal status with others. He advised them to select only that religion in which they would get equal status, equal opportunity and equal treatment.

Ambedkar considered that the untouchables occupied a "weak and lowly status" as they practiced Hindu religion and had been a part of the Hindu society. But this resulted in depriving them of their basic rights as human beings. Only because the untouchables were the followers of Hindu religion they were not enjoying human rights. Hence, to have human rights the low caste people had to choose and adopt such a religion which would guarantee equality and enjoyment of ordinary rights as human beings. When he failed to gain equal status and ordinary rights as a human being within the Hindu society, Ambedkar searched for another religion which he believed would give 'equal status, equal rights and fair treatment' to an untouchable like him. His statement in 1935 at Yeola Conference was quite revealing in this regard.

Ambedkar held the opinion that religion must recognize the fundamental principles of liberty, equality and fraternity; otherwise religion itself would be instrumental in dividing the society into different sections on the basis of inequality. To his mind, Hinduism had been doing just that. The Hindu society had been divided into different classes with the patronage of religion and the principle of inequality had been entrenched with religious sanction. He held the Hindu religion responsible for making some people untouchables and for all the sufferings of these people at the hands of the higher castes.

His search for a rational religion ended in Buddhism. Ambedkar regarded Buddhism as a much more rational religion compared to Hinduism, because Buddhism did not divide its followers into different strata on the basis of untouchability. He considered it the most rational religion as it practiced the principle of equality. His main objection to Hinduism was that it lauded inequality and untouchability through its dogma of *Chaturvarna* by dividing people according to their birth. Ambedkar considered Hinduism hostile to equality and opposed to freedom of all. According to Ambedkar, Buddhism on the other hand, propagated for equality among all its disciples and did not discriminate one follower from another as it considered all as equal human beings and, therefore, it was the only suitable religion for the world to be practiced by all.

By describing the evils of Hinduism he remarked that Hinduism deprived its followers of their freedom, it only emphasized conformity to commands of the higher caste people and its tenets were beyond scrutiny. All had to respect its principle without any protest even if those were inimical to their interests. It imposed many prohibitions on the ordinary followers but treated its interpreters above its codes. As the leaders of Hinduism interpreted the religious principles according to their own choice it was always favourable to them and disadvantageous to others. According to Ambedkar, "Hinduism was nothing but a multitude of commands and prohibitions".

Though many have viewed his renouncement of Hinduism and adoption of Buddhism in the last part of his life differently, it was his way of protesting against the principle of stratification of the Indian society. He praised Buddhism as he believed it to be a religion based on moral principles. Ambedkar pointed out that the founders of other religions considered themselves as emissaries of God; but Buddha regarded himself only as a guide and did not consider himself above its moral principles; thus, he gave a new meaning to the concept of religion. Therefore, Ambedkar thought Buddhism as the most rational religion of the world.

According to Ambedkar, Hinduism excluded the *Shudras*, people of low birth, from all religious practices and relegated them to a position of ignominy. They were allotted the lowest stratum in the social system according to the *Varna* system and they were also considered outside the *ashram* theory, which divided life into four stages, namely, *brahmacharya*, *garhasthya*, *vanprastha* and *sanyasa*; only to the "twice born" castes had the privilege to be included in these four stages of life. Thus, inequality was in-built into different schemes of Hinduism and as a result of which there were social as well religious inequality in Hindu society.

Ambedkar also questioned whether Hinduism recognized liberty. According to him, liberty to be real must be accompanied by certain social conditions, namely, (i) social equality, (ii) economic security, and (iii) availability of knowledge. If the society was devoid of equality, liberty had no meaning, because in such a condition the principle of liberty was applied differently for different people. According to Ambedkar, Hinduism denied equality and upheld inequality. "According to Ambedkar, the Hindu scheme of social structure based on the four *Varnas* or *Chaturvarna* breeds inequality and has been the parent of the caste-system and untouchability which are merely forms of inequality."[14]

Similarly, unless the people had economic self-sufficiency they would not think of liberty as people with empty stomach might not be in a position to avail their liberty and their liberty might be mortgaged with the people who provided them food. Ambedkar felt that three things in Hinduism worked against achieving economic security. First, Hinduism denied freedom of occupation in the scheme of Manu as each man had his occupation preordained for him even before his birth. Secondly, Manu directed the *Shudras* to serve the higher classes. Thirdly, Hinduism did not allow the *Shudras* to accumulate wealth. To seek equality and economic security and beware of their own limitations and potentialities people must have access to knowledge. But again, it was the monopoly of the higher caste people. In the Indian context, Ambedkar did not find the necessary requirements of liberty in society and thought that Indian society did not have congenial situations for the enjoyment of liberty. Therefore, he wanted to reform the Indian society.

Ambedkar raised his voice against exploitation of the backward people. He regarded that the caste system subjugated more than one-fifth of the population to levels worse than animals' and institutionalized inequality with the help of different religious principles. He attacked the Hindu religion from the standpoint of its victims—the untouchables. "Ambedkar was merciless in his denunciations of the pettiness, perversities and the hypocrisies of Brahmanism which, to him, was a wicked and mischievous agent of the social exploitation of the backward and untouchable sections of the Hindu Society."[15]

"Ambedkar has been the most renowned and the most militant champion of the untouchables"[16]. He directed his attention not only for the emancipation of all the untouchables but also towards annihilation of the entire caste system. "Ambedkar dreamed of an ideal society in which all would have justice. He envisioned his ideal in the famous three principles: liberty, equality and fraternity. They were the basis for the ideal society of his conception."[17] He wanted to establish a society free of any kind of exploitation.

Conclusion

Ambedkar had a multidimensional personality. He was a political leader, constitutional expert, statesman, administrator, social revolutionary, scholar, educationist, debater, thinker and champion of human rights combined in one. His name and views continue to command attention and respect even today.

Political parties of all hues invoke his name and try to garner mass support for their political programmes.

His principle of positive discrimination is based on the very concept of equality. But the operational aspects of this concept involved the need for some kind of autonomous institution, which was met by 'State' and 'religion'. He proposed radical transformation of the Indian society so that all could get justice.

The history of modern India will record the contributions of Ambedkar with ample awe because of his ability to awaken the subjugated and downtrodden people of India through his scholarly writings, inspiring speeches and competent leadership. *Dalits* could be eternally indebted to Ambedkar for whatever he has done for them. He had brought revolutions in social, economic and political fields for protecting their interests, saving them from the life of infamy and encouraging them to lead a life of self-esteem.

NOTES

1. Varma, V.P., *Modern Indian Political Thought*, Lakshmi Narain Agarwal, Agra, 1995, p. 578.
2. Ambedkar, *States and Minorities*, Thacker & Co. Ltd., Bombay, 1947, p. 3.
3. *Ibid.*, pp. 108-111.
4. Ambedkar, *Annihilation of Caste*, pp. 77-86.
5. *Ibid*, p. 32.
6. *Ibid.*
7. Ambedkar, *Ranade, Gandhi and Jinnah*, pp. 34-35.
8. Sandanshiv, S.N., *Reservation for Social Justice*, Current Law Publishers, Bombay, 1986, p. 7.
9. *Ibid.*, p. 8.
10. *Constituent Assembly Debates*, Vol. I, p. 59.
11. *Ibid.*, Vol. I, p. 333.
12. *Ibid.*, Vol. III, p. 330.
13. *Ibid.*, Vol. VII, p. 655.
14. Varma, V.P., *Modern Indian Political Thought*, Lakshmi Narain Agarwal, Agra, 1995, p. 580.
15. *Ibid*, p. 578.
16. *Ibid*, p. 579.
17. Moon, Vasant (Ed.), *Babasaheb Ambedkar Writings and Speeches*, Education Department, Govt. of Maharashtra, Bombay, Vol.1, p. 57.

13

Relevance of Dr. Ambedkar in Present Day Context

BINDESHWAR PATHAK

All his life Dr. Bhimrao Ramji Ambedkar, architect of India's Constitution and messiah of the downtrodden, fought against caste-based discrimination and inequalities which were responsible for step-motherly treatment and suffering of more than three-fourths of country's population for over 2,000 years. Since these evils derived their sanction from the caste system as laid down by *Manusmriti,* Ambedkar was deadly opposed to it. He was so strongly motivated that he went to the extent of making a bonfire of *Manusmriti* at Mahad near Bombay (Mumbai) in 1927 the immediate provocation for which was refusal of the upper castes to allow lower castes even to take water from a common village tank.

He roused the depressed classes to rebel against the caste system which confined them to play only mean, subordinate roles and thus by comparison enhance the dignity and prestige of the upper castes. He also asked them to throw overboard their fatalistic outlook that if they were the victims of social inequality and tyranny, it was because of their sins in the previous birth; and if they suffered in silence without any grudge or protest, at least after their death they would be liberated in their next life. What continues to make Ambedkar's teachings relevant even more than 50 years after his death is the still very stubborn attitude of the upper castes about their caste-based superiority over the downtrodden. Every other day newspapers report cases of honour killings from all over the country. The root cause of these crimes is the intolerance of one caste against another.

The caste system is a descending scale of contempt and is the fundamental cause of inequalities in Indian society. If you give education to the lower strata of the Indian society, which is interested in breaking social barriers, the caste-system will be blown up. At the moment the indiscriminate help given to education by the Indian Government and foreign foundations, which translated into simple language means grant of scholarships to top-notch students regardless of the fact that they come from lower or upper strata of society is going to strengthen the caste-system. This is so because the bulk of beneficiaries from such awards usually belong to the upper strata of society. However, giving education—scholarships etc.—to those who want to blow up the caste-system will improve the prospect of democracy in India and put democracy in safer hands.

Born as the 14th child of a Mahar family Ambedkar attained academic honours—doctorate degrees from the Columbia University in America and the London School of Economics in U.K. besides distinction of studying at Sorbonne and being called to Grays Inn in London—and thus demonstrated that *Shudhra* as he was could be as brilliant as any upper caste Hindu, although *Manusmriti* injunctions sought to belittle and denigrate them in every possible way. If he could accomplish and attain what was long thought impossible for Mahars and other untouchables amongst Hindus, what prevented others belonging to the Scheduled Castes and Scheduled Tribes in India from moving up in life instead of remaining confined and resigned to a low status?

Such lessons from Ambedkar's life need to be drummed into the ears of the lower castes in order to raise their hopes and aspirations. Their low caste does not diminish their faculties of learning. With his portfolio full of foreign degrees and testimonials by leading educationists of the Columbia University and the London School of Economics, Ambedkar returned home with a steel-like determination to awaken the underdogs and to infuse in them zeal and zest to make a bid for a better life. That Ambedkar did succeed, is a lesson most relevant for the vast number of lower castes caught in the rat race today.

Despite the imposing list of degrees and testimonials he had earned, Ambedkar was denied jobs, touched only with a barge-pole by the Hindu society. No wonder, young Ambedkar soon realized that his deliverance and the deliverance of the untouchables lay only in challenging the very foundation of India's caste system. He wrote books, published pamphlets, edited newspapers and formed powerful organizations of the Scheduled Castes to fight for their due place under the sun and not remain confined to *ghettos* marked for the poor. Reading of his writings is most relevant today.

Despite his monumental contribution to the Indian society—apart from being the architect of India's Constitution, he was mainly responsible for *dalit* resurgence all over the country—Dr. Ambedkar died as a miserable man. Talking to his private secretary, Nanak Chand Rattu, before his death he said: "My first worry is that I have not been able to fulfil my life's mission. I wanted to see my people as a governing class sharing political power in terms of equality with other communities. I am now almost crippled and prostrate with illness. Whatever I have been able to achieve is being enjoyed by the educated few, who, with their deceitful performance, have proved to be a worthless lot, with no sympathy for their downtrodden brethren. They have belied my expectations, they live only for themselves and their personal gains. Not even one of them is prepared to do any social work. They are only treading the path of their ruination. I now want to divert my attention towards the vast illiterate masses in the villages who continue to suffer and remain almost unchanged economically. But I don't seem to have many more days to live".

With tears in his eyes, Ambedkar said: "Tell my people, Nanak Chand, that whatever I have been able to achieve for them, I have done it single-handed, passing through crushing miseries and endless troubles, in the midst of abuses hurled at me from all sides, more so from the Hindu press, fighting with my opponents, all my life, as also with a handful of my own people who deceived me for their selfish ends. But I will continue to serve the country and my downtrodden people till my end. With great difficulty, I have brought the caravan where it stands today.

"Let the caravan march on and further on, despite the hurdles, pitfalls and difficulties that may come in its way. They must rise to the occasion, if they want to live an honourable and respectable life. If my people, my lieutenants are not able to take the caravan ahead, they should leave it where it stands today, but must not, under any circumstances, allow the caravan to lag behind. This is my message, probably my last message given in all seriousness, which I am sure will not go unheeded. Go and tell them. Go and tell them. Go and tell them." Such ideas need to be told and retold to the struggling lower castes so that they can justify the sacrifices made by their messiah.

Eleanor Zelliot, an American scholar, who has been in India for long and who has written extensively on the problems of the downtrodden in this country, says Ambedkar's life and work should be better known in the West for he was a leader who believed that the leadership of a people must come from within the group; religion must meet the needs of a people and reflect their greatness; education must be stressed and must reach the lowest. Those who have achieved elite status must remain concerned about their depressed brethren and courage is the essential element among those who wish equality; also, those who lead must be moral and pure of heart. If Zelliot feels Ambedkar's teachings are of great value to the people abroad, why should they not be propagated in our India where increasing number of the youths are struggling for a better deal?

Although in his own lifetime Ambedkar could see little by way of progress of all that he stood for and fought against, the ferment of his ideas and teachings has altogether changed the face of India's political scenario today. The U.P. chief minister, Mayawati and her mentor, the late Kanshi Ram, emerged as towering figures on Indian political horizon only because of the fire of revolt and rebellion ignited by

Ambedkar's teachings among the Scheduled Castes, Scheduled Tribes and Backward Classes who account for the overwhelming majority of country's population. No wonder Mayawati could seize power in U.P. because exploitation of the depressed classes here knew no bounds. Similarly Laloo Yadav emerged darling of the depressed classes in Bihar because of acute exploitation of the poor by feudal lords.

The caste-dominated Hindu society began to suffer jolts as the downtrodden aroused to fight for their rights refused to be dictated by the upper castes. But instead of winning over and pacifying the rising aspirations of the depressed classes, the upper castes sought not only to play down stirrings of revolts in their ranks but also paid no heed to roots of trouble they had started encountering. Unrest of the depressed classes who constituted the bulk of population started causing political disturbances as a result of which the Congress Party, which had led the freedom movement, began to lose their support. New political organizations claiming to champion the cause of *dalits* began sprouting in the country.

Traditional supporters of the Congress amongst the lower castes started switching loyalty. With a view to arresting erosion of their vote banks dominant political parties pushed through legislature bills and concessions to woo the backwards again. Since benefits intended for the downtrodden could not filter down to the ground level due to cranky and corrupt administrative machinery, resentment and suffering amongst the depressed classes remained widespread. Ambedkar kept on warning the upper castes that by neglecting the grievances and concerns of the poor they were only storing trouble for the future. And the trouble is there all over the country now.

Our polity was never so badly fractured as now: No party is in a position to command majority support all over India. Rising aspirations of the masses have given rise to new political formations which promise the moon but actually cannot be sure about their remaining in power until even the following day. There's total chaos. Centripetal forces are at full blast as a result of which the main casualty in the country is political stability. Could we not foresee this scenario. Certainly, we could, had we paid attention to warnings by Ambedkar and other leaders of his ilk. Since country's failure to rein in fissiparous tendencies is responsible for the spectre of political instability, there is urgent need to inculcate among the masses, unity and equality, which can happen only as Ambedkar argued with go-by to the caste system. Learn to love and sympathise your neighbour regardless of the fact that he belongs to lower or upper caste.

Ambedkar pleaded all along for concessions for the depressed classes so that they could come up and compete with the upper castes and thus contribute their mite to make India great. Political leaders mostly hailing from upper castes carefully listened to what Ambedkar was trying to impress upon them, but could never have the stomach to go out of the way to do anything which could end graded caste inequalities which had remained embedded in Hindu society for centuries. And because of this approach, see the results. The Congress which was the leading part all over the country is struggling for survival in many States. Why? Because the leadership did not own up the depressed classes, which had been their solid vote bank for decades.

Thanks to Ambedkar's teachings and propaganda, statutory provisions were made to assist the backward castes and depressed classes to come up and thus uplift themselves. But due to lack of sincerity among the leadership and bureaucracy presiding over implementation of government's plans and programmes, the benefits from statutory provisions could seldom percolate to lower levels. All this spawned misgiving and unrest amongst the masses. Of course, India has come a long way in so far as improvement in the lot of the depressed classes is concerned since Independence. But for restoration of political stability, for ending fractured electoral verdicts and for ushering an era of all-round growth and prosperity, the caste phobia has to be given go-by as Ambedkar argued all his life.

Ambedkar passed away on December 6, 1956, but the seeds of rebellion sowed by his teachings continue to arouse the masses with greater force and ferocity from year to year.

The downtrodden all over the country are making a blow for their rights, demanding recognition as equal. This *dalit* resurgence being witnessed all over the country is responsible for giving birth to new political formations. The erstwhile serving classes who used to vote for the Congress *en masse* are deserting and have already done so. Everybody is crying for a better deal. If the upper caste leaders had shown foresight and taken remedial measures for winning over and retaining the loyalty of the downtrodden earlier, this chaotic situation would not have arisen.

Whatever arguments one may advance for the current state of chaotic political situation, all this would not have happened had free India's leaders been acutely conscious of the disturbing trends that had started emerging soon after Independence. The Congress Party was the bandwagon of freedom struggle. It captured power after the British quit India in 1947. But instead of looking to the problems likely to arise with growing aspirations of the people, the party sought to sit on its laurels. No wonder growing unrest amongst the downtrodden is now creating insurmountable problems for the country.

Ambedkar's greatest contribution, apart from the laudable Constitution he gave to the country, was *dalit* resurgence he brought about. The Scheduled Castes, Scheduled Tribes and the Backward Classes, who account for more than three-fourths of India's population, virtually had no voice until Ambedkar came on the scene. The *Manusmriti,* bible of Hindu society, had not only relegated them to the fourth *Varna* called *Shudhra* in the caste hierarchy topped by *Brahmins* and followed in the second place by *Kshatriya* and the third by *Kayasthas* but also laid it down that they must remain subservient to the upper castes. They could not redeem themselves by their learning or scholarship, by devotion or service to the upper castes, nay even to gods.

For the first time in India's long history of post-Mauryan period, the depressed classes began to see light at the end of the tunnel, thanks to Ambedkar's teachings. For centuries they had not only suffered at the hands of the upper castes; they had also been denied basic human rights; and they had been told by learned Brahmins to acquiesce in their suffering as it was only a punishment for their misdeeds done in their previous births. Ambedkar's challenge to the edicts of the caste system infused fighting spirit amongst the downtrodden as a result of which at many places they began to make not only a blow for their rights but also demand equal treatment. All this is the product of what Ambedkar stood for.

Although free India's first Prime Minister, Jawaharlal Nehru, could rarely see eye to eye with Ambedkar, he was great enough to acknowledge that whatever Ambedkar had fought for all his life should not be dismissed lightly. Paying tribute to Ambedkar in the Lok Sabha on December 7, 1956, a day after his death, Nehru said: " Dr. Ambedkar is often spoken of as one of the architects of our Constitution. There is no doubt that no one took greater care and trouble over Constitution making than Dr. Ambedkar. He will be remembered also for the great interest he took over the question of Hindu law reform. But I imagine that the way he will be remembered most will be as a symbol of revolt against all the oppressive features of Hindu society. He used language sometimes which hurt people. He sometimes said things which were not wholly justified. But, let us forget that. The main thing was that he rebelled against something against which all of us ought to rebel. This Parliament itself represents in the legislation which has been framed, its repudiation of those customs or legacies from the past which kept down a large section of our people from enjoying their normal rights.

"When I think of Dr. Ambedkar, many things come to my mind, because he was a highly controversial figure. He was not a person of soft speech. But, behind all that was his powerful reaction and an act of rebellion against something that repressed our society for so long. Fortunately, that rebellion had the support, not perhaps in the exact way he wanted it, but in a large measure, the principle underlying that rebellion had the support of Parliament, and, I believe, every group and party represented here. Both in our public activities and in our legislative activities, we did our utmost to remove that stigma on Hindu society. One cannot remove it completely by law, because custom is more deep-rooted and, I am afraid, it still continues in many parts of the country even though it may be considered illegal. That is true.

"But, I have no doubt that it is something that is in its last stages and may take a little time to vanish away. When both law and public opinion become more and more determined to put an end to state of affairs, it cannot last long. Anyhow, Dr. Ambedkar, as I said, became prominent in his own way and most prominent symbol of that rebellion. I have no doubt that, whether we agree with him or not in many matters, that perseverance, that persistence and that, if I may use the word, sometimes virulence of his opposition to this did keep the people's mind awake and did not allow them to become complacent about matters which could not be forgotten, and helped in rousing up those groups in our country which had suffered for so long in the past.

Ambedkar rose on the horizon of the depressed classes like a lodestar who went on guiding them to fight for their human rights. But once the lodestar was gone, the zeal and zest to challenge India's caste system, which holds more than half the country's population in perpetual bondage, started losing momentum. There was at least a symbolic concern for the untouchables so long as Gandhi lived. But untouchability against which Ambedkar fought all his life never became an article of faith with the civil society in India. That is why Ambedkar wanted to reorganize civil society by disbanding the caste system: he wanted worth, but not birth, to determine one's place in society. No wonder against this background of social reality, Ambedkar's stature has grown and continues to do so. The downtrodden, irrespective of their social and political cleavages, are showing a proclivity to swear by Ambedkar's legacy.

Paying tributes to Ambedkar in Parliament, Mrs. Renu Chakravarti, Communist Party, said: "We, younger Members, never had the privilege of working with Ambedkar. But all of us cannot forget how he brought to the forefront of our people's conscience the disabilities suffered by a section of our people owing to our oppressive social system. Although we have passed the Hindu Code Bill in parts, the principles which Dr. Ambedkar had embodied in his original draft were wiser in many aspects. We pay our tribute to his outstanding intellect which rose against social inequality and narrow prejudices, and he become one of those who were known as the architects of our Constitution."

However, in Independent India, the untouchables and other weaker sections did make some gains. For instance, many of them started landing government jobs, even gaining entry into temples. But all this did not altogether change the social scenario. Earlier, they were openly hated, degraded and denigrated. Now animosity against them was under the surface. But here and there, instances did come to light that the society was undergoing a change now. People from the ranks of the untouchables and other depressed classes began to be noticed in offices, occupying generally low-level positions, something which had never happened before. But just as nobody could stop Ambedkar born in an untouchable family from conquering peaks of excellence in the academic world, highly educated and outstanding person even from the lower strata of society started doing well. Belonging to an untouchable family in Kerala, the late K.R. Narayanan, was elevated to be the President of India because of his outstanding performance as a diplomat in the country's foreign office.

Notwithstanding gains here and there, the fact is that even 60 years after Independence, untouchability stalks the land. The weaker sections continue to be hated and derided. Statutory provisions penalizing the evil of untouchability rooted in the caste system are not very effective. Even well-to-do people with university degrees occupying important positions in government or private offices fail to get proper respect and attention if they are the offspring of scavengers or other categories of people still suffering from the stigma of untouchability. The government has failed in breaking the caste mould, although it had set about the task with great zeal and determination. Reformers wanted *Manusmriti* injunctions which many in the country still believe had divine sanction to be forgotten. With the vast populace steeped in religion, no wonder neither the two great leaders, Gandhi and Ambedkar, nor the Independent India's government had any great luck in this regard.

Ambedkar's followers all over the country need to understand and do what he impressed upon the people sixty or seventy years ago. "Never regard yourselves as untouchables. Live a clean life. Dress yourselves like the touchables. Never mind if your dress is full of patches, but see that it is clean. None can restrict your freedom in the choice of your garments and in the use of the metal for your ornaments. Attend more to the cultivation of the mind and the spirit of self-help. You must abolish your slavery yourselves. It is disgraceful to live at the cost of one's self-respect. Self-respect is a most vital factor in life. Without it man is mere cipher. It is out of hard and ceaseless struggles alone that one derives strength, confidence and recognition."

After he had made a bonfire of *Manusmriti*, Dr. Ambedkar said: "It is not that all the parts of the *Manusmriti* are condemnable, that it does not contain good principles and that Manu himself was not a sociologist and was a mere fool. We made a bonfire of it because we view it as a symbol of injustice under which we have been crushed across the centuries. Because of Manu's teachings we have been ground down under despicable poverty. The counts in the indictment of the hereditary Hindu priests are numerous and appalling. He is a clog on the wheel of civilization. Man is born, becomes the father of a family and then in time dies. All along the priest shadows him like an evil genius."

Dr. Ambedkar told his followers that the sooner they stopped believing that their miseries were preordained, the better. "The thought that your poverty is an inevitability, and is inborn and inseparable is entirely erroneous. Abandon the line of thought that you are slaves. The appearance of *Tulsi* leaves round your neck will not relieve you from the clutches of money-lenders. Because you sing songs of Rama you will not get concessions in rent from the landlords. You will not get salaries at the end of the month because you are making pilgrimages every year to holy places. If you want to change your lot, you have to get out of the shackles of *Manusmriti* and adopt a new religion which does not condemn you the moment you are born.

"I do not think it is possible to abolish inequality in Hindu society unless the existing foundation of the Smriti-religion is removed and a better one laid in its place. I, however, despair of the Hindu society being able to reconstruct itself on such a better foundation. Go anywhere, fight is in store for us. It is foolish to suppose that in the event of conversion to Islam everybody from amongst us would be a Nawab or would become the Pope if we went over to Christianity."

Dr. Ambedkar said: "Many Hindus regard me as their enemy. But I have personal friends amongst even the Brahmin community. Situated as I am , it has fallen to my lot to lash the anti-social actions of the Brahmins who treat my people worse than dogs and impede their progress. I hate injustice, pompousness and humbug and my hatred embraces all those who are guilty of them. I want to tell my critics that I regard my feelings of hatred as a real force. They are the reflex of the love I bear for the causes I believe in and I am in no way ashamed of them."

REFERENCES

Book: Nanak Chand Rattu, *Last Few Years of Dr. Ambedkar.*

Maharashtra Government Publications on Dr. Ambedkar: 16 volumes.

Prof. Eleanor Zelliot's paper on Ambedkar in the Columbia University archives.

14

Chronology of Dr. Bhimrao Ramji Ambedkar

ANIL DUTTA MISHRA

1891 April 14: Born at Mhow (Mahu in ex-Indore State), presently district of Madhya Pradesh in the Mahar caste.

1893: Ambedkar's father Shri Ramji Sakpal, a Subedar-Major in the Army, was attached to the 2nd Grenadiers. Retired from service when Bhim Rao Ambedkar was only 2 years old.

1893-94: After father's retirement family settled down at Depoli Village in the Konkan district of Maharashtra. Ambedkar joined primary school at Depoli. Later they moved to Satara as his father secured a job in the military quarters at Satara.

1897: Mother, Smt. Bhima Bai expired when Ambedkar was only six years old.

1900: Entered the Government High School, Satara, in the first standard.

1904 November: In class V Ambedkar had to leave the Camp School at Satara because the family moved to Bombay and settled down there.

1905: At 14 married with Ramabai when he was in fifth standard and she was 9 years old.

1907-1908: Matriculation from the Elphinstone High School, Bombay.

1912: Graduated from Elphinstone College, Bombay.

1913 January: Joined the Baroda State forces as a Lieutenant. Served hardly for 15 days in January 1913, when he had to return to Bombay owing to his father's serious illness. He did not go back to Baroda to rejoin the service.

1913 February 2: Death of father, Shri Ramji Sakpal.

1913 June 4: Selected as a Gaekwad Scholar on an agreement to serve the Baroda State for ten years after his higher studies abroad. Ambedkar was one of the four students selected by the ruler of Baroda, Shri Sayaji Rao Gaekwad, for a scholarship for higher studies in the USA.

1913 July: Left for New York, USA, by sea in the third week of July 1913 as a Gaekwad Scholar on a Baroda State Scholarship and enrolled for three Summer sessions and three academic years at Columbia University, in New York, USA.

1915 May 15: Wrote thesis entitled "Administration and Finance of the East India Company" for partial fulfilment of the requirements of the Degree of Master of Arts, University of Columbia, USA.

1915 June 2: Took his M.A. in Economics from Columbia University, USA. The topic of thesis was: "Ancient Indian Commerce".

1916 June: Submitted his thesis "National Dividend for India: A Historic and Analytical Study" for Ph.D. to Columbia University.

1916 June: Left America for London and joined London School of Economics and Political Science.

1916 October: Admitted to Gray's Inn, London, for Law.

1917 June 8: Degree of Doctor of Philosophy for his dissertation from Columbia University.

1917: Had to discontinue his studies on the expiry of his scholarship and return to India and reached Bombay on August 21, 1917.

1917: Joined as Military Secretary to the Maharaja of Baroda as per Scholarship agreement made on June 4, 1913.

1917 November: Left Baroda and back in Bombay. At this time he published a brochure "Small Holdings in India and Their Remedies".

1918: Attended the Conference of the Depressed Classes held at Nagpur.

1919 November 11(1918 November 11-1920): Appointed as Professor of Political Economy in Sydenham College of Commerce and Economics, Bombay.

1919 January: Gave evidence before the Southborough Reforms (Franchise) Committee, claiming political rights for the Depressed Classes of India.

1919 December-1920 June: Started a Marathi fortnightly paper, the *Mooknayak* (the Leader of the Dumb) with the financial help of the Maharaja of Kolhapur. He could not, however, edit the paper as he was a Government servant. First issue in January 31, 1920.

1920 May: Presided over the All India Depressed Classes Conference at Nagpur.

1920: Again left for London to complete his studies.

1920 September: Rejoined the London School of Economics and Political Science and also entered Gray's Inn to qualify as a Barrister.

1921: Obtained the M.Sc. Degree in England. Thesis was "Provincial Decentralisation of Imperial Finance in British India".

1922 October: Submitted another thesis, "The Problem of Rupee: Its Origin and Its Solution" for D.Sc. (Economics) Degree to the University of London.

1922: After submitting the thesis Ambedkar went to the Bonn University, Germany, for study. And studied Economics in the University of Bonn till 1923.

1923: Was called back to London by Prof. Edwin Cannan, where he was asked to resubmit his thesis after rewriting it, which he submitted later on from Bombay in April 1923, for which he was awarded the D.Sc. Degree.

1923 April: Returned to India called to the Bar. Started practicing as a Barrister from June 1923 and joined the Appellate side of the Bombay Bar.

1923 (1924): *The Evolution of Provincial Finance in British India: A Study in the Provincial Decentralisation of Imperial Finance*, published by P.S. King & Sons, London, 1924.

1923 December: *Problem of the Rupee: Its Origin and Its Solution*, published by P.S. King & Sons, London, 1923. Reprinted in 1947 under the title *History of Indian Currency and Banking*.

1924 June: Started legal practice at the Bombay High Court. Started his active public career as a social worker, a politician, a writer and an educationist.

1924 July 20: Founded an organization in Bombay named the *Bahishkrit Hitkarini Sabha* for the moral and material progress of untouchables.

1925 January 4: A Hostel was inaugurated for the untouchable High School boys by *Bahishkrit Hitkarini Sabha.*

1925 April 11-12: Presided over the Provincial Depressed Classes Conference, held at Nipani, Bombay Presidency and gave Presidential Address.

1925 April 16: "The Present Problem in Indian Currency". Article. *The Servant of India,* April 16, 1925.

1925 December 15: "Statement of Evidence." Gave evidence before the Royal Commission on Indian Currency and Finance. The Royal Commission visited India in 1924-25 to examine the financial system and to suggest the reforms of the Indian currency.

1925: Publication, *Statement of Evidence.* Submitted to the Royal Commission on Indian Currency and Finance which visited India in 1924-25.

1926-1934: As nominated Member of the Bombay Legislative Council.

1926 April 29: "Report of the Taxation Enquiry Committee 1926". Review of *Report of the Taxation Enquiry Committee 1926. The Servant of India,* April 29, 1926.

1926: Met Dr. Sarvapalli Radhakrishnan first time. Who later on became the President of Independent India.

1927 February 18: Sworn-in as a nominated Member of the Bombay Legislative Council.

1927 March 19-20: Presidential address at the Conference of Untouchables—Kolaba District Depressed Classes Conference, at Mahad. Struggle for equality for untouchables began at this Conference.

1927 April 3: Started a Marathi fortnightly, the *Bahishkrit Bharat,* in Bombay.

1927 September: Started the 'Samaj Samata Sangh' to preach social equality among Untouchables and Caste Hindus.

1927 December 25 (1928): Led Chavdar Tank Satyagraha (Mahad Satyagraha) to establish the civic rights of untouchables to draw water from a public tank, "Chavdar Talen", at Mahad, District Kolaba.

1927 December 25: Ambedkar and the Untouchable Satyagrahis publicly burnt the *Manusmriti*.

1928: Appointed as Professor in the Government Law College, Bombay, and subsequently the Principal of the College.

1928 May 29: Statement concerning the state of education of the Depressed Classes in the Bombay Presidency submitted by Ambedkar on behalf of the *Bahishkrit Hitkarini Sabha* (Association for the Welfare of the Depressed Classes) to the Indian Statutory Commission (Simon Commission) on May 29, 1928, Damodar Hall, Parel, Bombay.

1928 August 3: Elected to the Bombay Provincial Committee.

1929 March: Started a paper the *Samata* which was the organ of Samaj Samata Sangh.

1929 May 17: Submitted 'Report on Bombay Presidency'. Member of the Committee appointed by the Bombay Legislative Council to cooperate with the Statutory Commission containing his views and recommendations regarding changes that should be made in the Constitution of the Government of the Bombay Presidency.

1929 May 25: Ambedkar expressed first time publicly his views on the subject of conversion of his religion—Hinduism to Buddhism in Jalgaon.

1930 March 2: As Chairman of the Depressed Classes Conference at Nasik.

1930 March 2: Kalaram Temple Entry Satyagraha—Led a Satyagraha to establish the right of untouchables to enter the famous temple of Kalaram at Nasik. Finally, the doors of the temple were opened to the untouchables in October 1935.

1930-33: Nominated as a delegate to the three Round Table Conferences in London and served on some of their Committees till 1934. He represented the Depressed Classes.

1930 August 8: Established the All India Depressed Classes Congress at Nagpur and presided over the First Session and delivered Presidential Address.

1930 October 4: Left Bombay for London as the representative of the Depressed Classes for the Round Table Conference.

1930 November 12: At the session of the First Round Table Conference. Demanded reforms from the British Government.

1930 November 12—1931 January 19: Political Safeguards: A Scheme of Political Safeguards for the Protection of the Depressed Classes in the Future Constitution of Self-Governing India, jointly submitted by Dr. B.R. Ambedkar and Rao Bahadur R. Srinivasan to the Minorities Sub-Committee No. III of the Round Table Conference, London.

1930: Started a weekly, the *Janata*.

1931 February 27: Returned back to India as the First Session of the Round Table Conference being over.

1931 September 7—1931 December 1: Settlement of the Communal Question: Provisions for a settlement of the Communal Problem put forward jointly by Muslims, Depressed Classes, Indian Christians, Anglo-Indians and Europeans to the Round Table Conference. Ambedkar (Depressed Classes), Aga Khan (Muslims), Rao Bahadur Pannir Selvan (Indian Christians), Sir Henry Gidney (Anglo-Indians), and Sir Hubert Carr (Europeans) agreed by the settlements.

1931 December 28: Returned back to Bombay after the Second Session of the Round Table Conference.

1931-1932: Depressed Classes and the Indian Franchise Committee: The Indian Franchise Committee, known as Lothian Committee, collectively defined the Depressed Classes and thoroughly examined their case for political safeguards. Ambedkar was one of the signatories. He also submitted a detailed note on the Untouchables (Depressed Classes) separately on May 1, 1932.

1932-1934: Was a Member of the Joint Parliamentary Committee on Indian Constitutional Reforms.

1932 August: Mukhed Village Satyagraha.

1932 August 17: British Government's Communal Award announced conceding separate electorate for the untouchables. Mahatma Gandhi felt that it would permanently divide the Hindu society and he declared to resist such a move.

1932 September 19: After the Communal Award's recommendations, a Conference was convened by Pandit Madan Mohan Malviya at Bombay as Mahatma Gandhi announced his intention to go on a fast unto death from 20 September 1932. Ambedkar was given the opportunity to speak in the Conference.

1932 September 19: Issued a Statement on Gandhi's fast.

1932 September 22: Ambedkar accompanied by other leaders met Mahatma Gandhi.

1932 September 24: Poona Pact with Ambedkar and other Depressed Classes leaders on the electorate for Depressed Classes.

1933 February 12: Letter from Ambedkar to Mahatma Gandhi relating to the revision of the Poona Pact.

1933 February 13: On Village Panchayats Bill in the Bombay Legislative Council Debates.

1933 February 14: On the question of Temple Entry for *Harijans* and the Temple Entry Bill of Ranga Iyengar.

1933 April 19: Letter from Ambedkar to Mahatma Gandhi relating to the revision of the Poona Pact.

1933 April 24: Left for London.

1933 April 27: Letter from Mahatma Gandhi to Ambedkar relating to the revision of the Poona Pact.

1933 May 6: Arrived in London.

1933 July 11-28 and 1933 October 3—November 7: Participated in the transactions of the Joint Parliamentary Committee on Indian Constitutional Reforms, under the Chairmanship of Lord Linlithgow.

1934 January 8: Returned to India from the Third Session of the Round Table Conference, London.

1934 June: Accepted the post of a part-time Professor in the Government Law College, Bombay.

1935: "Annihilation of Caste". An address which could not be delivered at the Annual Conference of Jat-Pat-Todak Mandal, Lahore, 1935. Made a complete exposition of caste in this lecture.

1935 May 27: Wife Smt. Ramabai died.

1935 June 1: Appointed as Principal of Government Law College, Bombay.

1935 October 13: Yeola Declaration: Made an announcement at a Provincial Conference of the Depressed Classes at Yeola, District Nasik, that the untouchables would leave the Hindu fold altogether and accept some other religion.

1935: He was made Perry Professor of Jurisprudence, a coveted distinction.

1936 May 31: At the All-Bombay District Mahar Parishad, stressing the need for conversion.

1936 July 11: Mahatma Gandhi wrote in *Harijan* about Ambedkar: "... a man who has carved out for himself a unique position in society. Whatever label he wears in future, Dr. Ambedkar is not the man to allow himself to be forgotten".

1936 August: Founded a new political party—The Independent Labour Party (ILP) of India, on the eve of the General Election of 1937.

1936 September 15: A group of sixteen Mahars was sent to study the Sikh religion at Amritsar. Ambedkar had also sent his son Yeshwant Rao and grandson Mukund to Amritsar.

1936: Published, Annihilation of Caste.

1936 November 11: Left for London *via* Geneva. He was on a mission to discuss with Constitutional Experts the situation that would arise on the conversion of the Depressed Classes to another religion.

1937 January 14: Returned from England to Bombay.

1937 March: Won the case in the Bombay High Court for establishing the civic rights of the untouchables to draw water from a public tank "Chavdar Talen" (Chavdar Tank). He led a *Satyagraha* for the same in December 1927 at Mahad.

1937 July 19: Elected to the Bombay Provincial Legislative Assembly from Bombay in the 1937 Elections with a thundering majority as a candidate of his Independent Labour Party. He was sworn in July 19, 1937. Retained this position till 1942.

1938-40: Turned to Sikhism.

1938: At the G.I.P. Railway Depressed Class Workmen's Conference, Manmad.

1939 January 29: "Federation *versus* Freedom". Kale Memorial Lecture, delivered at the annual function of the Gokhale Institute of Politics and Economics held in the Gokhale Memorial Hall, Poona. First published in 1939.

1939 March 19: Depressed Classes observed their Independence Day because on 19 March, 1927, their struggle for equality had begun at the Conference of Untouchables at Mahad. Ambedkar made a speech on the occasion.

1939 October: In his interview with the Viceroy, Ambedkar fully acquainted the Viceroy with the viewpoint of his community *vis-à-vis* the constitutional advance of India.

1939 December 16: A Conference of *Vatandar Mahar Vethia Parishad* held under Ambedkar's leadership.

1939 December 22: "Day of Deliverance". Ambedkar decided to join the celebrations on the appeal of Jinnah.

1940 December (1941): Publication, *Thoughts on Pakistan,* published by Thacker & Co., Bombay, 1941. A Committee of the Independent Labour Party requested Ambedkar to prepare a report on Pakistan. The Report on Pakistan prepared by Ambedkar was accepted by the Independent Labour Party's Executive Council and it resolved that the Report be published. First published in December 1940.

1941: The war-period (Outbreak of the Second World War on September 2, 1939) was of great significance in the public life of Ambedkar who, on behalf of the untouchables, lent total support to the British in the war-effort, even though he expressed his dissatisfaction that India had no voice in her foreign policy on war and peace.

1942 March 30-31: Convened a Conference of the leaders of the Depressed Classes at Delhi to discuss the Cripps

Proposals. The Conference was a landmark in the untouchables' history.

1942 April: Formed the All India Scheduled Castes Federation as an All-India Political Party to fight for the Scheduled Castes' interests.

1942 July 2: Was appointed Member of the Viceroy's Executive Council on 2nd July, 1942 in which he held the Labour portfolio till June 1946.

1942 July—1946 March: As Labour Member of the Executive Council of the Governor General of India (Viceroy's Executive Council), he secured adequate funds from the Central Government for the education of the Scheduled Castes and also reservations of posts in the Central and Provincial Government services for them.

1942 October 29: "Grievances of the Scheduled Castes". Memorandum submitted to His Excellency, the Governor-General.

1942: Demanded separate village settlements for the untouchables.

1943 January 18: "Ranade, Gandhi and Jinnah". Address delivered on the 101st Birthday Celebrations of Mahadev Govind Ranade held on January 18, 1943 in the Gokhale Memorial Hall, Poona. First published in the book form in 1943.

1943 May 7: Under his Presidentship the third meeting of the Standing Labour Committee set up the Tripartite Labour Conference met at the Bombay Secretariat.

1943 July: "What Ails the World Today". Article. *The Indian Reader's Digest*, July 1943.

1943 September 6 and 7: Under his Presidentship the Second Session of the Tripartite Labour Conference met at New Delhi.

1943 September 17: "Labour and Parliamentary Democracy". Speech delivered to the All-India Trade Union Workers' Study Camp.

1944 April: Moved an amending Bill proposing holidays with pay for industrial workers employed in 'perennial' factories.

1944 September 24: "Scheduled Castes ask for further Safeguards, Separate Electorates and Reservation in Public Services, Federation Committee on Fundamental Rights". *The Mail*, September 24, 1944.

1944 September 25: "Rationalism in India: Revolution and Counter Revolution". *The Liberator*, Madras, September 24, 1944.

1944 September 26: "Equal Place with Hindus and Muslims in Future Constitution. Dr. Ambedkar explains Scheduled Castes Demand. Gandhi-Jinnah Talks Criticised." *The Mail*, Madras, September 26, 1944.

1945 January 4: Got a Hostel opened at Banshi for the untouchables.

1945: *What the Congress and Gandhi Have Done to the Untouchables*, published by Thacker & Co., Bombay, 1945.

1945 July: Founded the People's Education Society, Bombay, which started a number of Colleges in the Bombay Presidency for Scheduled Caste students.

1945 November 27: Under his Presidentship the Seventh Indian Labour Conference met in Delhi.

1946 February: The outcome of the General Elections of February 1946 was a great blow to the Scheduled Castes Federation Candidates. With that, the position of Ambedkar had also become weak and shaky. Ambedkar was almost faced with a crisis in his leadership of the untouchables.

1946 March 15: Inaugurated the election campaign of the Scheduled Castes Federation for the Provincial Elections.

1946 April 5: Meeting between Cabinet Mission Delegation, Field Marshal Viscount Wavell and Ambedkar. Ambedkar appeared before the Cabinet Mission to plead the case of the millions of untouchables. Submitted a Memorandum.

1946 May 22: Letter from Ambedkar to Lord Pethick Lawrence.

1946 May 28: Letter from Lord Pethick Lawrence to Ambedkar.

1946 June 17: In a lengthy telegram to Prime Minister Attlee, Ambedkar drew the attention of Attlee to the developments and decisions at the Shimla Conference. He demanded three seats for the Scheduled Castes in the Interim

Government, but was persuaded to agree for two seats only.

1946 June 20: Submitted a Memorandum to the Cabinet Mission on behalf of the All India Scheduled Castes Federation.

1946 June 20: Started a College, Siddharath College, at Bombay.

1946 June: Came back to Bombay after the dissolution of the Viceroy's Council.

1946 July 20: Addressing a Press Conference at Poona, demanded an open declaration and a blueprint from the Congress as to how they proposed to safeguard the interests of the untouchables in the Future Constitution of India.

1946 August 1: Letter from Attlee to Ambedkar.

1946 August 12: Letter from Ambedkar to Attlee.

1946 August 24: When the Interim Government was announced on August 24, 1946, in which only one untouchable member of the Congress persuasion, Jagjivan Ram was included, Ambedkar was terribly disappointed and his immediate reaction was to demand one more seat for the Scheduled Castes in the Cabinet. It proved as a desperate appeal to Britain.

1946 August: Went to London and explained to Attlee how the Cabinet Mission trampled over the assurances given by the Government to the Scheduled Classes.

1946 September—November: In London, he pleaded for constitutional safeguards for the untouchables after the withdrawal of the British from India. He met Winston Churchill and also Attlee.

1946 November 5: Addressed a meeting of the Conservative Indian Committee in the House of Commons, London.

1946: In terms of the June 3 Plan of 1946, Ambedkar was elected to the Constituent Assembly of India first from Bengal and then from Bombay.

1946 December: Made his first speech in the Constituent Assembly and issued a call for a United India therein. On 15 December 1946, spoke on the Objective Resolution in the Constituent Assembly.

1946: *"State and Minorities"*. Memorandum on the safeguards for the Minorities in general and the Scheduled Castes in particular drafted by Ambedkar and submitted to the Constituent Assembly on behalf of the All-India Scheduled Castes Federation.

1946: *Cabinet Mission and the Untouchables*. 1946. A Pamphlet.

1947: Nominated by the Indian National Congress to the Constituent Assembly.

1947 June: Issued a statement as to what would be the position of Indian States on 15th August 1947—the Indian Independence Day.

1947 July 16: Again opened the topic of Joint *versus* Separate Electorate.

1947 July 16: "Joint *versus* Separate Electorate: Hindu Argument against Separate Electorate is Insubstantial and Unsupportable". *Jai Bheem*, Madras, July 16, 1947.

1947 August—1951: In the new Cabinet of Independent India, Jawaharlal Nehru included Ambedkar as Law Minister.

1947 August 29: Constituent Assembly appointed a Drafting Committee with Ambedkar as the Chairman to frame the Constitution of India and Ambedkar piloted the bill successfully.

1948 February 24: Appointed as Member of a Sub-Committee appointed by the Advisory Committee on Minorities, Fundamental Rights etc. at a meeting held on 24th February 1948.

1948 April 15: Married second time with Dr. Sharada Kabir (later named Savita). She was from a Saraswat Brahmin family of Bombay. Marriage took place at his residence in Delhi under the Civil Marriage Act. Ambedkar was 57 years old.

1948 October: Draft Bill of the Hindu Law Committee (Rau Committee), appointed in 1941, was introduced in 1943 and 1947. Ambedkar revised and submitted the Hindu Law Committee Report to the Constituent Assembly in October 1948.

1948 November: "Indian Constitution". Speech.

1948 November 4: Introduced the Draft Constitution in the Constituent Assembly.

1948 November 19: Speech on the significance of Directive Principles.

1949 September 14: Moved a bill, Abolition of Privy Council Jurisdiction Bill, in the Constituent Assembly.

1949 November 14: Presented the Report of the Drafting Committee together with the Draft Constitution of India as revised by the Committee, in the Constituent Assembly.

1949: "Marxism *versus* Buddhism". Address at the World Buddhist Conference in Kathmandu, Nepal.

1950 January 11: Was presented with a golden casket containing a copy of India's Constitution at a meeting at Parel, in Bombay, convened on behalf of the Scheduled Castes Federation.

1950: Took part in the first Modern Buddhist procession in Delhi.

1950 May 25: Reached Colombo accompanied by his wife Dr. Savita to attend the World Buddhist Conference convened by the Young Men's Buddhist Association. Participated in the World Buddhist Conference at Colombo in Ceylon (Sri Lanka). Spoke to the delegates on the "Rise and fall of Buddhism in India".

1950 June: Was instrument in getting the Milind Maha Vidyalaya opened at Aurangabad.

1951 February 5: Introduced the Hindu Code Bill in the Parliament.

1951 July: Founded the Bharatiya Buddha Janasangha.

1951 September 20: Vigorously defended the Hindu Code Bill in the Parliament.

1951 September 25: Resigned from the Nehru Cabinet as the Hindu Code Bill was abandoned by the Parliament.

1952 February: General Elections in January 1952. Contested from a Bombay Constituency. Lost his election to the Parliament.

1952 March: Nominated by the Bombay Legislative Assembly to the Council of States (Rajya Sabha), the Upper House of Parliament of India.

1952 June 2: Left Bombay for New York to receive the Honorary Degree of Doctor of Laws from the Columbia University.

1952 June 6: The Columbia University at its Special Convocation conferred the Honorary Degree of Doctor of Laws and Letters (LL.D.) on Dr. Ambedkar. The Columbia University hailed him as "One of India's leading citizens, a great social reformer and a valiant upholder of human rights".

1952 June 15: Returned from New York to Bombay.

1953: Lost his second election, by-election, to the Parliament.

1954 December: Ambedkar's choice of Buddhism came to be publicly known.

1954 December: Took part in the Conference of the Third World Federation of Buddhists in Rangoon, Burma.

1955: Founded the 'Bharatiya Buddha Mahasabha' for the spread of Buddhism in India.

1956-57: Started a Training School for the potential Legislators and Politicians and to invigorate the democratic forces in India. The School, the first of its kind in the country, worked with 15 students on roll from 1 July, 1956 to March 1957.

1956 May 8: Inclined towards Buddhism openly. Made a formal declaration of conversion.

1956 May 24: Declared on the day of Buddha Jayanti Celebrations at Nare Park in Bombay that he would embrace Buddhism in October 1956.

1956 June 16: Established 'The Bombay State Inferior Village *Watandar* Association'.

1956 September 23: Issued a press note announcing that his conversion to Buddhism would take place at Nagpur on 14 October 1956.

1956 October 14: At Nagpur, Ambedkar with his wife and 75,000 of his followers embraced Buddhism.

1956 November 20: Participated in the World Buddhist Conference in Kathmandu, Nepal. He spoke on "Buddha and Karl Marx". His speech was highly acclaimed where he was hailed as Nav Buddha.

1956 December 5: With his Private Secretary till 11.15 P.M. Ambedkar asked him to give him the Introduction and preface to his book *The Buddha and His Dharma*, which the former intended finishing before going to sleep. (A

Posthumous book, *The Buddha and His Dharma*, (Siddharath College Publication, Bombay), published by People's Education Society, Bombay, 1957.

1956 **December 6:** Dr. Savita Ambedkar at 6.30 A.M. found that her husband was no more. Thus passed away one of the greatest champions of the untouchables of India. Deeply mourned by the nation. Next day, on 7th December, his mortal remains were cremated on the Dadar sea-shore in Bombay amid thousands of his followers and admirers.

1990 **April 14:** The nation conferred its highest award 'Bharat Ratna' on him on 14 April 1990 as a mark of recognition of his services to the country. His wife Dr. Savita Ambedkar received this honour on his behalf from the President of India, Shri R. Venkataraman at a special ceremony in Rashtrapati Bhawan, New Delhi.

Bibliography

Sunita Gulati

Abraham, P., *Ambedkar's Contribution for Economic Planning and Development its relevance.* New Delhi: Kanishka, 2002. p. 254.

Ahir, D.C., *Dr. Babasaheb Ambedkar: Writings and Speeches,* a ready reference manual of 17 volumes, Delhi: B.R. Pub., 2007. p. 456.

Ambedkar, B.R., *Ambedkar and Social Justice,* New Delhi: Publications Division, Ministry of Information and Broadcasting, 1992. 2v.

Ambedkar, B.R. and Ram Ronki, From servitude to assertion: Ambedkar's subaltern approach to nationalism and dalit liberation, *Social Science Research Journal,* 9(2), 2001: pp. 146-70.

Ambedkar, B.R., *Ranade, Gandhi and Jinnah:* address delivered on the 101st birthday celebration of Mahadev Govind Ranade held on the 18th January 1943, Bombay: Thacker, 1943, p. 85.

Ambedkar, B.R., *States and Minorities: What are their Rights and how to secure them in the Constitution of India,* Bombay: Thacker, 1947. p. 70.

Ambedkar, B.R., *What Congress and Gandhi have done to the Untouchables,* Bombay: Thacker, 1945. vi, p. 399.

Ambedkar, B.R., *Untouchables: Who were they and why they became Untouchables?* New Delhi: Amrit Book, 1948. viii, p. 158.

Ambedkar, S. Nagendra, Panchayati Raj elections in Rajasthan, *Administrative Change,* 22(2), 1995 (Jan-Jun), pp. 177-82.

Ambedkar, S. Nagendra, Social fabric of legislative elite in Andhra Pradesh, *Journal of Constitutional and Parliamentary Studies,* 24(14), Jan.-Dec.90, pp. 155-75.

Ambedkar, S. Nagendra, Urban local self government in Andhra Pradesh, *Civic Affairs,* 40(7) Feb. 93, pp. 13-20.

Ambedkar: Autobiographical Notes, New Delhi: *Navayana*, 2004. p. 31.

Audi, M.J., Ambedkar's struggle for untouchables: reflections, *Indian Journal of Political Science*, 50(3), 1989 (July-Sept.), pp. 307-20.

Baisantry, D.K., Dr. Ambedkar: The Economist, *Yojana*, 36(6), 15 Apr. 92, pp. 21-22, 25.

Bakshi, S.R. (ed.), *Political Ideology of B.R. Ambedkar*, New Delhi: Deep and Deep, 2001, p. 263.

Bal, G.S. (ed.), *Understanding Ambedkar*, Delhi: Ajanta, 2000. p. 143.

Bandivedkar, P.M., A champion of human rights, *Social Welfare*, 38(3), June 1991, pp. 23-24.

Bellwinkel Schempp, Maren, From Bhakti to Buddhism: Ravidas and Ambedkar, *Economic and Political Weekly*, 42(23), 2007 (9 June): pp. 2177-183.

Beltz, Johannes, *Mahar, Buddhist and Dalit*: religious conversion and socio-political emancipation, New Delhi: Manohar, 2005. p. 309.

Chalam, K.S., *Modernization and Dalit Education: Ambedkar's Vision*, Jaipur: Rawat, 2008, p. 200.

Chandra Bipan, Gandhi and Ambedkar: Attitudes towards caste system, *Times of India* (13 Apr 1994), pp. 12.

Chandra, Ramesh and Sangh, Mittra, *The Ambedkar Era*, New Delhi, Commonwealth, 2003, p. 354.

Chatterjee, Debi, *Up against caste: comparative study of Ambedkar and Periyar*, Jaipur: Rawat, 2004, p. 235.

Chaturvedi, J.P., Ambedkar's contribution to national unity, *Mainstream*, 29(49), 28 Sep. 1991, pp. 29-32.

Chaturvedi, J.P., Ambedkar's contribution to national unity, *Mainstream*, 29(49), 1991 (28 Sep.), pp. 29-32.

Chavan, Sheshrao, *Gandhi and Ambedkar: Saviours of Untouchables*, Mumbai: Bharatiya Vidya Bhavan, 2001, p. 272.

Chavan, Sheshrao, *The Makers of Indian Constitution: Myth and Reality*, Mumbai: Bharatiya Vidya Bhavan, 2000. p. 254.

Dhani, S.L., *Dr. B.R.* (ed.), *Ambedkar: Man of Millennium for Social Justice*, Delhi: Kalpaz, 2007. p. 344.

Dhavan, Rajeev, Ambedkar's prophecy: poverty of human rights in India, *Journal of the Indian Law Institute,* (36(1), Jan-March 1994, pp. 8-36.

Dhawan, Shakuntla, Dr. B.R. Ambedkar: Apostle of social justice, *Yojana,* 35(6), 1991(15 Apr.), pp. 12-13.

Diwakar, G.D., Relevancy of the thoughts of Baba Saheb Dr. B.R. Ambedkar on small holdings in India and their remedies in present context. *Agricultural Situation in India,* 55(7), 1998(Oct.), pp. 431-35.

Dwivedi, H.S. and Sinha, Ratan, Dr. Ambedkar: The pioneer of social democracy, *Indian Journal of Political Science,* 66(1), 2005 (Jan-Mar), pp. 661-66.

Eminent Parliamentarians: B.R. Ambedkar, Lok Sabha Secretariat, New Delhi, 1991. p. 170+.

Fitzgerald, Timothy, Ambedkar Buddhism in Maharashtra, *Contributions to Indian Sociology,* 31(2), 1997 (Jul-Dec.), pp. 225-51.

Gaikwad, S.M., Ambedkar and Indian nationalism, *Economic and Political Weekly,* 33(10), 1998 (7 March), pp. 515-18.

Gangania, Ish, Cultural nationalism, humanism and Dr Ambedkar, *Mainstream,* 44(17), 2006 (15 April), pp. 21-25.

Gehlot, N.S., Dr. Ambedkar, Mahatama Gandhi and Dalit Movement, *Indian Journal of Political Science,* 54 (3 and 4), 1993 (Jul-Dec.), pp. 382-87.

Ghose, Kunal, Buddha, Vivekananda, Ambedkar: Progression in Indian thought, *Mainstream,* 1997 (Ann.20 Dec.), pp. 63-70, 78.

Ghosh, A.K., The relevance of Ambedkar, *University News,* 31(13), 29 Mar. 93, pp. 15-16.

Gopal Guru, Ambedkar's idea of social justice, *Administrator,* 42(1), 1997 (Jan-Mar), pp. 25-33.

Gopal Guru, Understanding Ambedkar's construction of national movement, *Economic and Political Weekly,* 33(4), 1998 (31 Jan-6 Feb), pp. 156-57.

Gupta, Dipankar, Positive discrimination and the question of fraternity: contrasting Ambedkar and Mandal on reservations, *Economic and Political Weekly,* 32(31), 1997 (2 Aug), pp. 1971-978.

Gupta, Rajesh, *Dr. Ambedkar aur Samajik Nayay* (Hindi), Delhi, Manak, 1994, p. 156.

Gupta, V.P. and Mohini Gupta, *Bhimrao Ambedkar: Vyakti aur Vichar* (Hindi), 2nd ed, New Delhi, Radha, 2006, p. 193.

Hancock, Virginia, New Buddhism for new aspirations: Navayana Buddhism of Ambedkar and his followers, *Manushi*, 145, 2004 (Nov-Dec.), pp. 17-25.

Harvani, Ansar, *Gandhi to Gandhi: Private Faces of Public Figures*, New Delhi, Gyan Pub., 1996, p. 258.

Illaiah, Kancha, The God of little men, *Young Indian*, 8(35-36), 1998 (4 and 11 March), pp. 13-16.

Inderjit, Common Civil Code: Ambedkar's middle path, *Times of India*, 1996, (16 Jul), p. 10.

Inderjit, Lok Sabha dissolution: B.R. Ambedkar's viewpoint, *Tribune*, 1997, (11 Apr), p. 8.

Jadhav, Praveen, *Ambedkar's People in India: with reference to "Chaityabhoomi"*, New Delhi: Rajat, 2007, p. 214.

Jaffrelot, Christophe, *Dr. Ambedkar and Untouchability: Analysing and Fighting Caste*, Delhi, Permanent Black, 2005, p. 205.

Jaganathan, N., Indian Constitution, economic development and social justice, *Monthly Commentary on Indian Economic Conditions*, 33(8), May 92, pp. 32-36.

Jaoul, Nicolas, Learning the use of symbolic means: Dalits, Ambedkar statues and the State in Uttar Pradesh, *Contributions to Indian Sociology*, 40(2), 2006 (May-Aug): pp. 175-207.

Jatava, D.R., B.R. *Ambedkar: Study in society and politics*, Jaipur, National, 1998. p. 223.

K.L. Chanchreek, *Dr. B.R. Ambedkar: Patriot, Philosopher, Statesman. Economic Writings*, volume-III.

K.L. Chanchreek, (ed.), *Dr. B.R. Ambedkar: A Rebel Dalit Leader*, New Delhi, Shree, 2006, 2 vols.

K.L. Chanchreek, Saroj Prasad and Rakesh Kumar, (ed.), *Dr. B.R. Ambedkar (1891-1991): Patriot, Philosopher and Statesman*, Delhi: H.K., 1991.

K.S. Chalam (ed.), *Relevance of Ambedkarism in India*, Jaipur, Rawat Pub., 1993, p. 209.

Kapor, S.D., B.R. Ambedkar, W.E.B. DuBois and the process of liberation, *Economic and Political Weekly*, 38 (51-52), 2003 (27 Dec.), pp. 5344-349.

Keer, Dhananjay, *Dr. Ambedkar: Life and Mission*, 2nd ed, Bombay, Popular Prakashan, 1962, p. 528.

Keer, Dhananjay, *Dr. Ambedkar: Life and Mission*, Bombay: A.V. Keer, 1954, p. 450.

Keer, Dhananjay, *Dr. Ambedkar: Life and Mission*, Mumbai, Popular, 1990, pp. 532, A99/Am16 K256.

Khare, Vijay S., *Dr. B.R.Ambedkar and India's National Security*, New Delhi: Kilaso Books, 2005, p. 319.

Krishna Iyer, *V.R. Ambedkar Centenary: Social Justice and the Undone Vast*, Delhi: B.R., 1991. p. 115.

Kuber, W.N., *Dr. Ambedkar: A Critical Study*, Delhi: People's Pub. House, 1973, p. 332, Rs. 30.00.

Limaye Madhu, Ambedkarism: fake and genuine, *Janata*, 49(14), 12 June, 1994, pp. 7-8.

Limaye, Madhu, Ambedkar and constitutional making, *Hindu*, 1995 (10 Jan.), p. 8.

Limaye, Madhu, *Manu Gandhi and Ambedkar and other essays*, New Delhi, Gyan, 1995. p. 180.

Lynch, Owen M., Ambedkar Jayanti : Dalit Reritualization in Agra, *Eastern Anthropologist*, 55(2-3), 2002 (Apr-Sept), pp. 115-32.

Malik, Bibhuti Bhushan, Ambedkar's view of Buddhism and civilization, *Third Concept*, 10(113), 1996 (Jul): pp. 48-51.

Mallaiah, L.C., *Relevance of Dr. B.R. Ambedkar's views on Indian agricultural development*, Delhi: Abhijeet, 2006. p. 216.

Mallick, Basanta Kumar, Ambedkar and his movement for social equality, *Mainstream*, 29(25), 1991 (13 Apr.), pp. 4-6, 34.

Mallik, Basant Kumar, Ambedkar on women's progress, *Mainstream*, 25(30), 1987 (11 Apr.), pp. 7-10.

Mallik, Basanta Kumar, Ambedkar as a builder of modern India, *Mainstream*, 30(25), 11 Apr., pp. 21-25.

Mandal, S.N., Dr. B.R. Ambedkar—The man and his mission, *Yojana*, 34(11), 1990 (16 Jun.), pp. 23-24.

Martin, Max, Baba Saheb Ambedkar: A versatile personality, *Yojana*, 39(6), 1995 (Apr), pp. 12-13.

Massey, James, *Dr. B.R. Ambedkar: A Study in Just Society*, New Delhi: Manohar, 2003. p. 123.

Maurya, R.D., Dalit liberation: The mission of Ambedkar for social justice, *Journal of Rural Development*, 11(2), Mar. 92, pp. 187-203.

Mishra, S.N., *Facets of Dr. B.R. Ambedkar*, New Delhi, Indian Institute of Public Administration, 2004. p. 161.

Mugekar, B.L., Dr. Ambedkar on India's Agrarian Problems, Janata, 46(12), 1991(14 Apr.), pp. 9-13.

Nagendra Ambedkar, S., Political elites: theoretical perspectives, *Indian Journal of Political Science*, 53(2) April-June 92, pp. 253-76.

Naik, C.D., *Social and Political Thought of Dr. B. R. Ambedkar*, New Delhi, Arise, 2008. p. 308.

Naik, C.D., *Thoughts and Philosophy of Dr. B.R. Ambedkar*, New Delhi: Sarup & Sons, 2003. p. 475.

Namishray, Mohan Dass, *Caste and Race: Comparative Study of B.R. Ambedkar and Martin Luther King*, Jaipur: Rawat Pub., 2003, p. 216.

Nandu Ram (ed.), *Ambedkar, Dalits and Buddhism*: Collection of Dr. Ambedkar memorial annual lectures, New Delhi, Manak and Dr. Ambedkar Chair in Sociology, 2008.

Nanheshwar Prasad, Dr. Ambedkar: a social reformist, *Yojana*, 40(5), 1996 (May), pp. 12-13.

Nazeer H. Khan, (ed.), *B.R. Ambedkar on Federalism, Ethnicity and Gender Justice*, New Delhi, Deep & Deep, 2001, p. 261.

Nikam, Shri Ram, Destiny of untouchables in India: Divergent approaches and strategies of Mahatma Gandhi and Dr. B.R. Ambedkar, New Delhi: Deep and Deep, 1998, p. 163.

Omvedt, Gail, *Ambedkar: Towards an Enlightened India*, New Delhi: Viking, 2004, p. 167.

Omvedt, Gail, *Dalits and the Democratic Revolution: Dr. Ambedkar and the Dalit Movement in Colonial India*, New Delhi: Sage, 1994, p. 348.

Padgaonkar, Dileep, Ambedkar and Gandhi, *Mainstream*, 45(18), 2007(21 Apr), pp. 7-8.

Pandit, Nalini, Ambedkar and the Dalits, *Seminar,* (461), 1998 (Ann. Jan), pp. 47-51.

Pandit, Nalini, Ambedkar and the demand for Pakistan, *Mainstream,* 36(17), 1998 (18 Apr), pp. 18-24.

Patil, Sharad, When Ambedkar call for caste-annihilation, *Mainstream,* 45(12), 2007 (9 Mar), pp. 16-20.

Pawar, I. Anand, Promoting weaker section in distance education: Dr. B.R. Ambedkar Open University experience, *University News,* 44(32), 2006 (7 Aug), pp. 11-17.

Pilchick, Terry, *Jai Bhim: Dispatches from a Peaceful Revolution,* Glasgow: Windhorse, 1988, p. 240.

Prakash, Deo, *Socio-economic Thoughts of B.R. Ambedkar,* New Delhi: Manak Pub., 2004. p. 292.

Prakash, Om, Economic Ideas of Bhimrao Ramji Ambedkar, *Indian Economic Journal,* 39(4) Apr.-Jun.92, pp. 82-89.

Prakash, Prem, *Ambedkar, Politics and Scheduled Castes,* New Delhi, Ashish, 1993. p. 181.

Radhakrishnan, P., Ambedkar's Legacy to Dalits: has the nation reverted on its promises? *Economic and Political Weekly,* 26(33), 17 Aug. 91, pp. 1911-22.

Raj Kumar, *Ambedkar and His Writings: A Look for the New Generation,* Delhi: Kalpaz, 2008. p. 301.

Raj Kumar, Relevance of Ambedkarism in India, *Mainstream,* 34(24), 1996 (18 May), pp. 21-25.

Rajagopalachari, C., *Ambedkar Refuted,* Bombay, Hind Kitabs, 1946, p. 38.

Rajasekhariah, A.M. and Jayaraj, Hemalata, Political Philosophy of Dr. B.R. Ambedkar, *Indian Journal of Political Science,* 52(3), Jul.-Sep.91, pp. 357-75.

Rajasekhriah, A.M. B.R. *Ambedkar: The Quest for Social Justice,* New Delhi: Uppal, 1989. p. 290.

Ramabrahmam, I. and S.N. Ambedkar, New Structures of Panchayati Raj: Issues and Challenges, *Journal of Rural Development,* 8(2), 1989 (Mar.), pp. 125-34.

Rao, Didla V. and Pulla Lakshmi, *Ambedkar's Thrust on Education and Reservation: Its Impact on Emancipation of Dalit, OBC and minorities,* New Delhi, Sunrise, 2007, p. 404.

Rao, Didla Venkateswara, *Dr. B.R. Ambedkar: Champion of Human Rights in India*, New Delhi, Manak, 2006, p. 218.

Rao, J.V. Raghavendra, Dr. Ambedkar, The Constitution and Reservation Policy: A Sociologists View, *Janata*, 57(13), 2002 (21 Apr), pp. 7-9, 15.

Rattu, Nanak Chand, *Dr. Ambedkar Important Messages, Sayings, Wit and Wisdom*, New Delhi: Rajgriha, 2001, p. 184.

Rattu, Nanak Chand, *Little Known Facets of Dr. Ambedkar*, New Delhi, Focus Impressions, 2001, p. 240.

Ravinder Kumar and Kamlesh Kumar, *Babasaheb Ambedkar ki Vani* (Hindi), New Delhi, Gyan, 2006, p. 139.

Ravindra Kumar and Kamlesh Kumar, *Voice of Babasaheb Ambedkar*, New Delhi: Gyan, 2007. p. 139.

Reddy, S.V. Rajashekar and Reddy, G. Malla, Profile of distance learners: a case study of Dr. B.R. Ambedkar Open University. *University News*, 35(4), 1997(27 Jan), pp. 13-17, 20-21.

Rodrigues, Valerian, Buddhism, Marxism and the conception of emancipation in Ambedkar: [In] *Dalit Movements and the Meanings of Labour in India*, edited by Peter Robb, Delhi, Oxford, 1993. pp. 299-338.

Roy, Ramashray, *Gandhi and Ambedkar: A Study in Contrast*, Delhi, Shipra, 2006, p. 243.

S.N. Mandal, *Dr. B.R. Ambedkar: His Thoughts and Observations*, New Delhi, National, 2004, p. 193.

S.R. Bakshi, *Social Ideology of B.R. Ambedkar*, New Delhi, Deep and Deep, 2001, p. 325.

Sahay, Mohan, Dalit politics: the relevance of Ambedkar, *Statesman*, 1997 (9 Aug), p. 8.

Sahay, S., The founding father : Ambedkar in perspective, *Tribune* (4 October, 1994), p. 8.

Sangharakshita, *Ambedkar and Buddhism*, Delhi, Motilal, 2006, p. 181.

Sanjay Prakash Sharma, *Dr. B.R. Ambedkar: A Crusader of Social Justice*, Jaipur: RBSA Publishers, 2003. 2 v.

Sardesia, S.G., Ambedkar and the emanicipation of the scheduled castes, *Mainstream*, 35(19), 1997 (19 Apr), pp. 9-12.

Shabbir, Mohammad (ed.), *Ambedkar on Law, Constitution and Social Justice*, Jaipur, Rawat, 2005, p. 403.

Shourie, Arun, *Worshipping False Gods: Ambedkar, and the Facts which have been Erased*, New Delhi, ASA Pub., 1997, p. 663.

Shyamlal, *Ambedkar and Dalit Movement: Special Reference to Rajasthan*, Jaipur, Rawat, 2008, p. 248.

Singh, Awadhesh Kumar, Relevance of Ambedkar's Philosophy of Social Justice, *Third Concept*, 9(104-105), 1995 (Oct.-Nov.), pp. 51-57.

Singh, M.K., *Ambedkar on Caste and Untouchability*, New Delhi, Rajat, 2008, p. 288.

Singh, M.P. and Sufia, Ahmed, Ambedkar and social justice, *Gandhian Perspectives*, 13(1), 2004 (July-Dec.), pp. 23-33.

Singh, Man Mohan, Ambedkar: The relentless crusader, *Janata*, 35(6), 1991 (15 Apr.), pp. 10-11.

Singh, Shriprakash, *Dr. Ambedkar on Minorities*, New Delhi, India First Foundation, 2005, p. 168.

Sinha, Jogendra, Dr. B.R. Ambedkar: a critical study, Patna: Vijay, 1993. p. 217.

Social justice: Gandhi and Ambedkar, *Gandhian Perspectives*, 11(1-2), 1998(Spring-Fall): pp. 55-66.

Sontakke, Y.D. (ed.), *Thoughts of Dr. Baba Saheb Ambedkar*, New Delhi: Samyak, 2004. p. 344.

Surendra Jondhale and Johannes Beltz, Reconstructing the world: B.R. Ambedkar and Buddhism in India, New Delhi: Oxford Univ. Press, 2004. p. 316.

Surendra, Mohan, Contribution of Dr. Ambedkar, Janata, 47(8), 12 Apr. 1992, pp. 12-13.

Thorat, Sukhdeo and Aryama (eds.), Ambedkar in retrospect: essays on economics, politics and society, Jaipur: Rawat, 2007. p. 360.

Thorat, Sukhadeo and Narendra Kumar, *B.R. Ambedkar: Perspectives on Social Exclusion and Inclusive Policies*, New Delhi, Oxford Univ. Press, 2008, p. 386.

Thorat, Sukhadeo, Ambedkar's role in economic planning, water and power policy, 2nd ed, Delhi, Shipra, 2006, p. 238.

Tiwary, Shailendra K., *B.R. Ambedkar and Indian Constitution: Configurating the Indian Constitution: Explorations in the Ideas of B.R. Ambedkar*, Gurgaon: Shubhi, 2008, p. 220.

Tiwary, Shailendra K., Crusader, *Yojana*, 35(6), 15 April 91, pp. 10-11.

V.T. Patil, (ed.), *Studies in Ambedkar*, Delhi: Devika, 1995, p. 395.

Valerian Rodrigues (ed.), The essential writings of B.R. Ambedkar, New Delhi, Oxford Univ. Press, 2002, p. 559.

VALMIKI Ambedkar Awas Yojana (VAMBAY), *Shelter*, 5(1), 2002 (Jan.), pp. 96-99.

Vasant Moon, *Dr. Babasaheb Ambedkar Writings and Speeches*, Vol. 7, Bombay, Education Department, 1990, p. 382+.

Venugopal Rao, C., Dr. B.R. Ambedkar's economic philosophy: a critical analysis, *Asian Economic Review*, 37(3), 1995 (Dec.), pp. 524-27.

Verma, D.K. and A. Sohrot, *Ambedkar's Vision and Education of Weaker Sections*, New Delhi: Manak, 2004. p. 199.

Vibhute, K.I.,Ambedkar's sense of social justice and constitutional sprint, *Mainstream*, 31(22), 10 Apr. 93, pp. 25-7.

Yadav, Sushma, *Social Justice Ambedkar's Vision*, New Delhi: Indian Institute of Public Administration, 2006. p. 94.

Zelliot, Eleanor, *From Untouchable to Dalit: Essays on the Ambedkar Movement*, New Delhi: Manohar, 2005, p. 350.

Index